Ida Lupino, Filmmaker

Ida Lupino, Filmmaker

Edited by
Phillip Sipiora

BLOOMSBURY ACADEMIC
NEW YORK • LONDON • OXFORD • NEW DELHI • SYDNEY

BLOOMSBURY ACADEMIC
Bloomsbury Publishing Inc
1385 Broadway, New York, NY 10018, USA
50 Bedford Square, London, WC1B 3DP, UK
29 Earlsfort Terrace, Dublin 2, Ireland

BLOOMSBURY, BLOOMSBURY ACADEMIC and the Diana logo are trademarks of
Bloomsbury Publishing Plc

First published in the United States of America 2021
This paperback edition published 2023

Each chapter © of Contributors

Volume Editor's Part of the Work © Phillip Sipiora, 2021

For legal purposes the Acknowledgments on p. ix constitute an extension
of this copyright page.

Cover design: Ben Anslow
Cover photograph: Ida Lupino in a surrealist portrait, 23 April 1943 © Bettmann / Getty
Images

All rights reserved. No part of this publication may be reproduced or transmitted in any form or by any means, electronic or mechanical, including photocopying, recording, or any information storage or retrieval system, without prior permission in writing from the publishers.

Bloomsbury Publishing Inc does not have any control over, or responsibility for, any third-party websites referred to or in this book. All internet addresses given in this book were correct at the time of going to press. The author and publisher regret any inconvenience caused if addresses have changed or sites have ceased to exist, but can accept no responsibility for any such changes.

Library of Congress Control Number: 2021936496.

ISBN: HB: 978-1-5013-5208-9
PB: 978-1-5013-8133-1
ePDF: 978-1-5013-5210-2
eBook: 978-1-5013-5209-6

Typeset by Deanta Global Publishing Services, Chennai, India

To find out more about our authors and books visit www.bloomsbury.com
and sign up for our newsletters.

To my dear wife, Cary, who graciously coexisted with Ida Lupino for a long time in the planning, research, and completion of this volume.
—Phillip Sipiora

CONTENTS

Acknowledgments ix
Foreword xi
Preface 2

1   Introduction: All Sides of the Camera 3
    Phillip Sipiora

2   Beyond the Performance: Ida Lupino, American Stages, and the Business of Show 17
    Karen McNally

3   Ida Lupino: A Life in Hollywood 35
    William T. Ross

4   Overlooked and Underrepresented: The Essential Lupino 51
    Courtney J. Ruffner Grieneisen

5   "A Big Family of Little Failures": Postwar America's Children and Ida Lupino's *Not Wanted* 63
    Julie Grossman

6   (Not so) "Vicious and Depraved": Ida Lupino's Portraits of Men 77
    Marlisa Santos

7   Accidental Outlaw: Agency and Genre in *The Bigamist* 95
    Michael L. Shuman

8   Ida Lupino's Moral Filmmaking: *The Bigamist* and *The Trouble with Angels*   113
    Ashley M. Donnelly

9   Ida Lupino's Manipulation of Age Conventions   127
    Valerie Barnes Lipscomb

10 Ida Lupino and Acting: Situating Performance in Cinematic Context(s)   147
    Curtis LeVan

11 Against the Grain, Within the Frame: The Double Consciousness of Ida Lupino   165
    Mary Lynn Navarro

12 *Outrage* and Trauma: A Reconsideration and Reevaluation   181
    Kathleen "Kat" Robinson

13 Ida Lupino, Hitchhiking into Darkness   193
    Phillip Sipiora

14 Unsolicited Bequest: Ambivalent Inheritance in Ida Lupino's 1960s Mysteries   213
    Ann Torrusio

15 A Subtle Subversion: Ida Lupino Directing Television   227
    Adam Breckenridge

16 Ida Lupino's Thrillers: The Terror of the "Lethal Woman"   243
    Fernando Gabriel Pagnoni Berns

Contributors   257
Index   261

ACKNOWLEDGMENTS

I first became aware of Ida Lupino when I was a teenager. I do not recall exactly when I came under Lupino's spell, but I was probably in my early teens. I grew up on the west side of Chicago in a large family, and we huddled most evenings in front of our small television, three generations glued to episodes of mysteries on the small screen. My earliest memories of Lupino were of her in *The Twilight Zone*. However, it was her work in film that was most enduring for me, especially *Beware, My Lovely* (1952), *The Bigamist* (1953), and *The Hitch-Hiker* (1953). Lupino's presence was compelling to me in her markedly diverse roles, and my return to her work years later, as a film specialist, has only energized my enthusiasm for her power of presence, creativity, and imposing originality as both performer and filmmaker. Ida Lupino is infectious in so many strategic ways, and my reading of film has been significantly altered because of her influence. Her professional life was characterized by a distinct enthusiasm for cinematic performance, an unrelenting work ethic, and a lifetime commitment to improving her art(s).

Assembling this volume has been a labor of love and has enriched my life, far beyond a better understanding of Lupino's lasting contributions to film and television. I am grateful to so many individuals for their support and assistance in bringing this book to life. First and foremost, my wife Cary has lived with Lupino, on screen and in our lives, much more than she had ever anticipated when I first began this project. Our daughters, Jessica and Austin, and our son, Phillip, were enthusiastically supportive from the very beginning. My heartfelt thanks to Mike Shuman, a dear friend and contributor to this volume, who was invaluable in lending his technical expertise and wide grasp of cinematic history when relevant issues came up, as they often did. In addition, I gratefully acknowledge Shannon Zinck's deft editorial assistance. Further, I am most appreciative of Julie Grossman, who was particularly helpful with her wise counsel and kind friendship. And my film students, numbering more than 20,000 over the years, have been so very insightful in their reactions to Lupino's films, and they contributed significantly to my ongoing exploration into her cinematic spirit and technique(s). To them I will forever be indebted.

As the editor of a scholarly journal for two decades, I keenly understand how important editorial counsel and support are to the successful completion and launch of any writing project. Hence a special thank you to Katie Gallof and Erin Duffy for their dynamic professionalism, patience, and prudence in guiding the birth of this book. I would like to acknowledge the fine contributors to this volume for their dedicated, penetrating, and insightful work, and I would like to extend my deep gratitude to Cynthia Miller, who graciously provided a Foreword. My kindly thanks to acclaimed film historian, Gary D. Rhodes, for contributing a Preface. And there are two dear film pals of mine who were always available to listen and offer their wise counsel in addressing complicated and sticky issues inherent in exploring a cinematic artist as complex and beguiling as Ida Lupino.

FOREWORD

Cynthia J. Miller

Until quite recently, far too little scholarly attention has been focused on media trailblazer Ida Lupino. With a career that spanned over forty years, we have really only begun to scratch the surface in considering a woman who railed against stereotyping and continues to defy easy definitions. She worked as an actor, writer, director, and producer in an era when the range of such options was limited and resistance was considerable; becoming part of a handful of women—like Virginia Van Upp, Dorothy Arzner, and Maya Deren[1]—who challenged studio-era hierarchies and worked on the "other" side of the camera or outside the studio system entirely. Examinations of her life and career in recent years have raised as many questions as they have answered.[2]

Among audiences, Lupino has been primarily recognized for acting roles in films such as *They Drive By Night* (1940), *High Sierra* (1941), and *The Hard Way* (1943), but her impact on the film industry was so much more, and so much more complex. Dissatisfied with her acting career, Lupino knew all too well that she was referred to as "the poor man's Bette Davis"[3] and sought to unyoke herself from the superficiality of an industry that privileged hype over thoughtfulness and façade over depth. "I don't want to smile all the time," she complained. "After all, you can't act your life away."[4] Her determination to do more—be more—than another in a long line of actors used and discarded by the studio system led her to abandon a lucrative contract with Paramount Studios and establish her own independent production company, The Filmakers. Hollywood columnist Hedda Hopper noted the young actress's integrity, and applauded her desire to avoid being just another blonde Hollywood bombshell, recalling that, in 1939,

> I told her . . . If you want to be an actress, throw your contract in the ash can and wait for the good parts. If you go on playing these blonde tramps for another year, you'll lose all that time and maybe the courage to battle for something better.[5]

Her words had clearly resonated with Lupino, who had, by then, transformed herself from just another platinum blonde into a respected actress. Her discomfort at the objectification of female stars in the construction of motion picture spectacle was a driving force in her career and would shape the trajectory of her next several decades as a multifaceted filmmaker.

Lupino's midlife career change in the 1940s left an indelible mark on motion picture history, as she became the only female director in the immediate postwar era. Her work was animated by themes that have retained their relevance to the present day; chief among them, critiques of American social institutions and inequality, the restrictive limitations of gender roles, the pitfalls of American consumerism, and the role of Hollywood films in obscuring certain lives and perspectives while privileging others.[6] From unwed motherhood in *Not Wanted* (1949), to rape in *Outrage* (1950), family strife in the wake of fame in *Hard, Fast, and Beautiful* (1951), and bigamy in *The Bigamist* (1953), Lupino's early directorial work found companionship in the social problem or "message movie" genre of the day, as she strived to focus her films on lived realities, rather than Hollywood's high gloss. Throughout that work, and into her later directing and her endeavors on television in series such as *Thriller, The Twilight Zone, General Electric Theater*, and numerous others, she proved herself powerful force for relevance, social awareness, and women's place in the film industry.

The chapters in this volume deftly explore Lupino's life and legacy from a wide variety of perspectives and focal points. Phillip Sipiora has carefully crafted an important collection of chapters which, both individually and together, spotlight the complexities of Lupino and her work—from her refusal to conform to industry norms, to her use of complex, intimate narratives, to her precise and highly developed skill as a visual storyteller—examining them in the context of their era, as well as with the benefit of hindsight. Each of the authors approaches Lupino's work with a thoughtfulness that highlights the ways in which it was unique and influential, as well as the ways in which it was a product of the time in which it was produced. Because she was a woman that agitated social and industry norms, of particular interest is the volume's treatment of Lupino's complex relationship with gender roles and related issues such as images of aging, the use of social power, and portrayals of possibility. While Lupino has often been cited as not framing herself or her work as "feminist," she has been co-opted as such. Yet, as several of the volume's chapters illustrate, her life and work transcended such easy definition.

While the conversation around Ida Lupino is far from finished, the chapters that follow provide a valuable and important foundation for understanding and continuing to examine the immeasurable contribution of one of the studio system's most notable and multifaceted figures.

Notes

1. Also, Lois Weber, in the silent era.
2. For an excellent and complex discussion of Lupino's directing career, see Therese Grisham and Julie Grossman's *Ida Lupino, Director: Her Art and Resilience in Times of Transition* (New Brunswick, NJ: Rutgers University Press, 2017).
3. Grisham and Grossman, *Ida Lupino, Director: Her Art and Resilience in Times of Transition*, 158.
4. "Ida Wants to Be Herself," Warner Bros. Studio Publicity Materials, c. 1942. Margaret Herrick Library, Academy of Motion Picture Arts and Sciences, Beverly Hills, CA.
5. Hedda Hopper, "Ida's Ideals," *Chicago Sunday Tribune*, September 4, 1949. Margaret Herrick Library, Academy of Motion Picture Arts and Sciences, Beverly Hills, CA.
6. For a thorough discussion of these themes in Lupino's work, see Grisham and Grossman, *Ida Lupino, Director: Her Art and Resilience in Times of Transition*.

PREFACE

Gary D. Rhodes

The car screeched to halt on the 101. That was when she came up.

Veteran film actor Robert Clarke and I were on the way to the Smoke House, our favorite restaurant in the City of Angels and Traffic Jams. We jabbered incessantly about the old days of Hollywood, but never before about her. Motion to non-motion to emotion.

Bob began talking about Ida Lupino, the actor and filmmaker that Martin Scorsese has rightly called "essential."

My pals Cary and Toby Roan had recently been working with Lupino to secure access to 35mm print material on her unforgettable film *The Hitch-Hiker* (1953). Their company, the Roan Group, undertook the first major restoration of it. I introduced them to Bob, who shared his memories of Lupino in a bonus feature on their laserdisc release.

Onscreen text at the beginning of *The Hitch-Hiker* warns us, "What you will see in the next seventy minutes could have happened to you." And of course, it did, and it does, over and over again. We are trapped there, in Lupino's gloriously frightening, superbly awful, existential nightmare.

In his eulogy for Lupino, Scorsese wrote, "There's a sense of pain, panic, and cruelty that colors every frame."

Barely moving on the freeway, I scanned the scene furtively for suspicious hitchhikers while Bob regaled me with regal stories.

A friend had recommended him to Lupino's production company, The Filmakers, and soon he auditioned for *Outrage* (1950). Bob viewed Lupino as a dramatic personality, akin to Tallulah Bankhead and Bette Davis.

"You're it, dah-ling," she told Bob, hiring him on the spot. He became the second male lead in *Outrage* and subsequently costarred in *Hard, Fast and Beautiful* (1951).

Once filming began, Bob saw Lupino in a new light. Yes, she was glamorous, and yes, she was a great actor, but she was so much more. She focused with precision on all of the performances, treating actors as more important than herself.

Lupino worked directly with Bob, reassuring him that nothing else mattered. Only their work, only his performance. She acted out his role, reading the dialogue as she wanted him to do.

Lupino knew exactly what she wanted, so much so that the cast put her on something of a pedestal, referring to her as "Miss Lupino," Bob recalled, out of respect. And that respect lasted for the rest of his life.

Alas, Robert Clarke, Cary Roan, and Ida Lupino are now deceased.

But never was being trapped in a car more wonderful than hearing Bob's memories of the great director, the "essential" Ida Lupino.

1

Introduction

All Sides of the Camera

Phillip Sipiora

> Ida Lupino is an extremely talented maverick—a situation which has frustrated stereotype-demanding Hollywood.¹

Impact, Reception, and Reputation

This volume has been a nourishing source of inspiration for me, providing insight into Ida Lupino and the film, stage, and television media that she participated in for nearly five decades, and now is an important time to participate in the renaissance of interest in the life and work of Ida Lupino.²

Indeed, Lupino breathed life into every art form that she touched, as the chapters in this collection suggest. Ida Lupino never lost her passion and dedication to artistic performance, beginning when she was entering her teen years in London, the proud daughter of veteran theater and film professionals, Stanley Lupino and Connie Emerald. Ida Lupino was born for cinema, both through the nurturing professional guidance of her parents and for the creative and performative passion that characterized the fiber of her being, bursting forth at a very young age. In 1936, Ida graced the May cover of *True Story* when she was only eighteen years old, yet could reasonably be taken for someone twice her age. This international exposure was a harbinger of things to come (Figure 1.1).

FIGURE 1.1 *Teen idol at eighteen.*

Lupino's first film experience, in a very minor way, was in *The Love Race* (1932), starring her father (Stanley Lupino) and directed by her uncle (Lupino Lane). Her first serious film acting was in *Her First Affaire* (1932) when, amazingly, she was given the role that her mother had auditioned for. This twist of fate was a foreshadowing of the frenzied life that Lupino would lead for so long and in so many ways. In 1934, at the age of sixteen, Lupino made her first American film appearance in *Search for Beauty*. In spite of her early success as an actor, the drive to direct was present from early on, and she reveals her enthusiasm for directing while, still in her twenties, she was quoted in a 1945 fan magazine interview: "I see myself, in the years ahead, directing or producing or both. I see myself developing new talent, which would be furiously interesting for me. For I love talent. Love to watch it. Love to help it. Am more genuinely interested in the talent of others than I am in my own."³ Her subsequent career directing film and television bore out her youthful prediction. Yes, Lupino clearly led a tumultuous, eclectic life, as this volume suggests. There is no question that Lupino could be difficult to work with, as husband Collier Young has noted: "Things aren't normal unless Ida resigns three times on every picture—once before it starts and twice during production."[4] Ida, like many other celebrated directors, could clearly be bossy and unrelenting at times, yet her enthusiasm and dedication to her work, whichever form it took, surely overshadows her idiosyncrasies of personality.

The chapters in this volume are arranged thematically, and, necessarily, there are overlaps and interconnections among the analyses. The first section, **Impact: Reception/Reputation**, provides historical and evaluative context to the career of Ida Lupino, flowing from Martin Scorsese and his moving eulogy of Ida Lupino upon her death in 1995. This tribute, "Behind the Camera: A Feminist," calls attention to Lupino's pioneering work as a director, and Scorsese identifies her directorial production as a "singular achievement in American Cinema."[5] He recounts her cinematic narratives as "intimate, always set within a precise social milieu,"[6] a synoptic, poignant précis encapsulating of the power of her art. She never forgot the importance of "poor bewildered people,"[7] with whom she intimately identified. Further, Scorsese recounts that Lupino never fails to movingly capture the "psyche of the victim"[8] in her special concern for "women trying to wrestle with despair and reclaim their lives."[9] The spirit of the eulogy reminds us that Ida Lupino lived her life explicitly revealing an empathetic tenor, especially in her directorial work, which is the informative architecture for so many of the chapters in this volume.

Karen McNally details, with precision and sentience, Lupino's interest and experience in performance—and the business of show, particularly the importance of supervising the business end of things. This interest is especially apparent in the ways in which Lupino manages Filmakers, the production company that she formed with husband Collier Young. They deliberatively made the decision to aim for independence as they self-distributed *The Bigamist*, resulting in the collapse of their arrangement with Howard Hughes. Two films in Lupino's career take the challenging dynamic of business and performance as a central theme, articulating its oppositions and crossovers within the settings of American popular theater and amateur tennis. Directed by Lupino, *Hard, Fast and Beautiful* is a Filmakers production that explores the encroachment of commercialization on the amateur game of tennis and considers the development of star players through a variation on the stage mother Hollywood narrative. In *The Hard Way* (1943), directed by Vincent Sherman, Lupino plays an ambitious older sister who crafts her sibling's career on the musical stage and, in the process, destruction, death, and career suicide follow. The significance of Lupino's intervention as both director and producer is emphatically clear in a number of ways that articulate the business/creative dynamic that

Lupino continually negotiates as a filmmaker. Ida Lupino's mercurial career demonstrates an explicit intent to promote creative over economic priorities in an often-controlling industry.

William T. Ross offers a probing discussion of the critical moments and stages in Lupino's career in his detailed analysis of the formative changes that took place over half a century. Ross deftly examines issues of family legacy, Hollywood context, gender, and strategic career challenges, including a strong streak of independence and he articulates, with careful precision, Lupino's original contributions that expanded the boundaries of cinema, as so often illustrated by her ability to personally negotiate artistic limits. Ross chronicles Lupino's transition to television directing and her history of success in a medium that was experiencing growing pains in the 1950s and 1960s. Ross crystalizes her complex life with simplicity: Ida Lupino of Hollywood led a life worthy of respect, admiration, and study.

Courtney Ruffner Grieneisen chronicles the qualities that made Ida Lupino essential in film history as she fervidly followed her own set of rules, especially character transcendence, tenderness of subject matter, and equity of gender. Lupino's intimate, precise use of the camera, seductively drew viewers into her films, often becoming emotionally and morally invested, particularly in films like *On Dangerous Ground*. Characters like Jim Wilson are softened by his preoccupation with inhumanity and his genuine care for others. Further, Lupino shapes the way that the characters of Jim and Mary stand equal to one another as gender representations. In short, the use of the handheld camera, employing medium and close-up shots, and the equality of gender with sexualized scenes are only a few of Lupino's masterful touches that help to create a place in the story line where the viewer is seamlessly able to escape reality and become one with the character(s) (Figure 1.2).

Culture and Gender, Aging, Acting, Performance

Julie Grossman introduces readers to a diverse series of readings of Lupino's artistry that reframe her work within a contemporary context by focusing on the ways in which Lupino captures the brutality of social conformity and the alienation of those who stand apart from mainstream culture. In particular, these motifs are revealed through Lupino's analysis of gender trauma and the failed institution of family, both symptoms of the breakdown of social roles in postwar America. One film, in particular, addresses the social context of repression: In *Not Wanted*, Lupino establishes what would throughout her career be her authorial stamp: a thoroughgoing critique of imprisoning social and familial roles and a noir representation of the bleak prospects for happiness for men and women in modern America. The American

FIGURE 1.2 *Ida as early performer.*

dream is not what it promises to be in the works of Lupino and gender and family roles are presciently portrayed as distortions of conventional ideals. (It should be noted Julie Grossman and Therese Grisham have coauthored a superb volume that examines Lupino's directorial work: *Ida Lupino, Director: Her Art and Resilience in Times of Transition*, Rutgers UP, 2017.)

Marlisa Santos explores the challenges and complications facing Lupino as she addresses issues of gender in an increasingly complex world. More specifically, Santos analyzes how Lupino interrogates complex narratives in which characters are caught in various traps of contemporary gender ideology: male husband as provider, female wife as homemaker and mother, and female mistress as seductive siren. In *The Bigamist*, for example, the weaknesses and foibles of bigamist Harry are also the deficiencies of Eve and Phyllis, as all of them are culpable in the eventual multi-marriage mess in which they find themselves. Santos sees Lupino as a humanist, rather than solely a feminist, and her films affirm her efforts to reveal the foibles and challenges of characters in a changing world, regardless of gender. In her treatment of *Outrage*, Santos explores the uncanny display of the familiar becoming the unfamiliar as it gains force with the actual sexual assault of Ann Walton, victim and main character, resulting in a damaged psyche that remains unhealed. Lupino's desire to show the complexity of human emotion is never oversimplified in this complex film. Santos continues to explore these intertwined representations of gender and conflict in several television episodes directed by Lupino (Figure 1.3).

Michael Shuman keenly examines *The Bigamist*, as a legacy of film noir, in arguing that Lupino, as actor and director, complicates the noir landscape further by introducing a distinctively feminine perspective into a genre of film otherwise universally dominated by a masculine creative vision. *The Bigamist* is a film about gender identity, loneliness, and infidelity, which immediately follows *The Hitch-Hiker*, an exemplary representative of Hollywood film noir. Lupino, while adopting oblique camera angles, brooding sensibility, and a persistent feeling of impending tragedy in *The Bigamist*, imports the style and conventions of film noir into a different context, thus illuminating her "softer" social concerns through techniques already familiar to the moviegoing audience. Barriers of space and characters, Lupino suggest, are never secure, whether physical, psychological, or emotional, and the sanctity of personal space is a fabrication we enjoy in an attempt to protect our individuality. Lupino's refusal to provide thematic and narrative closure both emphasize the moral uncertainties of *The Bigamist's* plot and further define her status as an outlying filmmaker in a Hollywood predicated on niche markets, proven narrative formulas, and powerful advertising rhetoric.

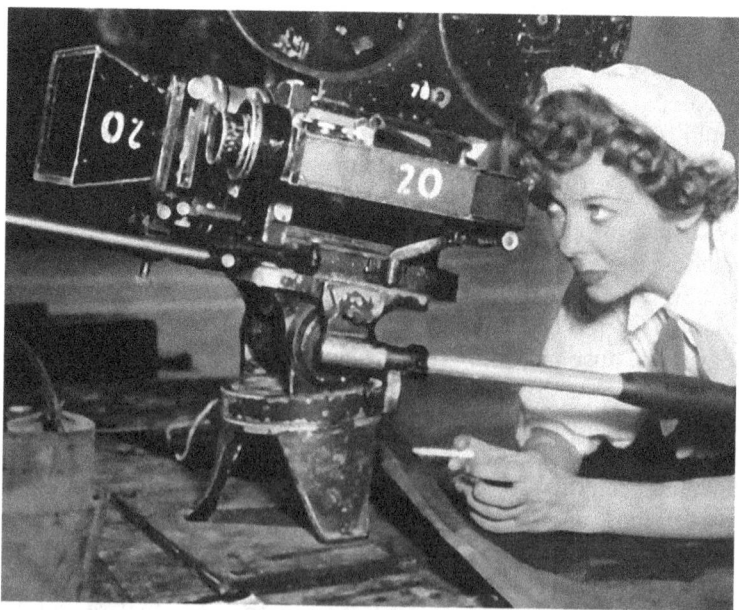

FIGURE 1.3 *Lupino directing* The Hitch-Hiker.

Ashley M. Donnelly argues that *The Bigamist* is *not* a conventional film. This film, influenced heavily by both noir and neorealism, is an intricate, subtle, and well-crafted work of art that exemplifies Lupino's stylistic integrity as a director and her unique way of presenting moral subjects. *The Bigamist*, Donnelly suggests, is heavily influenced by Italian neorealism and is not representative of American noir. Lupino's vision and distinct visual style are two critical reasons for this assessment. Although the tone of *The Bigamist* is dark, the film itself is not. There is significantly more natural and produced lighting in it than in standard film noir. The excessive use of shadow is avoided, and, notably, there is no femme fatale (as is the case in *The Hitch-Hiker*). There are several distinctive characteristics of Lupino's directorial and acting skills: her use of crossed lines and/or patterned backgrounds, her linear narration and linear character motion, and her careful control of actors' proxemics and body language. The entire film is a linear story of the past until the very end, when the audience watches Harry face the grim consequences of his double life. Mirroring the linear style of the script, Lupino shoots the film in a linear manner. Reminiscent of Italian neorealism, which depends on location shooting, natural lighting, long shots, use of nonprofessional actors, and scenes emphasizing the uglier side of Italy's glamor after the Second World War, *The Bigamist*, while employing professionals and light kits, does employ long shots to emphasize atmosphere and place. *The Bigamist* is arguably a beautiful, touching movie. Her treatment of both men and women in the film brings forth a world that seems so real, so normal, and so humane that condemnation is lost within the narrative she shoots, and human concern flourishes instead. Lupino's cinemagraphic emphasis on broken lines, obscured blocks, and disrupted parallels is also evident throughout *The Trouble with Angels*, which raises such questions as the following: How can women change the world working within undeniable patriarchy? How can they "fix" things without abandoning tradition? These questions are, once again, large, difficult to answer, and are ultimately left to the resolution of the audience.

Valerie Barnes Lipscomb sentiently probes the issue of age stereotypes in her analysis. In films such as *Outrage*, *The Hitch-Hiker*, *The Bigamist*, and *Hard, Fast and Beautiful*, Lupino does not challenge stereotypical portrayals of age. Rather, these works from the Filmakers (a production company formed by Lupino and her husband Collier Young) skilfully illustrates conventions of age performance that leads to a heightened cinematic effect. As a director, Lupino always assumed the stance of an older woman, someone who could mother the cast and crew. It was not for nothing that Ida, as Director, was often indentified under the rubric of Mother in more than one metaphor, a tribute to her powerful, "in control," yet simultaneously nurturing sensibility, which revealed her complex cinematic sensibility. Hence her nickname on set: "Mother" and "the female-Hitch." And "Mother of Us All" was embroidered on the back of her director's chair. Lupino's characters encounter traditional cultural authority figures, particularly in the more melodramatic films *Outrage*

(1950) and *The Bigamist* (1953), which include, respectively, an older doctor who cares for Phyllis during her pregnancy and a judge who has the last say regarding the legality and morality of Harry Graham's bigamy. To the societal authority conferred upon figures such as doctors and judges, Lupino adds the authority of age. In these instances, authority is associated with males at the height of their professional and earning power, which typically occurs toward the end of middle age. By the same token, the San Francisco adoption agency administrator in *The Bigamist*, Mr. Jordan, appears to be nearing the Third Age threshold (nearing retirement), and he clearly wields power over the lives of the late thirty-something Grahams. This narrative structure calls for an age-casting approach that differs from the doctors and judges who are simply the voices of authority and social convention in Lupino's films. In *Outrage*, Ann Walton at twenty is becoming engaged, indicating that this film could ultimately follow the arc of a traditional female Bildungsroman, ending in marriage. Similarly, Florence Farley is just out of high school and meets an eligible young man early in *Hard, Fast and Beautiful* (1951); hence, the audience might reasonably expect another female coming-of-age plot. Each film focuses on a young woman's innocence at the beginning, which it contrasts with increased maturity by the narrative's end, even if the woman has not realized full assimilation into adult society. Lupino carefully employs age conventions to illustrate how characters progress toward the Second Age (independence, maturity, and responsibility). The audience is allowed to envision a typical mid-century happy ending, although the films themselves do not provide that neatly tied denouement. Lupino's films make use of all the stereotypes of age across the continuum from younger to older, rather than challenging those perceptions. Young women start as naïfs who need shepherding, often by paternally oriented men, while older men are authority figures who represent social norms. Critics tend to overlook or silently accept such portrayals, as age has been the last of the "identity" categories to garner critical attention in the humanities.

Curtis Le Van explores the acting of Ida Lupino, as revealed by patterns emerging not only through overall performances, but also within specific contexts. Three roles played by Lupino, each in a different decade, illustrate her acting in relation to the situations' contextualizing production. These circumstances involve numerous dimensions of cinema, including legal requirements and studio traditions. Lupino's early work in English film provides the grounds for understanding her later work in America during the Golden Age of Hollywood. Later, her performances were informed by the rise of method acting and its influence on presentation. In the early 1930s, *The Ghost Camera* (1933) demonstrates two dominant active narratives: the film was shot quickly and clearly exhibits English life and popular tastes in comedy. Further, the film is remarkably self-aware, with characters commenting routinely on melodrama (or genre in general), filmmaking and tastes in film, and even the issue of "haste." These combined components point to a film that made use of character roles, a practice not uncommon in 1930s England, and the role of Mary (Lupino) is no exception. Lupino always has her eyes wide open and speaks only in the upper register of her voice. She is young in this film, but her character demands a particularly overt depiction of innocence. She is courteous, proper, and not without an explicit appearance of sensuality. Lupino's acting, which was not overly dynamic, substantially contributes to the overall artistry and disposition of the film. Lupino's acting in the Golden Age reveals a rich, intense character portrait as Marie in *High Sierra* (1941). Lupino distinguishes herself revealing the principles and manifestations of method acting in her 1954 film *Private Hell 36*, a crime drama that relies on hidden motives and emphatic secrecy for its narrative trajectory. Lupino's performance, not unlike a police officer engaging in detection, construes meaning in other characters' words and motions, responding appropriately as dictated by the exigencies of immediate circumstances.

Breaking New Ground

Mary Lynn Navarro examines the challenging context(s) of women breaking into the men's club of Hollywood directors, past and present. As the owner of her own production company in the 1940s, Lupino's subsequent transition to television direction extended her talent, for in television her career spanned decades and contributed to a variety of shows such as *The Twilight Zone, Alfred Hitchcock Presents, The Fugitive,* and *Bewitched*. Although she blazed a trail, Lupino garnered critical acclaim mostly in retrospect (sadly). Navarro critiques Lupino's work by using the concept of "double-consciousness" to examine how Lupino's films both mask and reveal constructs that go against the standard Hollywood grain, defy conventional expectations yet also invoke societal mores and values. Her characters, plotlines, and various realities frame the cultural moment but also distinguish a break from the "ordinary," and one may question whether her unique talent can be measured by her groundbreaking work as a woman. Navarro analyzes *The Hitch-Hiker, The Bigamist,* and The *Twilight Zone* episode of "The Masks" (1964) to advance the argument that Lupino transcends being pigeonholed into a category of "feminist director" to emerge as a strong female director.

Kathleen "Kat" Robinson argues that, many decades earlier, the culture and times were ready for a film about rape, and Ida Lupino exposes the risk that she made to direct such a film. In the face of production codes, cultural insecurities, and gendered thoughts on feminine roles, Lupino asserts a stance in her film that provides a basis for conversation and discussion. The representations and portrayals in *Outrage* attempt to capture and portray a sense of trauma's effect on the film's narrative structure. Further, the film also captures and presents insightful commentary on trauma and rape. However, one of the more salient observations connected to the film is the impulse to examine how this narrative functions cinematically from the feminine perspective provided by Lupino, instead of a more traditional masculine perspective, often privileged, crafted, and presented in cinematic narrative. This privileging of message is yet another illustration of the dominant male narrative that structures and reinforces a misguided understanding of rape. However, Lupino's work refuses to justify this gendered presupposition, and her 1950 film is sadly overlooked due to its common branding as simple melodrama or an attempt at film noir. Yet, the film examines not only the violent rape but also the subsequent wrestling with the pain of that rape by the main character, Ann Walton. Her traumatic presence in the film confounds and confronts an existing narrative that cannot handle the rupture and rapture caused by the act of rape, anymore than it can handle the agency or victimization that will disrupt the societal, ontological network in the film. The narrative presentation of Ann's involvement with her memory of the rape trauma illustrates how the abject experience of trauma contributes to the altered representation of space and time expressed in the film. Lupino interrogates and integrates trauma in her films, and the subsequent evolution(s) in her narrative structures reflect the experiences and effects of trauma. In many Lupino films, the narrative structure offers an opportunity to capture and to explore the witnessing of the experience and effects of trauma. Lupino's narrative evolution uses elements of trauma to reflect on a range of motifs, while simultaneously creating a fiction that captures the external and internal experience of coming to terms with the trauma of rape. *Outrage* is infuriating, haunting, and demanding of attention as Lupino addresses elements of trauma's effect on the narrative structure, yet in such a unique yet applicable fashion that the film emphatically stands as a solid example that deserves reconsideration and, most definitely, reevaluation.

In an examination of phenomenological moments and movements in *The Hitch-Hiker*, **Phillip Sipiora** explores phenomenology as a strategic part of exploring what it means to probe the human experience in relation to other human experiences, what it means, fundamentally, to be human. Lupino understands this complex matrix of existential angst and her exposition of this phenomenon is an essential part of her film *oeuvre*, particularly in her darkest film. Lupino's shots of displacement and disjuncture are potent metaphors at work that convey violence more violent than if viewers viewed complete gore-laden bloody bodies. These teaser tastes are not original with Lupino, of course, but they do demonstrate her sense of irony and powerfully intense visual metaphor. The film is structured on a matrix of phenomenological dependencies. Myers depends on Gil and Roy, captured good citizens, and they codepend on him (and each other), all for the same reason: they desperately need one other to stay alive. Codependency is one of the film's driving motifs and plot segmentation is relatively simple in the diurnal experiences of captor and captives. The deep structure of the film reveals a complexity more interwoven and philosophical than superficial, storyboard representations. Film subjectivity is always a complex issue, and in *The Hitch-Hiker* (as well as in *Outrage* and *The Bigamist*) Lupino surgically probes fundamental issues of agency, intersubjectivity, and the ways in which they interrelate to call to attention two fundamental interpretive questions: How does one learn from experience and how does one act based on acquired knowledge? Gil and Roy's ordeal is an illustration of how their collective, exploratory responses to the sociopathy of Myers transform them individually as well as their relationship to each other. Lupino deftly presents their analytical and interpretive experiences in a series of scenes demonstrating her rich cinematic powers, which lead viewers to salient interpretive inferences. Hence, *The Hitch-Hiker* chronicles a loss of ethical values, but also depicts the reclamation of those values precisely through narrative encounters, lending to the illustration of tangible ethics as a direct result of cinematic engagement on a personal level between and among characters.

Television Directing

Ann Torrusio examines Ida Lupino as a director who has received limited serious critical attention, and her neglect from scholars has, in part, been due to her inability to fit within a feminist framework. Torrusio examines the made-for-television mysteries Lupino directed from the early 1960s, including "Sybilla" (1960) from *Alfred Hitchcock Presents*, "Trio for Terror" (1961) from the *Thriller* series, and "The Masks" (1964) from *The Twilight Zone*, all of which demonstrate a preoccupation with the unsolicited—even abject—aspects of inheritance. A conflict that can be negotiated but never fully resolved, the question of ambivalent inheritance depicted in Lupino's television mysteries reflects a postwar ideological tension over gender norms and Lupino's position as the first female director during the formative years of American television who resisted the frames of a feminist agenda. Lupino's television directing is a rich source to explore her rich breadth and depth of talent.

Adam Breckenridge begins by noting that if we plumb the depths of her television work, we find that Lupino did much of her best work in this medium. Her television directing is clearly an extension of the motifs and style that she explored in her film work, especially when we bear in mind that Lupino was free to choose which scripts and shows that she directed. Therefore, she was free to choose scripts that explored ideas that were of strong interest to her, which makes it much easier to argue for her television work as an extension of themes and motifs explored in her cinema. Lupino deserves serious commendation for the remarkable variety of her television work as she was involved in directing dozens of shows that span many genres, including Westerns, sitcoms, horror/suspense, crime/gangster, detective shows, medical dramas, and historical adventures. Further, Lupino directed a number of "teleplay" shows such as *Screen Director's Playhouse*, *Climax!*, *General Electric Theater*, *Kraft Suspense Theater*, and *Bob Hope Presents the Chrysler Theater*. Two of the principal reasons Lupino's directing work has been neglected stem from the ironic conjunction of sexism and feminism. To Lupino's credit, there is still a clear streak in her television work of choosing scripts that challenged gender stereotypes, at least for their time (which may not all seem quite so progressive now). *Honey West* (1965–66) is the only female-led show she worked on that was not a sitcom (sitcoms, of course, often advocate for the domesticity of women). *Honey West* is a detective show with something of a *Mission Impossible* perspective (high-tech gadgets are a key element), with the titular character working as the head of the organization with mostly men working for her. To see women working in such positions of power was rare in the popular entertainment of this time, but Honey West (Anne Francis) is also smart, resourceful, and usually the one having to rescue her male employees. In the context of the mid-1960s, the show is positively progressive. Thus, a strong case can made for viewing Lupino's television production as an extension of her film work and, therefore, an important key to understanding Lupino's interests and motivations as a director.

Fernando Gabriel Pagnoni Berns examines representations of women in Lupino's television episodes according to common stereotypes in the culture at that time. A primary concern is the issue of subjectivity and self-determination; in these series there is an emphasis on the displacement of characters from the binary categories of good woman/bad woman that patriarchy had forced upon society and the masculine/feminine distinction that feminism, as an intellectual movement, attempts to challenge. Lupino directed nine episodes of the *Thriller* series in the early 1960s, and six of them are analyzed closely for depictions of aggressive and sexuality-charged women in comparison to other episodes that focus on more passive women. In addition, while many of the Lupino-directed episodes of *Thriller* are concerned with female sexual deviance as monstrous, subversive to a patriarchal social order, other episodes focus on a more literal representation of monsters, an extension of the popular horror film motifs of the mid-twentieth century. Lupino delivers an imposing challenge to women of her era: either demonstrate self-determination and confidence in all thought and action or prepare to be labeled as a social outcast subject to emotional marginalization and physical outrage. In "The Closed Cabinet" (1961), arguably one of her more feminist episodes, Lupino features Evie, a female character who is both strong-willed and decidedly princess-pure. Evie emerges as a sympathetic character and communicates Lupino's vision of strong womanhood most effectively to an audience accustomed to uncomplicated messages in popular culture.

This volume is directed toward those readers and viewers who have an interest in the directorial and acting work of Ida Lupino, as well as scholars of Ida Lupino in particular and cinema in general, as exemplified in the publication of *Ida Lupino: Her Art and Resilience in Times of Transition* as well as the release of Lupino films on Blu-Ray, such as Nicholas Ray's *On Dangerous Ground* in 2019. (Anecdotally, Lupino is sometimes noted as an uncredited codirector of *On Dangerous Ground*). We have attempted to gather together a diverse assembly of probing and discerning interpretations of Lupino's inspirational, pioneering work in film and television. This experience has been particularly rewarding for me because Ida Lupino has so much to tell us about gender, ethics, relationships, responsibilities, and the constant human challenge to learn how to lead our lives in a more meaningful way. No filmmaker can ever answer the eternal question of "how to be," but surely there are deep, complex insights in the films of Ida Lupino that may help us to more closely interrogate ourselves and the world around us in our struggle to perceive "the challenge of being" with compassion and understanding.

Notes

1. James Robert Parish and Don E. Stanke, *The Forties Gals* (Westport, CT: Arlington House, 1980), 132.
2. In diverse ways, the legacy of Ida Lupino is bursting with enthusiasm, judging by recent scholarship devoted to Lupino's life and work, including the recently published strikingly original, impressively analytical volume, *Ida Lupino: Her Art and Resilience in Times of Transition* by Therese Grisham and Julie Grossman (New Brunswick: Rutgers University Press, 2017).
3. Qtd. in Christoph Huber. Available at http://cinema-scope.com/features/mother-of-all-of-us-ida-lupino-the-filmaker (accessed August 16, 2017).
4. Gladwin Hill, "Hollywood's Beautiful Bulldozer," *Collier's*, May 12, 1951, 77.
5. Martin Scorsese, "Behind the Camera: A Feminist." *The New York Times*, December 31, 1995, 43.
6. Ibid., 43.
7. Ibid., 43.
8. Ibid., 43.
9. Ibid., 43.

2

Beyond the Performance

Ida Lupino, American Stages, and the Business of Show

Karen McNally

Ida Lupino's wide-ranging career, which combines directing with screen performances and film production, film with television, and studio contracts with independent filmmaking, illuminates essential ideas of creativity, performance, stardom, and the business of show business that are often simultaneously represented within the narratives of her work. Lupino's various statements regarding professional independence and creativity attest to the ways in which she sought to define her career. Her refusal to renew the contract she signed with Paramount in 1933 due to a dissatisfaction with roles, and her subsequent agreement with Warner Bros. in 1940 to sign a one-year rather than seven-year contract, allowing Lupino to continue working elsewhere, indicates a determination to maintain a creative and professional distance from the business of the major studios. Lupino's regular refusal of particular roles while under contract underlines the notion that, as Marsha Orgeron contends, "From the beginning, hers was a directorial impulse, even in relation to her attempts to control her own reputation as an actress."[1] At the same time, the routes Lupino took in seeking professional control, as both star and director, and studio employee and independent filmmaker denote the kind of consistent negotiation between performance/performer and business/industry evident also as a thematic concern.

Lupino was hardly alone in attempting to navigate this essential Hollywood dynamic, from stars' struggles to assert creative choices under the tight controls of long-term studio contracts, to the achievement of increasing independence through the establishment of production companies that challenged the major studios' industry dominance. The 1948 Supreme Court Paramount Decision, which required that the Big Five studios divest themselves of the exhibition arm of their businesses, combined with the studios' increasingly precarious financial position and the consequent departure from the strategy of long-term contracts to open up a more viable space for both independent production and stars' control of their careers. Kirk Douglas' Bryna Productions and Burt Lancaster's Hill-Hecht-Lancaster, in which the star collaborated with agent Harold Hecht and producer James Hill, are among the best-known examples of the star-led production companies created out of this opportune set of circumstances. In 1949, Lupino formed Emerald Productions, named after her mother, actress Connie Emerald, with husband and production executive Collier Young and producer Anson Bond. The departure of Bond and entrance of screenwriter Malvin Wald initiated both the era of The Filmakers (1949–53) and Lupino's formal directing career.[2] As Dan Georgakas explains:

> They emphasized their desire to make substantial films of a sociological nature that challenged contemporary norms without being preachy. *What* was in a film was thought to be more important than *who* was in the film. Thus, rather than relying on the existing star system, they would develop new acting talent. Lupino often referred to her films as being documentary in nature.[3]

This narrative of distinction from the business-driven operations of the studios and big business underpins much of Lupino's commentary concerning the Filmakers' history. Lupino consistently denied any active ambition to direct. In relating to Hedda Hopper the path to her first formal directing role, The Filmakers' first official production *Never Fear* (1949), Lupino posited this as a choice between stardom under the control of a major studio, 20th Century Fox, and creative freedom through her independent production company: "The money men said they wouldn't finance our second picture unless I directed it. Now I'm faced with whether I'll sign with Zanuck as an actress—or direct. I decided to go independent. I decided I didn't want to be a movie star—with all it entails—and live that way."[4] Even a positive creative decision to direct, Lupino suggests, is instigated by the controlling strategies of business. Lupino went further in distinguishing creativity from business when explaining the ultimate demise of The Filmakers project. Following *Never Fear*, the partners agreed a distribution deal with Howard Hughes whereby RKO would additionally finance their next three films to the tune of $250,000 while The Filmakers retained creative control.[5] While *Outrage* (1950) and *Hard, Fast and Beautiful* (1951) were produced and distributed under this agreement, The Filmakers took the decision to aim for additional independence and self-distribute *The Bigamist* (1953), resulting in the collapse of their deal with Hughes and contributing to the financial failure of the film and ultimately the company. Tellingly, in her 1967 article for *Action*, the in-house magazine of the Directors' Guild of America, Lupino related these events in terms which distanced her from the business decision which secured the fate of The Filmakers: "We got talked into going into the distribution business. I opposed the move every step of the way. 'We're creative people, we're picture makers,' I argued. 'We know nothing about distribution. Let's stay away from it.' But I was outvoted and pretty soon we were out of business."[6] Through this narrative, Lupino explicitly expresses the creative function of the company in opposition to a disruptive notion of business. Moreover, by outlining her opposition to The Filmakers' decision, Lupino clarifies her creative role, insisting further upon the transparency of a creative/commercial divide.

Backstage Revealed

The kind of distinctions between business and the creative evident in Lupino's remarks are apparent in a number of her films as both star and director, as the narratives work through the troublesome dynamic of business and show and its essential intersections. Often depicting a contrast between the cold ambition and immorality of the backstage business and the manipulated performer in its grasp, the films still present this notion with ambivalence, through weary noir chanteuses and stars of the stage and sporting world whose own sins are not entirely displaced onto the narratives' industry representatives. While the narratives as played out ultimately maintain a separation of business and performance, depicting the former as a destructive force, the fluid imaging of ambition and unethical behavior prevents too stark a line being drawn between the performer and the ways and means of the backstage characters. *The Man I Love* (1947) and *Road House* (1948) both exemplify the obsession of film noir with the dark hinterland of American entertainment. Sexual exploitation and violence are the markers of the business, and Lupino's chanteuses demonstrate the cycle's concern with moral ambiguity. Her straight-talking singers move freely between front of stage and back, but ultimately their cynical edges earned through repeated experience of the backstage world are classically a mask for an essential vulnerability and higher moral aspirations.

The Big Knife (1955) focuses on Hollywood during its period of decline following the Paramount Decision, becoming one of a number of films of the postwar period which explored the workings of the movie industry through both explicit critique and nostalgia for a studio system in the throes of change. *Sunset Boulevard* (1950), *The Bad and the Beautiful* (1951), and *Two Weeks in Another Town* (1962) each depicts filmmaking as a cold and ruthless business while simultaneously celebrating Hollywood's creativity and excesses. In *The Bad and the Beautiful*, the relentless drive of producer Jonathan Shields (Kirk Douglas) is seen to result in the theft of his director's screenplay, the broken heart of his movie's star, and the death of the wife of an author writing a screenplay adaptation. Despite this narrative depiction of the negative results of single-minded ambition, the representation of Shields as the charismatic creative force behind his movies links the creative and financial, and points to a wistful nostalgia for the industry's powerhouse individuals. As James Naremore explains, "*The Bad and the Beautiful* was a film about the tawdry absurdities and operatic splendours of a strangely admirable industry. Thus in the completed picture, the characters are less like Hollywood sharpies and more like frustrated dreamers, yearning for art, glamour, and sophistication. Sometimes they actually achieve moments of transforming intensity by working in Tinseltown."[7] *The Big Knife* contrastingly is bereft of nostalgia, drawing a distinct line between the artistry of those with directing or acting skills and the bald financial agenda of the studio head. The film's narrative depicts the internal struggle of Hollywood star Charlie Castle, played by Jack Palance, as he attempts to assert his independence from studio boss Stanley Hoff (Rod Steiger) and refuse another seven-year contract. Hoff's physical brutality and propensity for blackmail, the pimping of starlets like Shelley Winters' Dixie Evans, and even murder are unsuccessfully masked by manicured nails and his famed Mayer-style tearful conversations with his stars. Charlie's resistance therefore becomes futile, as he comes to recognize that the studio's cover-up of his hit-and-run accident that saw a studio employee serve jail time for him has left him a puppet of the unethical and illegal business practices of Hoff. Charlie is described in the opening narration as "a man who sold out his dreams, but he can't forget them," and it is his desire for creative control which drives his struggle for independence. As the star of swords and sandals epics and boxing movies, Charlie's value to the studio is as a physical object, emphasized by images of him trading punches with his trainer or laid out for a massage.

His attempt to rediscover his lost dreams of creativity is encouraged by his estranged wife Marion, played by Lupino, who acts to voice the film's critique of the business of show. When Marion suggests that Charlie leave Hollywood and find roles on television or in the theater, Charlie counters that he could wait years for a decent role in the theater: "And anyhow, what is all this, this, this arty buck. You know that this, this industry is capable of turning out good pictures, pictures with guts and meaning." Charlie's championing of Hollywood's filmmaking artistry is acknowledged by Marion but only via its creative personnel, as she cites a list of directors including Stevens, Mankiewicz, Kazan, Huston, Wyler, and Kramer in Hollywood's defense. Her insistence that producer Stanley Hoff is incapable of a similar artistic role reinforces the narrative's essential industrial division between the financial and the creative. Marion is ready and able to express her distaste for the representatives of the industry, like Hedda Hopper-style gossip columnist Patty Benedict, who questions Marion on the couple's sleeping arrangements and is bluntly told, "I'm the one in this town who's not afraid to tell you to mind your own business." When Hoff attempts to deny any plot to murder starlet Dixie, claiming to be "a simple man," Marion diffuses his power and false humility, asking him, "Mr Hoff, can't you stop talking about yourself?" Ultimately, however, the business forces that have been depicted throughout as cruel, manipulative and violent win out, when the film concludes with the knife-slashing suicide of the powerless and creatively stifled star.

Attempted Displacement in *The Hard Way* (1943)

Two films in Lupino's career take the challenging dynamic of business and performance as their central theme, articulating its oppositions and crossovers within the settings of American popular theater and amateur tennis. Directed by Lupino, *Hard, Fast and Beautiful* is a Filmakers' production that explores the encroachment of commercialization on the amateur game and considers the development of star players through a variation on the stage mother Hollywood narrative. In *The Hard Way*, directed by Vincent Sherman, Lupino plays an ambitious older sister crafting her sibling's career on the musical stage as in the process relationship destruction, death and career suicide follow. In the latter film, narrative depictions of star ambition mitigate against the sharper distinctions between industry and performer that are at work in *The Big Knife*. *The Hard Way*'s essentially family tale means these harsh dividing lines are less easily drawn as the narrative proceeds through the sisters' close relationship rather than through the disconnections of industry figure and star. It is, in turn, through a suggested distortion of the family relationship that the film targets a more conflicted and gender-specific critique of the entertainment business.

The film's opening credit sequence points to both the specificities of the critique and its blurred character boundaries, showing the image of a headless torso of a bejewelled woman in evening dress and furs, suggestive of the monetary ambitions of either sister in the narrative that follows. As Jeanine Basinger points out, the following scene can be likened to the beginnings of the later *Mildred Pierce* (1945), which similarly depicts a fur-coated woman by the dockside whose suicide attempt is halted by a policeman, although Lupino's character goes further by jumping into the water.[8] In the same way, this scene becomes the catalyst for the film's flashback framework and for Helen Chernen's (Lupino) voice-over narration, which immediately establishes a narrative of escape that, in comparison with Mildred's, is explicitly more class than gender-based. While Mildred explains her feeling of having "been born in a kitchen and lived there all my life," Helen's voice-over is accompanied by images of slagheaps and factories billowing smoke as she relates a mining town's frustration: "Many of us had dreams of a different life, a better life, but what could we do? Not even the sun could break through that prison of smoke and grime." Helen has already made one unsuccessful attempt to leave, as we learn from her husband Sam, whose contrasting passivity can be likened to that of Mildred's first husband, Bert. The voice-over and early scenes set the characterization of Helen apart from that of Mildred, immediately outlining her personal desires rather than attaching them solely to her aspirations for her sister. Therefore, while Mildred carves out a career in order to provide daughter Veda with the lifestyle she covets, Helen is immediately established as a character with personal ambitions who makes use of sister Katherine "Katie" Blaine's (Joan Leslie) pretensions to the stage to secure an escape route for them both.

The Hard Way follows sisters Helen and Katie as they move beyond small-town America through Vaudeville to success on the New York stage. Bumping into a Vaudeville act, Runkel and Collins, after their show at a local theater on the night of her high school graduation, Katie convinces Albert Runkel (Jack Carson) of her promising talent. After Helen intervenes to arrange both an engagement and Katie's place in the act, the sisters skip town and go on the road where Runkel, Collins & Company soon becomes Runkel and Runkel. Led by her sister, Katie moves on to solo stardom as a musical comedy star on Broadway, along the way discarding her husband who resorts to suicide. Katie eventually turns on her sister when Helen moves from manager to producer, steering an exhausted Katie toward a new future in drama and away from the marriage proposal of Albert's ex-partner, Paul Collins (Dennis Morgan). The loss of her sister leads Helen to the dock and the hospital bed where the film began and where she passes away in the closing scene.

The depiction of Helen's determined guidance of Katie's career, while constructed as a sibling tale, positions the film alongside Hollywood's stage mother sagas, from baldly titled *Stage Mother* (1933), to *I'll Cry Tomorrow* (1955) and *Gypsy* (1962). According to Vincent Sherman, the story was loosely based on the biography of Ginger Rogers and her mother Lela, who famously managed her daughter's acting career. The film even cheekily alludes to this reference point when, at their first encounter, Albert tells Katie that she reminds him of a young Ginger Rogers. Rogers' first husband, in addition, was a Vaudeville performer whose career faded after their marriage and who reportedly attempted suicide following their divorce. This real-life framework appears to have been acknowledged by Rogers herself, who was offered the lead by producer Jerry Wald but refused it, commenting, "This could be the story of my life."[9] Each of the stage mother films presents the relationship between performer and manager/unofficial adviser as a conflicted one, defined by the problematic combination of a business and personal relationship and the performer's ultimate desire to free herself (since it is invariably a female character) from her mother's control over her career and private life. In the mentioned examples, the mother character is depicted as a destructive influence whose ambition and lack of interest in the mother-daughter relationship (or even, initially, in her less favored daughter's career in *Gypsy*) impacts negatively on her blameless daughter's life, for example through alcoholism in *I'll Cry Tomorrow* or a decadent lifestyle and career as a stripper in *Gypsy*. *The Hard Way* bears a similarity to these films in its representation of the damaging results of Helen's calculating mastery of Katie's career. The film refrains, however, from absolving Katie of responsibility for her own demise, suggesting instead the essential connectedness of the business and performance of American entertainment.

Helen, as Katie's manager, is the film's central representation of the deal-making business of show, Lupino's lead role emphasizing its prominence as a theme. The image of a cold and aggressive business that the film presents through Helen comes through her activities in pursuance of Katie's career. The apparent ease with which she leaves her husband, her readiness to see Katie marry Albert as "a meal ticket" (having previously warned her sister off early marriage), pushing Paul then Albert out of the act, coercing an obviously unwilling Katie into legitimate drama, all together casts Helen in a harsh light.

Probably the most unpalatable episode occurs when Helen encourages the fading star of Katie's first solo show to become intoxicated, thereby moving her sister from the chorus to a starring role. In fact, the pitiless nature of the business is most consistently attributed to Helen as its narrative representative, even where other characters lead the events. Producer Jack Shagrue (Paul Cavanagh) proposes breaking up Runkel and Runkel to put Katie in the chorus of the aforementioned revue, and later drops musical star Katie from his Broadway drama, but in both situations it is left to Helen to deliver the news, associating her rather than Shagrue with the cold detachment of business. There is more than a tinge of gendered critique in the depiction of Helen's single-minded ambition for Katie and herself, but equally a class-based disapproval, so that Helen's desperation to escape a life of drudgery and coal dust forms the background to the explicit portrayal of business efficiency in these scenes. In contrast, Shagrue's middle-class refinement, to which Helen aspires, means that his business decisions are articulated behind closed doors or seem forced upon a sentimental business by Helen's overreaching for Katie's career. As he explains to Helen in dismissing Katie from her planned dramatic role: "Helen, let's face it, she just can't do the part. I don't want to be cruel about it. I'm crazy about Katie, but I've got a play to produce, and I just can't do it with her in the lead. I'm too good a businessman." Even playwright Laura Britton (Leona Maricle), who combines middle-class artistic credentials with business capability, and with whom Helen subsequently coproduces the play in which Katie will star following Shagrue's departure, turns on her when Katie collapses with exhaustion, accusing Helen of the calculating exploitation of her sister. Unlike Vincente Minnelli's Jonathan Shields, whose creative genius becomes the means through which all is forgiven, Helen remains distinguished from the artistic, whether through failing to recognize that Runkel and Runkel's act is too vaudeville for a supper club or trying to shoehorn Katie as a musical comedy star into a dramatic play.

Helen's form of business is lacking either the middle-class mask of caring professionalism displayed by Shagrue, or Laura's creative and business mix, ensuring that she becomes the focus of negative commentary. The film's main critique is framed by Paul Collins, who confronts Helen about her methods and aims, refers to her as "poisonous," blames her for Albert's suicide (likening her to a murderer) and accuses her of controlling Katie, calls her "Lady MacBeth," and eventually divides the sisters, convincing Katie to marry him and leave both the stage and Helen behind, leading to the latter's suicide. *The New York Times* review of the film recognizes this overriding depiction of Helen, referring to her as "a female Svengali . . . etched in venom" to Katie's "little Trilby."[10] According to Sherman, Lupino was so concerned by the characterization that a scene was inserted with the intention of creating audience sympathy for Helen through an explicit injection of feminine vulnerability.[11] When Shagrue's offer for Katie splits up Runkel and Runkel, Paul coolly express his admiration of Helen's handling of the situation: "You're marvellous, a regular machine—no heart, no blood, no feelings. . . . I'll bet you couldn't fall in love if you wanted to." Pulling Helen in for a kiss to which she responds, Paul repeats the line already set up in the film as his standard brush-off—"Write me in Duluth"—which earns him a slap and positions Helen momentarily as the unsuspecting victim of his manipulation, suggesting a chink in her emotional armor.[12]

This early moment of intended sympathy for Helen, however, is surpassed by the film's relentless criticism of her business identity. Helen's ambition, the film suggests, ultimately results in her sister's loss of a traditional female romantic life. A montage sequence that occurs when Katie and Paul latterly develop a relationship points to this stolen life as the couple are shown horse-riding, swimming, and riding in a speedboat, and Paul suggests Katie's missed destiny is having "ten kids." The onslaught of disapproval of Helen's business methods is reinforced by Katie's casting of herself as an unknowing victim of Helen's ambition. When Albert can only gate-crash Katie's party after her first appearance in a starring role, he accuses Helen of being the cause of Katie's change in behavior. At this point Katie defends her sister, pointing to the sacrifices made by Helen that have brought her a stream of offers from Broadway and Hollywood. After deteriorating into an undiscriminating party girl and an exhausted, disinterested performer, however, Katie denies her own ambition and culpability for what she calls the "fighting and cheating and lying and double-crossing," displacing her guilt in the creation of show business onto her sister.

Yet the film resists enabling this kind of blunt line drawing between business and performance that would deny the essential fluidity in the relationship that creates American entertainment. Unlike the stage mother films referred to earlier, *The Hard Way* depicts a close relationship between the sisters that deteriorates only toward the end of the narrative, indicating that Helen's ambitions are intended to improve the fortunes of both her sister and herself. The lack of drive exhibited by each of the male characters, save Shagrue, from Helen's passive husband, to Albert, and to Paul, whose management of Runkel and Collins comes second to his professional womanizing, is seen to result in a lack of both creative and financial success. It is only through Helen's haunting of talent agencies and establishing professional relationships that Runkel and Runkel moves, if briefly, to the more sophisticated environs of the supper club and Katie proceeds onward to the musical stage. Moreover, Katie's ambitions are outlined throughout the narrative, working against the simplistic industry critique that occurs around Helen. As Jeanine Basinger notes, Katie's ambitions are writ large in the after-party scene during which she refuses to return to marriage and life on the road with Albert.[13] Her contempt for her unambitious husband is evident in her suggestion that he give up working and join her in New York, and it becomes evident that stardom has been a goal which she now revels in having achieved when she tells him: "Everything is so wonderful for me now. I'm living in a bath of champagne. This is what I've dreamed about all my life."

This scene is far from the first point at which the film characterizes Katie as a driven performer, as the early scenes of the film establish links between Katie's acting pretensions and her desire for fame and financial reward. Katie's hankering for a graduation dress displayed in a shop window becomes the catalyst for Helen's arguments with her husband, who refuses to purchase it, and for the sisters' ultimate determination to escape their small-town fate (Figure 2.1).

Frustrated by her limitations, Katie imagines herself to be a rich European with suitors and/or written up in a newspaper article: "Miss Katherine Blaine was at the Ambassador's Ball last night in her usual dirty rayon." The film presents a compelling visual image of Katie's economic frustrations and her determination to be center stage in a scene during which a photographer takes the class graduation photo. Initially positioned front and center in the shot, Katie is moved to a less prominent space by the photographer once he notices that her "dirty rayon" is ruining his shot of preened graduates in white dresses. By pushing Katie "off stage," the photographer unwittingly suggests the fate to which the shabbily dressed Katie and her sister suspect unless they *both* take swift action. It is no surprise then that it is Katie herself who immediately affects change that evening when Albert spots her impersonation of Runkel and Collins' act in the local ice-cream parlor after their performance. Katie's determined ambition, therefore, is apparent throughout the film, from the ease with which she marries Albert to flee the small town, immediately recognizing and exploiting his sexual attraction to

FIGURE 2.1 *Consumerism inspires escape in* The Hard Way.

her, to her readiness to usurp a string of performers from Paul, to Albert, and then fading star Lily Emery (Gladys George). While Helen brokers the deals and becomes the visible and audible representation of the business of show, Katie's ambitions, and further her actions, act as a central inspiration for what occurs. Moreover, Helen refuses to countenance Katie's denial of her own ambition and refusal of agency in own demise, directly arguing what the film often veils through its more explicit critique of Helen: "You wanted it alright, and don't pretend you didn't. Your eyes were open. You realized what I was doing all the time. You've come every step of the way with me, and if you didn't like it, you could have said so."

The film comes full circle when the sisters gaze at a dress in a shop window just as they had when a similar dress initially spurred them to action, serving as a reminder of the economic incentives that brought about Katie's success and of the involvement of both sisters in that endeavor. Katie's ultimate denial of either ambition or responsibility, however, is reinforced in her dismissal of her sister from her life, so Katie departs for marriage and a family with Paul and Helen is the recipient of narrative censure through her death in the final scene. The film's depiction of the business of show is, therefore, a fluid one, which both critiques industry methods and their impact on the performer and disallows the notion of strict boundaries between the economic and entertainment, alluding to the essential working connections between the imperatives of business and the creative, while ultimately condemning the former through narrative closure.

Despoiling the Sporting Stage in
Hard, Fast and Beautiful

Produced and directed by Lupino, *Hard, Fast and Beautiful* provides an opportunity to consider her creative perspective on the show/business dynamic. Set in the arena of amateur tennis, the film connects directly with ideas of performance versus business in its representation of an increasingly conflicted sport drawn to the needs of commercial entertainment. In some ways a standardized melodrama, the narrative follows young tennis discovery Florence Farley, played by Sally Forrest, as she plays her way to US Champion, pushed along by her mother Millie (Claire Trevor) and smooth operating ex-player and coach Fletcher Locke (Carleton G. Young). A powerless, sick husband and earnest fiancé are left in the women's wake until Florence rejects the path of acquisition on which she has been set by her mother and retreats to marriage with her forgiving fiancé. The film's melodramatic narrative combines with Lupino's semi-realist style of filmmaking through scenes that show Florence playing at various tournaments, including Forest Hills with accompanying documentary footage. This realist aspect suggests a more abrasive critique than is apparent in *The Hard Way*, linked to the contemporary postwar context of the commercialization of amateur sport. The Forest Hills setting, in fact, roused Bosley Crowther's only positive comments regarding the film, even as he slated the scenes themselves.[14] Indeed, the film takes a more damning approach than does *The Hard Way*, focusing on business as an intrusive and unethical force in the creation of a sporting performer. Like *The Hard Way*, the narrative can be located within the stage mother genre, and again the family relationship becomes the means through which the lines separating entertainment from business are drawn, and the latter is negatively critiqued as the public impacts on the personal.

    The significance of Lupino's intervention as both director and producer is clear in a number of ways that articulate the business/creative dynamic that Lupino negotiates as a filmmaker. Ida Lupino's stardom immediately comes into play in the opening titles announcing "The Filmakers Present An Ida Lupino Production" against an image of an empty tennis arena. The clear intention to exploit Lupino's star status seems reinforced by the title line "Produced by Young." The idea of giving star boost to the film is enhanced by Lupino's Hitchcock-style appearance alongside Robert Ryan in the stands at one of Florence's matches. The realist visual backdrop at the same time establishes the on-location filmmaking style which, according to Dan Georgakas, became "a Lupino trademark, driven in part by budgetary constraints but more so by the artistic desire to achieve sociological realism."[15] The expressed intent of The Filmakers to tackle controversial social topics sees its visual illustration in Lupino's directing style signposted by the backdrop of the opening title sequence. At the same time, the mainstreaming of the film via a melodramatic narrative and noir-like visual touches highlights the complex negotiation of roles undertaken by Lupino, even as the film itself presents the relationship between business and show as an undesirable intrusion.

The narrative launches with Millie's voice-over set against a shot of a tennis ball being hit against a garage door as the camera soon reveals. Unlike Helen's voice-over, which promotes a level of empathy as she articulates her dreams of escape from the soot-ridden hills of a mining town emphasized in *The Hard Way*'s accompanying imagery. Millie is immediately condemned by her own words as a mother driven by ambition: "Listening to you drive that ball against the garage door used to drive me crazy. That's because I always wanted something better for you, and I made up my mind to get it, no matter what I had to do." No scenes of urban deprivation follow, but instead a typical postwar suburban family home gained as a result of Millie's aggressive social climbing forced upon the husband she clearly views as a passive irrelevance to her plans. When an acquaintance from high school and member of one of the town's prominent families, Gordon McKay, invites Florence to play tennis at the country club where he is working. Millie eagerly encourages the relationship, recognizing the opportunities for social advancement that it may provide.

In the scene that follows, Millie expresses to husband Will her dissatisfaction, similar to Helen in *The Hard Way* and Mildred in *Mildred Pierce*. In the latter films this confrontation starts the process of separation, but Millie's manipulation of her relationship will continue throughout as she maintains the appearance of a marriage while engaged in the single-minded promotion of her daughter and, it is intimated, an affair with Fletcher. An early scene in the marital bedroom establishes Millie's self-interest and cold indifference toward her husband, who unsuccessfully attempts both physical and emotional closeness. Millie's thoughts are on moving home so that Florence might "meet the right people," while she simultaneously rebukes Will for his readiness to "rot in a place like this." The scene's unusual visual imagery clearly points to the irretrievably broken marriage between the Farleys. Rather than an image of two single beds positioned alongside each other, familiar due to Production Code guidelines, the beds are positioned with the headboards back-to-back, leaving the couple lying opposite each other and out of each other's vision. It is in this manner that Will questions why Millie seems unable to love both husband and daughter and Millie, unconcerned, paints her nails and contemplates Florence's next move. Florence's arrival in the room again separates the couple as Millie advises her daughter not to try too hard to beat Gordon in their match—making the right social impression is more important than performance—and Will attempts to remind Florence "it's only a game." The scene additionally hints at the ambition and acquisitiveness with which Florence will be only minimally associated, resulting in the narrative's much more easily drawn boundaries of manager and performer, aggressor and victim. Florence's response to her father's reasoned comment is, "Well, sure, but maybe I can beat him," suggesting her personal ambitions as a player have been lit. Before leaving the room, she returns to a tailor's dummy that bears an evening dress that her mother has been sewing for her, giving it one last touch before she leaves the room, suggesting her individual desire for the consumer items her mother will seek to acquire. Millie's willingness to exploit her daughter's talent becomes the overriding narrative concern, however, so that when Florence is invited to join the country club and take part in an out-of-state national championship, Millie ensures her own invitation and initiates her direct control over the business of Florence's career.

The film makes explicit connections between the sports world and the entertainment business through its representation of emerging notions of tennis stardom. Pointing to the ways in which performance as entertainment in the mid-twentieth century led to the mainstreaming of Italian-American identity, Ellen Nerenberg notes that this occurred not only through dance on the movie screen but also through the fact that "sports for entertainment had created household names out of such athletes as Joe DiMaggio, Yogi Berra, and Rocky Graziano, with Rocky Marciano and Jake LaMotta recognizable as well."[16] *Hard, Fast and Beautiful* draws on the increasing celebrity status of sports people, exploring the blurring of lines between amateur and professional that simultaneously occurs in the tennis arena. Mandy Merck explains the culture of "shamateurism" in tennis that existed prior to the official switch to the professional game considering, in particular, the impact that it had on female players who often aimed to combine career success with the financial benefits of expenses and designer dresses, which allowed them to dilute an image of ambition with illustrations of their femininity. Merck points to a changing room scene during Florence's first tournament when a player proudly shows another competitor her new frilly underwear beneath her tennis skirt, referencing the 1949 Wimbledon scandal when American Gertrude "Gorgeous Gussie" Moran was reprimanded for wearing similar clothing deemed too provocative.[17] As Merck suggests, this kind of sexualized display associated with the sportswoman and her work resulted in "the spectacle of the woman tennis star—athlete and erotic object."[18] Direct parallels can be drawn to Hollywood studios positioning particularly female stars as erotic objects, not only for the purposes of film narrative and audience appeal, but also in their role as idols of consumption and the promoters of a lifestyle of affluence as well as of the dresses and lipsticks that might be purchased after the movie. The appeal of Florence's homemade evening dress is an early indication of consumerism's power, and the arrangements that are subsequently made for Florence to wear branded sportswear and be photographed in designer dresses become both evidence of her and the game's unstated slide into professionalism and an essential factor in the creation of her stardom.

In representing this Hollywood-style combination of business and performance in the form of the female tennis star, the film maintains the damaging nature of the union by clearly distinguishing between Millie's active ambition and Florence's naivety about her mother's behind-the-scenes machinations. When Gordon rebukes Florence for receiving a $50 payment for playing tennis with an oil heiress, this acts as the only explicit critique of Florence as an active participant in what occurs. In contrast, by Millie's own words in her voice-over, the audience is left in no doubt as to her ambitions for her daughter and, essentially, for herself, which are made real by her unholy alliance with Fletcher Locke. A tournament official's description of Fletcher as "combination coach and promoter, if you know what I mean" immediately signals the unethical behavior through which the film defines him, and through which business triumphs over performance as sports people are restyled into stars. His slippery manner articulates an untrustworthy image of business in the same way that the suggested affair between Fletcher and Millie suggests a lack of honor between the coconspirators and the abuse of both the personal and the professional in their relationships with Florence. It is through Fletcher that the narrative underlines that Millie's consumerist desires are personal rather than maternal. In a scene preceding Florence's ascent to the US Championships, Millie tells Fletcher, "Florence needs so many things," while the audience is in no doubt that it is of her own needs that she speaks. Success will create "a buzz," Fletcher assures her, leading to "hotel chains all over the world, press syndicates, a million angles and they all work." For both characters, Florence's successful performance rates only as a marker of stardom and the financial and consumerist rewards this will afford, and the unprincipled route they take to achieve this is necessary and inconsequential (Figure 2.2).

In the aforementioned scene, the frame moves from two-shots to close-ups of Millie's face as she responds to Fletcher's promises. Just as the close-up of Barbara Stanwyck in *Double Indemnity* (1944) shows Phyllis Dietrichson react with relish as Walter Neff (Fred MacMurray) murders her husband in the car seat behind her, Lupino's direction makes Millie the guilty party via this explicit visual focus, despite the dialogue illustrating Fletcher's active lead. Lupino uses similar contrasting techniques to bind the narrative's individual story to a wider social critique. Discussing the visual elements of some of Lupino's films including *Outrage* and *Hard, Fast and Beautiful*, Ronnie Scheib points to the ways in which these films find "a balance between the dynamic stylistic impetus of drama and the open-ended 'documentary' autonomy of real location space."[19] Lupino utilizes these juxtapositions of style throughout, preceding tournament matches with martial music as Millie and Fletcher march Florence to court. Before Florence's US Championship match, off-kilter shots depict Florence crouching to tie her laces while Millie and Fletcher tower above her firing instructions (Figure 2.3).

In a further scene Florence is pictured in shadow as Fletcher coaches her, again contrasting with the bright realism of the tournament scenes. The sense of anxiety and unease created through these noir-like scenes

FIGURE 2.2 *Dark deals in* Hard, Fast and Beautiful.

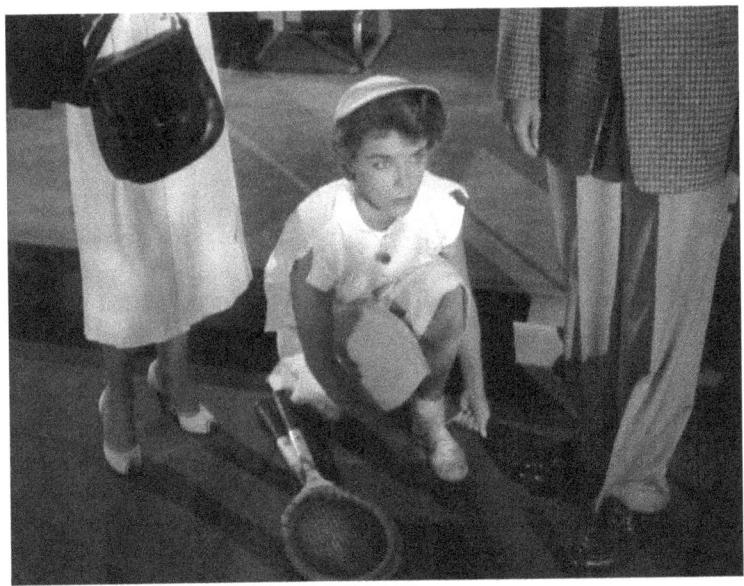

FIGURE 2.3 *Professional power looms over the amateur game.*

works against any clarity of realism achieved through a documentary style, pointing to the essential conflict between performance and business that the film stresses thematically. By connecting these contrasting styles through individual scenes, the film moreover combines the drama of the individual with the broader context of documentary, reinforcing its theme as social critique.

As a film drawn from the stage mother genre, the narrative depicts the damage done to familial relationships through Millie's aggressive pursuit of success via Florence. Millie's emasculation of her husband is apparent, from the new car she purchases that he was unable to provide, to her acceptance of red roses from Fletcher in front of him in the family home. She, in turn, encourages similar behavior in her daughter who, on becoming US Women's National Champion, dismisses her fiancé's request for an immediate wedding in favor of a European tour and, at her mother's suggestion, offers Gordon a job writing articles about her for one of the news organizations with which Fletcher has brokered a deal. The obvious warmth of the father/daughter relationship is contrasted with the increasing distance between Millie and Florence until, in a scene reminiscent of *The Hard Way*, Florence expresses her sudden recognition of and disgust at her mother's business transactions. In London as part of the European tour, Florence returns to the hotel room drunk, having received a proposal of marriage from a European playboy, the kind of socialite to whom Millie has been keen to introduce her. Florence's meltdown, like that of Katie, articulates her awareness that her initial ambition to perform has been despoiled by the objectives of business. Disrespected by her competitors, to whom her fur coats and expensive hotel rooms openly signal her flouting of sporting ethics, Florence accuses her mother of "playing it dirty for money," and the film's consistent depiction of Millie's cold ambition and her cynical alliance with Fletcher Locke mean that Florence remains detached from responsibility for her own demise, separated as an unknowing performer from the business of show. Florence's subsequent decision to emulate her mother and openly play for financial reward leads to an icy professional relationship that suggests the intrusion of business into sport results in both the disintegration of the family and the death of the performer.

The closing scenes of *Hard, Fast and Beautiful* suggest a sport wholly infiltrated by unethical business practices. When Millie and Florence sit down with a female journalist, the scene plays like an interview with a Hollywood columnist, with Florence scripting a star image of herself as a family-loving girl just "lucky to have such a wonderful mother." The journalist's comment—"They'll love that angle—a girl's best friend is her mother and all that sort of thing"—indicates her cynical recognition of the press manipulation in which she plays her part. Similarly, when Florence proposes the journalist advise her readers to "play fair, play hard, play clean," the journalist's retort that some players "make a profession of it" hints at her awareness of Florence's business arrangements, and equally implies that the practice of amateur sport has essentially become a sham.

Once Florence has reunited with her sick father, whose rejection of Millie is absolute, she successfully defends her title and announces her retirement to the waiting media, handing the cup to her mother and departing with fiancé Gordon. Millie's astonishment turns to desperation as her calls after Florence are ignored and she observes Fletcher talking with the young pretender her daughter has just defeated. After Fletcher dismisses her suggestion that they go somewhere to discuss their plans, Millie is pictured alone with the championship cup in the darkness of the stands as pages of old newspapers blow across the court like tumbleweed. This wretched image leaves Millie both the film's tragic victim and the bearer of narrative guilt. The loss of her family becomes the result of her unflinching desire to acquire, which supplanted an essential maternal ambition for a daughter to achieve through performance. Fletcher's immediate switch of allegiance to Florence's successor, meanwhile, alludes to continuity in the professional overpowering of sporting performance, and as the screen returns to the opening image of an empty tennis arena, the film reiterates its theme of the unhappy fusion of business and show.

Conclusion

Ida Lupino's career demonstrates an explicit intent to promote the creative over the economic priorities of an often-controlling industry. Her stated attempts to distance herself from commercial interests and her negotiation of the roles of star, director, and independent producer pointedly illustrate the indivisible, yet challenging dynamic of creativity and business that exists as American show business. Lupino's starring roles frequently dramatize this bond, revealing the off-stage forces of business and their impact on the individual performer. As director and producer, Lupino likewise tackles this essential issue, accentuating her take through her directorial style and a hardened critique of unethical business practices. In both *The Hard Way* and *Hard, Fast and Beautiful*, performance and business are represented as two distinct arenas, the merging of which results in turmoil and the destruction of the performer until that star chooses to depart the stage. Complicated by displacement and the stage mother narrative, business is ultimately the bearer of guilt in these films that end with suicide and family relationships in ruins. Beyond the narratives of their leading characters, however, both films leave the structural bond between performer and industry in place, as the background noise of the films suggests that the dynamic remains, simply expressed by other players. While depicting the relationship as fundamentally flawed, Lupino's films ultimately point to the unending endurance of the American business of show.

Notes

1. Marsha Orgeron, *Hollywood Ambitions: Celebrity in the Movie Age* (Middletown, CT: Wesleyan University Press, 2008), 171.
2. The Filmakers' declared intent was to produce films that were stylistically and creatively distinguished from the product of the major studios, utilizing the financial independence that freed them from the strategies and business imperatives to which Lupino had felt subjected.
3. Dan Georgakas, "Ida Lupino: Doing It Her Way," *Cineaste*, 25, no. 3 (2000) 33.
4. Orgeron, *Hollywood Ambitions*, 177. Lupino took over direction of *Not Wanted* (1949), an Emerald Productions film, following Elmer Clifton's heart attack but was not credited.
5. Wheeler Winston Dixon, *Lost in the Fifties: Recovering Phantom Hollywood* (Carbondale, IL: Southern Illinois University Press, 2005), 140.
6. Ida Lupino, "Me, Mother Directress," *Action!* May–June 1967, 14–15, in Richard Koszarski (ed.), *Hollywood Directors 1941-1976* (Oxford, London and New York: Oxford University Press, 1977), 375.
7. James Naremore, *The Films of Vincente Minnelli* (Cambridge: Cambridge University Press, 1993), 114.
8. Jeanine Basinger, *A Woman's View: How Hollywood Spoke to Women, 1930-1960* (London: Chatto & Windus, 1993), 436.
9. Vincent Sherman, *Studio Affairs: My Life as a Film Director* (Lexington, KY: University Press of Kentucky, 1996), 110–11.
10. T. S., "Film Review: The Hard Way (1942) at the Strand," *The New York Times*, March 13, 1943, www.nytimes.com/movie/review (accessed April 26, 2014).
11. Sherman, *Studio Affairs*, 113–14.
12. Katie and Laura, in fact, both suggest at later points that Helen is in love with Paul.
13. Basinger, *A Woman's View*, 438.
14. Bosley Crowther, "Hard, Fast and Beautiful (1951) The Screen in Review," *The New York Times*, July 2, 1951, www.nytimes.com/movie/review (accessed April 26, 2014).
15. Georgakas, "Ida Lupino," 33.
16. Ellen Nerenberg, "Overlooking and Looking Over Ida Lupino," *Voices in Italian Americana*, 7, no. 2 (Fall 1996), http://alljournals.com/via/ViaVol7_2Nerenberg.htm (accessed November 18, 2013).
17. Mandy Merck, "*Hard, Fast and Beautiful* (1951)," in Annette Kuhn (ed.), *Queen of the 'B's: Ida Lupino Behind the Camera* (Trowbridge: Flicks Books, 1995), 79.
18. Merck, "*Hard, Fast and Beautiful*," 82.
19. Ronnie Scheib, "*Never Fear* (1950)," in *Queen of the 'B's*, Kuhn (ed.), 42.

3

Ida Lupino

A Life in Hollywood

William T. Ross

I

The Trouble with Angels, the last feature film Ida Lupino was to direct, was released in 1966. She was forty-eight. She would direct her last episode for a television series one year later and make her last guest appearance as an actor in a TV series (*Charlie's Angels*) in 1977, having experienced, on the set, a great deal of trouble remembering her lines. Toward the end of his biography of her, William Donati uses "borderline personality disorder" (plus alcohol dependency) to explain the many examples of erratic behavior occurring with more frequency in the last few years of her professional life and on into retirement.[1] All in all, a sad and premature end for the only woman motion picture director of the 1950s and one of the pioneer women directors in television.[2]

If Lupino did not provoke interest because of her pioneering role as a female director, we would probably view her relatively early demise simply as another sad story of a former Hollywood diva who had been done in by her own internal demons. But because she has historical importance as the second female member of the Directors Guild (after Dorothy Arzner) and the only working female director in the 1950s, we really are more interested in her active years: how she managed to succeed, what kept her from going further, why she was forced to turn to directing television instead of continuing in feature films, and what brought those years to a premature close. Interesting questions, but those asking them—and those also more interested in the auteurist possibilities of her work—must often be embarrassed by various public statements she made, starting at just about the time she stopped directing. Frankly, she often sounds pretty much like any other representative of an "old" Hollywood, the Hollywood that could not adapt to the new sort of films coming out, and certainly could not adjust to aesthetic departures like *Bonnie and Clyde, The Graduate* (both 1967), *The Wild Bunch*, or *Easy Rider* (both 1969).

Gerald Mast and Bruce F. Kawin give several reasons why the "old" was being replaced by a "new" Hollywood. The first and most obvious was the loss of the traditional mass audience to television which, as they recognize, actually began in the 1950s and, as we shall see later, had already impinged upon Lupino's career. What "new" Hollywood saw was that the "sexual and social values of American film audiences" of the 1960s were changing. In other words, people who actually went to movies were fans of foreign filmmakers like Fellini, Godard, Bergman, and Antonioni, all of whom treated sexuality and other behavior differently from traditional American models and were more inclined to encourage "elite" American directors' forays into more self-consciously "artistic" film. (They have in mind directors like Arthur Penn and Mike Nichols.) In an attempt to cover every base, Mast and Kawin throw in pornography (e.g., *Deep Throat*), underground cinema (Warhol), and cult films (*Pink Flamingo, Rocky Horror*). These categories probably say more about influences on young directors than on profit-minded producers.[3]

Lupino was certainly a product of the "old" Hollywood, of directors like Raoul Walsh, Jean Negulesco, and William Wellman, all of whose techniques she studied while she was in front of their cameras, and of the editing techniques of Warner Brothers, whose cutting room let her serve an unofficial apprenticeship. Although she was at least a generation younger than the old directorial hands mentioned earlier (and only four years older than Arthur Penn), she never showed any signs of wanting to join the "younger" crowd. When we see her in the *New York Times* in 1969 denouncing "film nudity," saying that it "embarrassed teenagers out on a date" and praising David Lean (b. 1908) for his treatment of "bedroom scenes" in *Doctor Zhivago* (1965), we can assume that she neither understood the new film aesthetic nor contemporary teenagers.[4] And she allegedly refused to appear in any "R"-rated movie.[5] In short, her comments show her dissatisfaction with any new postcode treatment of sexuality and no real appreciation for anything else in the "new cinema."

It is much the same with her comments on woman's place in Hollywood and in the world. In fact, she had been making such comments ever since her first marriage in 1938, comments about how making a marriage work is mostly a woman's responsibility.[6] But in 1972 she indicates a distaste for the women's movement, which reveals a fairly crude misconception of what it is all about. She is not "one of the ladies who go in for women's lib. Any woman who wishes to smash into the world of men isn't very feminine.

... Baby, we can't go smashing." And then she goes on to claim that she had turned down (directing) jobs in Europe because "I'd have to leave my husband and daughter."[7] There is no evidence of these multiple offers, but the point is to emphasize her subordination of career to husband and child.

Even students of Hollywood with a sense of humor would be faintly embarrassed by how she praises the two queens of Hollywood gossip, Hedda Hopper and Louella Parsons, long after both were safely dead.[8] But such praise suggests a way of understanding both Lupino's successes and failures. To an auteurist/aesthete, Hedda Hopper and Louella Parsons represent the commercial crassness of Hollywood at its worst. To a feminist, the two are simply tools of patriarchy, keeping women, even successful women, in their places. To Lupino, gossip columnists were as much a part of her community as Jack Warner, John Ford, Marlene Dietrich, Humphrey Bogart, her friend Errol Flynn, and all the lesser studio employees. That community was her home, and its values were her values. And I would suggest that Ida Lupino's life is best seen, not as a narrative of patriarchal repression or of an auteur trying to break free from the conforming pressure of the studio, but rather as a life lived within the confines of a very specific community. It was not the most caring community in the world, but it was one whose values could be intuited. Those values were the only ones she had, and she never really deviated from them. And that community allowed her to thrive in a lot of ways, and, far from punishing her, as Annette Kuhn claims,[9] it supported her as she tried to develop her talents in all kinds of different directions.

Ida Lupino did not start out in Hollywood, but she did start out in show business. Her father was Stanley Lupino, a very popular singer/comedian/ actor, and her mother was a stage dancer. Her godfather was the popular composer Ivor Novello, who was also a leading man on the English musical stage and in British musical film. There does not seem to have been a time when she was not aware of her parents and extended family's occupation, or any chance that she would not follow them. More important for the future, the family had already acquainted itself with the new medium of film. Her first appearance in a film came in 1931 when she was thirteen. She was an extra in a crowd scene in *The Love Race*, directed by her uncle Lupino Lane and featuring her father.[10] At the same tender age she posed for a publicity or portfolio portrait, dressed as a member of a chorus line with top hat, short skirt, and barebacked halter. The shortness of the skirt and the lift of the high heels show off a comely set of legs. Her biographer titles the picture "star at thirteen."[11] She was not yet a star, but the picture is certainly a sign of the difference in the times: today there would be a major flap over posing an adolescent to look like someone who has reached the age of consent, as well as complaints about the "commodification of sex."

In fact, she would play sexually attractive, "older" parts in all five of her British films. How sexual the parts were can be inferred from an anecdote involving Ivor Novello, her costar in *I Lived With You* (1933). In a scene with Lupino, he suddenly stopped the camera. "I can't stand this ... it's ridiculous what with my godchild lying on top of me trying to rape me."[12] Her first real part was in *Her First Affaire* (1932), directed by Alan Dwan, who had also worked in Hollywood. He predicted that she would be in Hollywood before the year was out. He was not far wrong. With the experience of having substantial parts in five films with five different directors under her belt, she arrived in New York on August 29, 1933.[13] It was a privileged arrival. The fifteen-year-old traveled with her mother and a contract in hand from Paramount Pictures. Paramount arranged a press conference for her, claiming she was sixteen, apparently a significant difference in 1933. (Officially, she was signed as one of the "new faces" competing to play the lead in *Alice in Wonderland*, a part Lupino did not want and did not think that she could play.) The press conference was a success. A week after she left London, she arrived in Hollywood. It would be her home until her death sixty-one years later.[14]

She might have been notably underaged but she was not underprepared. Ida had all the wisdom a show business family could give her (and an experienced mother chaperoning her), and she had the familiarity with filmmaking that meaty roles in five feature-length films could provide. Hollywood and the American motion picture industry was where she wanted to be, and that desire was not based on fantasy. She also carried with her the memory of something her father had said when he gave her a tour of London's Elstree studio: "Ida, the player whose likeness appears on those pieces of film is important; the man who determines *what* pieces is the most important of all. He is the director."[15]

As she had enough sense to know, her five years at Paramount were not particularly auspicious. Her career began with the head of production telling her that the studio was planning for her to be the next Jean Harlow, and a special script was being written for her.[16] The script never materialized, but they did manage to pluck her eyebrows and turn her already-light hair platinum. The parts she was actually given were mostly pedestrian. She would have to wait until 1939, after she had left Paramount, to have her first significant role, that of the cockney model opposite Ronald Coleman in *The Light that Failed*, directed by William Wellman. Wellman's name is a reminder that though she may have had unimpressive roles in often insignificant films, she managed to work with several talented, well-known directors during the Paramount years, including Raoul Walsh (whom she would work with again in the 1940s and whose influence she acknowledged), Henry Hathaway, Lewis Milestone, and Rouben Mamoulian. In the next decade, in addition to Walsh (twice), she would work with a clutch of famous immigrants: Jean Negulesco, Michael Curtiz, and Anatol Litvak. Just as important, probably, she received permission to visit the studio's editing rooms, where she got hands-on practice in cutting.[17]

While still a minor under contract with Paramount, she learned several of the survival skills every successful Hollywood star seemed to possess. The first was how to manipulate the press, both in keeping your name in the public's eye and in avoiding any scandal that could sink your career. She knew how to be outrageous without being scandalous. For example, On March 18, 1934, the *Los Angeles Times* carried a story in which Lupino claimed her father "kicked me out when I was twelve," that she completely dominated her mother, choosing "her clothes and everything," and that she had insisted that her sister be sent to a convent school. The interviewer was left breathless by this "deliciously arrogant child."[18] Her claims were nonsense, proof that she was learning that truth was not required to get public attention. She certainly skirted with scandal. Howard Hughes courted her. She let him give her an expensive pair of binoculars on her sixteenth birthday. But she was wise enough to avoid any sexual entanglement. Later, during her marriages, she routinely called Hedda and/or Louella at the first sign of marital difficulties to make sure they got the story first. This staying on the good side of the powerful was normal and strategic: it was not only important to keep one's name in the public eye, but also to divert that eye from anything truly scandalous. There was a certain quid pro quo involved: feed the publicity machine most of the time, and it will sometimes give you a pass. Much later in her career, for example, it could not have been a secret that Mrs. Ida Lupino Young was in Las Vegas for a quickie divorce from Mr. Young so that she could marry Howard Duff, the father of the baby she was carrying. But the obliging press said nothing.

She was often suspended for refusing to accept studio assignments. Perhaps this far-from-unique behavior gained her a reputation for toughness that made her entrance into the all-male domain of directing more acceptable. Some of that time on suspension or between films was spent in developing other talents useful to filmmaking. If her biographer, who provides no documentation, can be believed, she composed several musical pieces in a classical or semiclassical vein; one piece was broadcast by the Andre Kostelanetz Orchestra, and several other compositions were performed by the Los Angeles Philharmonic.[19]

As far as we know, this musical inclination did not impinge directly on the scoring of her films, but she was also learning aspects of filming that did pay off. For example, her presence was almost always felt in either the script or the original story of the majority of the films she directed and/or coproduced in the 1950s. Thus, it is significant that by the time she became a director she had already published a short story in *Colliers* magazine and that she had sold scripts to one of her favorite radio series, *Suspense*.[20] (Acting in radio dramas was one of her favorite and profitable occupations while under suspension and off payroll.) She also, in the mid-1940s, wrote one screenplay by herself, and with the actress Barbara Reed she wrote *Miss Pennington* and optioned it to RKO for $5,000.[21] Apparently neither work was ever actually filmed. Clearly, an apprenticeship, no matter how informal, was being served.

Meanwhile, the 1940s saw her acting career peak. By 1946, she was making $4,000 a week, more than $2,000,000 per annum in today's dollars. She received the New York Film Critics' Best Actress award in 1943 for her performance in Vincent Sherman's *The Hard Way*, which was filming when she got word that her father had died in England. The trauma of his death probably intensified her dislike of the script, her performance, the director, and everything else about *The Hard Way*. But in a press release meant to accompany the film, she announced to the world that she wanted to be a director.[22] She was twenty-four years old. (Eventually, she and Sherman patched things up and remained friends for life.)

II

In February, 1949, Lupino met Roberto Rossellini at a party. He observed to her (and apparently to a nearby reporter), "In Hollywood movies, the star is going crazy, or drinks too much, or wants to kill his wife. When are you going to make pictures about ordinary people, in ordinary situations?" His question, we are told, made a "profound impression on Lupino."[23] It is best to stick with the impression rather than trying to parse a statement made by a man whose most famous movie featured a far-from-ordinary martyr-priest in a far-from-ordinary political and social situation, and one of whose last films was about the court of Louis XIV. If Lupino had seen any of Rossellini's early movies, she may very well have been impressed by what Mast and Kawin call the "unvarnished look of non-studio reality."[24] Certainly some of the exteriors in *The Hitch-Hikers* and the last shot in *Hard, Fast and Beautiful* of the empty tennis court seem to have that look (Figure 3.1).

In any case, Lupino was not interested in or very well equipped to push the aesthetic, philosophical, or sociopolitical boundaries that Italian neorealism was famous for. But she was interested in "ordinary" people in realistic situations. It is unfortunate that in 1949, when she met Collier Young and formed an independent production company, they quickly decided to define what they wanted to produce as "documentary" films. They did not have the tradition of Robert Flaherty or Pare Lorenz in mind. Instead, as they later told the *New York Herald-Tribune*, they were "trying to make pictures of a sociological nature to appeal to older people who usually stay away from theaters." They were "out to tackle serious themes and problem dramas." They eschewed "melodramas."[25] A cynic might say that melodrama is exactly what unwed motherhood, rape, and polio (the subjects of three of their films) was sure to lead to. It seems fair to say that what they were after were well-plotted stories with realistic, if somewhat sensational, conflict in

FIGURE 3.1 *The empty court.*

realistic, contemporary settings. Their expectation, as explained to Hedda Hopper, was that those older ticket-buyers were "more interested in what's in a picture than *who's* in it."[26] This was no major revolt from ordinary Hollywood fare; after all, the late 1940s had seen topics like race and anti-Semitism covered in films like Kazin's *Gentlemen's Agreement* (1947), *Pinky* (1949), and Clarence Brown's *Intruder in the Dust* (1950).

Independent producers were not especially rare in Hollywood, with David O. Selznick being perhaps the most famous. The studios were perfectly willing to work with independents (leasing equipment and sound stages and handling publicity and distribution) as long as the arrangement was profitable. What is interesting is that Lupino's last film before going independent involved some degree of personal negotiation. The film was *Road House*, released in 1948. According to Sean Axmaker in notes to the movie on the Turner Classic Movies website, Lupino "discovered the original unpublished story (then called *The Dark Love*), bought and developed the property, and sold it to Darryl Zanuck at 20th Century Fox as a package with herself attached as star."[27] Donati's account has both Collier Young and Lupino discovering the story, and assigns more responsibility to her new agent, Charles K. Feldman.[28] Either version shows Lupino apparently ready to step out of her role as "mere" actress and take a greater hand in shaping her own future. The story also serves to remind us that, though academic interest today centers on Lupino's role as director, her "breakout" from acting was far more comprehensive. In the eight films that she and

Collier Young finally turned out, she made appearances in four, received credit for coscripting five and producing one. She probably should have received coproducer credit on most of the films, and without doubt she was responsible for casting on the majority of them. Furthermore, as Diane Waldman has shown, Lupino's delicate negotiations with the Breen office were all that enabled *Never Fear*'s subject matter of illegitimate births to arrive on the screen at all.[29] The same could be said for *Outrage* and its treatment of rape. Lupino was proving to be talented in all aspects of filmmaking. She was making herself a very well-rounded member of the community (Figure 3.2).

Thus, while her first opportunity to direct was a result of chance, there is no indication that anyone was particularly surprised that she could do it or upset that she was allowed to. That chance or lucky break begins in 1948 or 1949 when Lupino and Collier Young, her new husband, found the ideal script for their first feature. The subject was illegitimate birth, a far more sensational topic then than today. Lupino, like a director-to-be, "added a few touches written with a shrewd eye for camera angles." Eventually, the couple would form their own production company, but for this first feature they teamed up with independent producer Anson Bond, with whom Lupino was to be coproducer.[30] Robert Eggenweiler was hired as her assistant and became the first experienced film hand to "idolize his boss as a brilliant woman." The partners hired Elmer Clifton to direct. As assistant director, Maurice Vaccarino also proved to be a fervent admirer.[31]

FIGURE 3.2 *Jefty's new attraction in* Road House.

Clifton suffered a mild heart attack before shooting began. On the first day of filming, he was hardly in shape actually to take charge. It was up to Lupino to get things rolling. Darr Smith, from the *Los Angeles Daily News*, happened by the crew shooting on a Los Angeles street. Smith clearly knew a great deal about the industry.

In Donati's words, "Smith was impressed by the fast and efficient method of Lupino's directorial skill." He knew that she was not a member of the Directors Guild. Lupino denied that she was directing. "Heavens no! I wouldn't think of directing." She was just giving Elmer Clifton a hand, since he was not feeling well that day. Smith played along, concluding his story with "Lupino isn't really directing this picture. She says so herself. But it's difficult to tell just what she's doing if it isn't directing."[32]

That Clifton got screen credit fooled no one in the business. Word quickly got around that Lupino had done a fine job. In short, the film was a success, and its actual director rewarded with membership in the Directors Guild. And, seemingly, her success was applauded by many different sections of her community. First, she was not only accepted into the Guild, but she was asked to present the award for best director at the 1950 Academy Awards. The award went to Joseph Mankiewicz for *A Letter to Three Wives*. Mankiewicz took notice of the presenter by saying, "Miss Lupino is the only woman in the Directors Guild and the prettiest." Today the comment would be branded as "sexist," but 1950 is not today.[33] The invitation to present the award coupled with the winner's acknowledgment of her membership in what had been an all-male club suggests that Hollywood had no trouble accepting Lupino in her new roles. The wider film community, according to Harry Mines, a journalist friend who did publicity for *Not Wanted*, was "electrified." One of his proofs of this enthusiasm is that Joan Crawford, not one of Lupino's circle, called and "asked if I could bring a print to her house." Indeed, Mines claims, "Everyone clamored to see it"[34] (Figure 3.3).

The enthusiasm of the upper reaches of the community was matched by the respect of those in the trenches. While *Not Wanted* was doing well at the box office, Lupino was already directing her second film, *Never Fear*. The cinematographer was Archie Stout, who had worked with John Ford (and just about everyone else). Lupino was proud to have him working with her, and he apparently was happy to be there. A *Colliers* story on Lupino quotes Stout as saying, "Ida has more knowledge of camera angles and lenses than any director I've ever worked with, with the exception of Victor Fleming. She knows how a woman looks on the screen and what light that woman should have, probably better than I do."[35] Stout's second point was hardly surprising to anyone who had worked with Lupino in the past, since she was always concerned with the way she was lit, felt free to give suggestions, and thought of James Wong Howe as her favorite cinematographer just because he taught and inspired her better than anyone else.[36]

FIGURE 3.3 *"You Said You'd Call Me" in* Not Wanted.

After this acceptance by her peers and admiration by her supporting professionals and technicians, it is not surprising that the backers of *Never Fear* insisted that she direct. With Lupino accruing all of this encouragement and validation, it is hard to construct a narrative of gender discrimination or patriarchal obstruction in charting Lupino's early success as a director. There may even be a smidgen of truth in the overstated claim by Mary Ann Anderson, presumably based on something Lupino told her late in life, that after *Not Wanted* and *Never Fear*, she "had offers from all the studios."[37]

In any event, she went on directing for her own company for the next few years, turning out several respectable films such as *Hard Fast and Beautiful*, *The Bigamist*, and *The Hitch-Hiker*. Walter Winchell is quoted in an ad for *The Bigamist* as saying Lupino should "get an Oscar" for directing and acting in the film. Such a multi-category award would have been a unique Oscar indeed.[38] The actual award for Best Director in 1953 went to Fred Zinnemann for *From Here to Eternity*. While at least most of their films made more than they cost to produce, a disastrous contract that Young had signed with Howard Hughes meant RKO got most of that profit. In an attempt to get out of that arrangement, Young and Lupino tried to distribute *The Bigamist* on their own, an unfortunate decision that led to bankruptcy.

And, like that, Lupino's career as a feature-film director was over. Given her success with her own company, it is certainly puzzling that another directorial assignment did not somehow materialize. And there is no totally satisfactory answer as to why one did not. By 1955, when her company had released its last film, Hollywood studios were in retrenchment, cutting overhead by slashing payrolls, adapting to the falling attendance that would presage Mast and Kawin's "New Hollywood." Fewer titles were being filmed, meaning less directing assignments to go around. And, to paraphrase Howard Hawks, one of the old workhorses who kept busy, directors, unmoored from long-term studio contracts, spent more time negotiating than directing.[39] In effect, Lupino lost her negotiator when Young, by now divorced from her, moved on to other things. It is also true, as Mast and Kawin remind us, that the studios were not exactly looking for small-budget, black-and-white films on "social" issues.[40] In the age of television, those films would not get people out of their living rooms and into the theaters. For all her expertise, Lupino had no experience in directing color or wide screen or the kind of grand "spectacle" that Hollywood seemed to want. (Hawks, for example, directed *Gentlemen Prefer Blonds*, a lavish musical, and *Land of the Pharaohs*.) For whatever reason, it would take sixteen years for her to "negotiate" another feature film assignment as director.

We should not think of her situation as unique. Things were not a whole lot better for some of the male directors she had worked with. If one looks at the last dozen or so of the men who directed her before *Not Wanted*, one sees amazing variety. Death claimed one or two, and "blacklisting" hurt several others. Admittedly, some seemed to have no trouble getting assignments, including Don Siegel and (at least in the 1950s) Nicholas Ray. Others, less lucky, wound up switching their attention to television. As did Lupino.

But first, she entered television as an actor, with an appearance on *Four Star Playhouse*.[41] Most "movie stars" entered television in the 1950s for the same reason most directors did: movie jobs were hard to find. (Her old friend David Niven, one of the "four stars," was the one who suggested she might try out the new medium.) All in all she made nineteen appearances on *Four Star Playhouse*. And, after 1956, she did not appear in a theatrical film for thirteen years, when she began returning to the big screen occasionally for "character" parts. She also started writing scripts for television, including "The Stand-in" for *Four Star Playhouse* in which she also appeared. In 1957–58, she and Howard Duff starred in a situation comedy called *Mr. Adams and Eve*, more or less based on their lives. She received an Emmy nomination for best leading actress in a comedy series but lost to Jane Wyatt of *Father Knows Best*.

III

"I loved shooting for television. I'd learned to shoot lean and fast in the 1950s. In television there's no running over. If you are slow and go over budget, you will get fired. I loved the tension and the excitement and the people. Each show was a new challenge to Mother."[42]

Several sources follow Lupino in crediting Richard Boone with starting her career as a television director, because he encouraged her to direct an episode of *Have Gun Will Travel*. But her first television show was broadcast before *Have Gun* came on the air. It was a half-hour noirish drama, based on a story she provided for a series called *Screen Director's Playhouse*. The anthology series' title accurately describes its content: works for television filmed by movie directors. To be included was for Lupino a confirmation of her status. *No. 5 Checked Out* was televised on January 18, 1956. It featured Teresa Wright, William Talman, and Peter Lorre. The item shows every sign of being made in a hurry, but there is much to praise. Auteur critics will be delighted to find that the center of menace is shifted from the female to the male. Those wishing to praise her technique will marvel at how well she handles location shots in a cheap motel office and guest room and how well she does with the exterior scenes at a lake. The only fair criticism is that she could not keep Peter Lorre from giving a terrible imitation of Peter Lorre, as he was wont to do.

"The Man Who Lost," Lupino's first of eight episodes for *Have Gun Will Travel*, was broadcast on April 25, 1959. By that time, she had directed at least four episodes in other series, and during 1959 would direct another four. Given the speed at which these thirty-minute episodes were filmed—three days for rehearsal, three days for shooting is the stock description—there is very little opportunity for individual expression or stylistic distinction. One must assume that Lupino was valued for the qualities she points out herself. She knew how to shoot lean and fast, which implies not only the technical competence—knowing what setups are required, what shots are possible, what lighting the cinematographer will be able to accomplish, what conditions the sound man must have—but also how to keep egos and personalities on an even keel so work can proceed. She must have been good at it, for by one count between 1958 and 1969 she directed a total of sixty-nine scripts for thirty-one different series.

The futility of searching through all sixty-nine episodes to try to define an auteurist perspective is made clear by Mary Celeste Kearney and James M. Moran.[43] In a series, "creative efforts are shaped and controlled almost exclusively by producers rather than directors."[44] In other words, the reason *Have Gun Will Travel* managed to look like the same show for six seasons, despite having fourteen different directors, was that scripts and production were overseen by a producer intent on continuity, on squelching any deviation from the "concept." While "craft" and "efficiency" can certainly be rewarded under such a system, originality cannot prevail.

In their quest for sexist (mis)treatments of the first woman director in television, Kearney and Moran take umbrage over a publicity picture of the director in the "arms of the Skipper and Gilligan as she is about to be tossed into the 'lagoon'."[45] This picture somehow indicates that the female director is being taken as an "exotic spectacle" rather than as a "director." But in worrying over their subject being demeaned by a photograph, they miss the contribution that Sol Saks, head of all CBS comedy series, insists Lupino made to *Gilligan's Island*. When rehearsals for the pilot of *Gilligan* started to go bad, Saks asked her to step in. "Where they [that is, the cast] had grumbled, Ida's presence quieted them," Saks claimed. Her "appearance had a lot to do with that show going on and becoming a success."[46]

Ida was clearly aware of how she projected herself. Kearney and Moran are upset by Lupino's style of directing a virtually all-male crew by acting like the "damsel in distress": *You can do this for mother, can't you?* One might instead congratulate her on the successful discovery of how to keep a crew working harmoniously and on schedule or one might celebrate her superior ability for conflict avoidance. Lupino herself says in a contemporary statement quoted by Donati, "I try never to blow it—they're just waiting for you to do it. As long as you keep your temper, the crew will go along with you."[47] There is ample evidence that Lupino did have a fiery temper, and not just in the company of her various spouses. One would think Kearney and Mean would commend her for recognizing both her shortcomings and the sexist situation she confronted and neutralized, but all they can do is criticize her for being unaware that "damsel in distress" is "not the only alternative to being aggressive on the set."[48] However much Lupino's work habits did not suit certain critics, they seem to have made a good impression on the producers of her day who kept calling her back for repeat assignments.

In 1965, she was finally offered a chance to direct another theatrical film. Since William Frye, who made the offer, had been executive producer for several series that Lupino had worked on, they must have had at least something of a professional relationship.[49] Apparently Rosalind Russell, the leading lady, had final say on choice of director, and Lupino had a difficult first few weeks before their relationship gelled. In the end, Lupino turned out a professional product on time and budget. Russell even publicly acknowledged her talent and pioneering status.[50] The only problem, according to Lupino, was directing Hayley Mills, a "child" actor who in real life was approaching twenty.[51]

A sequel was quickly ordered indicating the film was a financial success. Frye and Russell both returned for *Where Angels Go Trouble Follows*. "I was not asked to direct the sequel," Lupino recalled later, implying surprise and disappointment.[52] The sequel was directed by James Neilson, a director with experience directing child actors at Disney. Perhaps that experience was why he was chosen, perhaps Lupino had more problems directing younger actors than we know, but it is odd that the producer who chose her for the first film and the star who praised her would not have insisted on her return. (Hayley Mills was not in the sequel.)

But not being offered the sequel was not her only disappointment. In fact, writing of the late 1960s, her biographer can say, "The demise of her directing career was startling and quite unexpected"[53] Later, seeming to contradict himself, he says, "scripts and offers poured in," which, if true, means those "offers" must have been very tentative or insincere.[54] One of her friends told Donati that she did not "promote" herself enough, but that would seem to contradict the claim that she was constantly receiving (presumably feature length) "scripts and offers." (Lupino, as we have seen, says that some of the "offers" were for jobs overseas, perfectly acceptable except that she did not want to leave her family.) Possibly she just ran into a streak of bad luck during which no "deal" actually closed. Most directors do so at some point in their career.

But if one looks at how active she was in television after 1966, a puzzling number pops up. After 1966, she only directed three more episodes for television. It is possible that she deliberately withdrew from television in order to signal that as the director of a box office success, she was now ready to resume her career as a director of feature films. Numerically speaking, very few television directors ever moved up to feature-length films (and those that did, like John Frankenheimer or Sidney Lumet, made their reputation directing live dramas). If that was her gambit, it failed. If there is another explanation, it appears to be lost in history.

Her acting career lasted longer, and indeed she stayed relatively busy in the decade following 1967. By one count, she appeared in eleven movies (five of them shot for television) and twenty-three episodes of television series. But in 1976, disaster struck. In that year, she was cast as the female lead in *The Thoroughbreds*, a film shot on location in Kentucky. Unfortunately, because of emotional distress caused by the most recent separation from Howard Duff, plus her alcoholism, she was fired from the picture and replaced by Vera Miles. (The film was released as *Run for the Roses*.)[55] Although the official explanation for her dismissal was "artistic differences," one can be sure that the true reason was soon known throughout the industry. Her acting career in television ended the next year with the painful appearance, as noted earlier, on *Charlie's Angels* when she again had trouble with her lines. Seven years later, at the age of sixty-six, a conservator was appointed to oversee her financial arrangements.[56]

Obviously and sadly, after a certain point in time, Lupino's personal problems made any more successes in film impossible. And there is a certain regret that the talent demonstrated in the five films she directed in the early 1950s was not allowed to flourish. And possibly Hollywood's gendered expectations held her back, though her career shows no more disappointments than those of many male directors from the same era. But it is also true that nothing about her life or expressed attitudes shows that she was ready for the "new" Hollywood that dominated filmmaking after 1969. In order to appreciate her real accomplishments, it may be necessary to remove our own blinders. We tend to privilege the feature-length film director and the transgressor of absolute gender barriers. Lupino fits both categories, but she also fits many other categories as well. It may be more rewarding—that is, fairer to her and more revealing of the real world to us—to see her as a person who led a most interesting life. From the show business ambiance of her father's world to the life of a diva (with even a Japanese butler, at one point) to the woman who worked with her hands in the Warner Brothers editing room, to the story and scriptwriter, to the actor who understood lighting and camera angles, to the producer and casting director, and, finally, to the respected television director, Ida Lupino of Hollywood had a life worthy of respect, admiration, and study.

Notes

1 William Donati, *Ida Lupino: A Biography* (Lexington: University Press of Kentucky, 1996), 259–62.
2 The presence and culture of American experimental filmmakers like Maya Deren or Shirley Clarke should be noted.
3 Gerald Mast and Bruce F. Kawin, A *Short History of the Movies*, 7th ed. (Boston: Allyn and Bacon, 2000), 432–3.
4 Ida Lupino, "Me, Mother, Directress," in Richard Koszarski (ed.), *Hollywood Directors: 1941-1976* (New York: Oxford University Press, 1971), 376–7; Donati, *Ida Lupino*, 236–7.
5 Donati, *Ida Lupino*, 244.
6 Ibid., 73.
7 Ibid., 240–1.
8 Ibid., 254.
9 "Introduction," in Annette Kuhn (ed.), *Queen of the 'B's: Ida Lupino Behind the Camera* (West Port, CT: Praeger, 1995), 7.
10 Donati, *Ida Lupino*, 18.
11 Ibid., photograph between 144–5.
12 Donati, *Ida Lupino*, 23.
13 Ibid., 25.
14 Ibid., 24–6.
15 Ida Lupino, with Mary Ann Anderson, *Ida Lupino: Beyond the Camera* (Albany, GA: Bear Manor Media, 2011), x.
16 Donati, *Ida Lupino*, 26.
17 Lupino, *Beyond the Camera*, x.
18 Donati, *Ida Lupino*, 27.
19 Ibid., 50.

20 Ibid., 158.
21 Ibid., 126.
22 Ibid., 97.
23 Ibid., 146.
24 Mast and Kawin, *Short History*, 317.
25 Donati, *Ida Lupino*, 156.
26 Ibid.
27 "Road House (1948)," Turner Classic Movies, http://www.tcm.com/thismonth/article/253214%C0/Road.House.html (accessed October 23, 2013).
28 Donati, *Ida Lupino*, 139.
29 Diane Waldman, "*Not Wanted* (1949)," in Kuhn, *Queen*, 13–39.
30 Ibid., 148.
31 Ibid., 149–50.
32 Ibid., 150–1.
33 Ibid., 178.
34 Ibid., 15.
35 Ibid., 164.
36 Ibid., 79.
37 Lupino, *Beyond the Camera*, 145.
38 See the advertisement reproduced in Ibid., 96.
39 Mast and Kawin, *Short History*, 286.
40 Ibid., 286–8.
41 Donati, *Ida Lupino*, 204.
42 Lupino, *Beyond the Camera*, 148.
43 Mary Celeste Kearney and James M. Moran, "Ida Lupino as Director of Television," in Kuhn, *Queen*, 147, note 9.
44 Kearney and Moran, "Ida Lupino," 138.
45 Ibid., 145.
46 Donati, *Ida Lupino*, 231.
47 Ibid., 232.
48 Kearney and Moran, "Ida Lupino," 144.
49 Donati, *Ida Lupino*, 232.
50 Ibid., 233.
51 Lupino, *Beyond the Camera*, 123.
52 Ibid.
53 Donati, *Ida Lupino*, 237.
54 Ibid., 242.
55 Ibid., 246.
56 Ibid., 257.

4

Overlooked and Underrepresented

The Essential Lupino

Courtney J. Ruffner Grieneisen

Martin Scorsese wrote in his eulogy, "Ida Lupino: Behind the Camera, a Feminist," that Lupino's "work is resilient, with a remarkable empathy for the fragile and the heartbroken. It is essential."[1] To simply say that her work is exceptionally important and extremely necessary is to assume that the audience not only knows Lupino and her work but is also familiar enough with the time period in film from which she hails. Perhaps, after a cursory search through a biography on Lupino, she becomes more recognizable in our current day in terms of her work in *High Sierra* (1941) or *The Hitch-Hiker* (1953) or, more specifically, she may be even better known today for her work on *The Twilight Zone* (1959). Subsequently, we should be acquainted with Lupino and her work for many other reasons, which include the fact that she was the second woman to be inducted into the Director's Guild of America and that she has not one but two stars on the Hollywood Walk of Fame (for both television and film). Further, she branched out on her own in the early 1950s, when Hollywood was downsizing, to "form her own production companies so that she could direct her own films."[2] In the industry, Lupino is known for her moxie and her boldness. Tapping into a male-dominated field in the 1940s and 1950s was no easy feat, yet Lupino "understood the cultural state of the decade in which she worked,"[3] and that is what allowed her to flourish in her career at this time. Critics want to feminize her as she stands as a symbol for female strength in the male-dominated world of Hollywood. However, Lupino's work was not about gendering and attaching the appropriately stereotyped characteristics to males or females or even playing the role of the hard businesswoman wearing pants to make a point. Robert Kolker states that Lupino "understood that gender was not something defined by movies, only stereotyped by them,"[4] and Lupino, herself, has made clear, "[w]hile I've encountered no resentment from the male of the species for intruding into their world, I give them no opportunity to think I've strayed where I don't belong. I assume no masculine characteristics, which can often be a fault of career women rubbing shoulders with their male counterparts, who become merely arrogant or authoritative."[5]

When we delve into her work as actress and as director, we must come armed with the knowledge that Ida Lupino was not our everyday feminized symbol of the 1940s and 1950s working woman. Instead, this article asserts her contribution to the academe if we take the time to see exactly what has made her "essential" in our vast film history: her own set of rules concerning character transcendence, tenderness of subject matter, and equity of gender.

Many of Lupino's more readily accessible films like *High Sierra* (1941) and *The Hitch-Hiker* (1953) have been analyzed by critics and film enthusiasts. However, two equally underrepresented yet vastly different Lupino films have been resurrected (just in time) and are now available for download or purchase. *Never Fear* (aka) *The Young Lovers* (1949) and *On Dangerous Ground* (1952) capture the viewer and implore a sense of genuine interest in the male and female characters and the plight that they experience interacting with the story line.[6] To say that Lupino has a "nice effect" on her audience is to make light of the seriousness of her commentary within these two films. But to not acknowledge that something transcendent happens to the viewer during these films is to undermine Lupino's abilities in acting and filmmaking, and this woman is far too talented to disregard her any longer in the academic canon.

To begin, *On Dangerous Ground* immediately situates the viewer in a dim-lighted room characteristic of 1940s and 1950s film noir. At the onset of *On Dangerous Ground*, the viewer is immediately reminded of the opening scene in Mervyn LeRoy's *Little Caesar*. While LeRoy aims to concentrate the camera on the clock foreshadowing/marking the time Rico has left in his world, Nicholas Ray (with Lupino's uncredited part in directing) focuses the viewer on a holster and gun symbolizing the harshness of the life of main character Jim Wilson (played by Robert Ryan), who lives in a world that he feels is unjust and inhumane. We learn from Robert Kolker's comments on Lupino's female perspective that she is "interested in gazing closely at both male and female faces of loss and loneliness" and she "gives their neediness equal attention."[7] *On Dangerous Ground* opens with the feel of a gangster film because we immediately see weaponry and crime at Jerry's Liquor Store. We are not privy to Jim's occupation until after we see him scraping food into the garbage from his own dishes and heading off to work, when we find out that he is a police officer. When we are introduced to Jim's partners, Pop (Charles Kemper) specifically, we begin to feel the "masculine softness and vulnerability [that] indicate a strength that comes from places other than male braggadocio and a puffed-up sense of the heroic."[8] Jim is genuinely concerned for Pop when he asks, "How's your shoulder, Pop?" and then insists that they drop by to see the doctor. Jim's masculine softness is highlighted when Pop mentions to another officer on duty that "Jim takes it [the cop's life] harder than the rest of us," and our sensibilities as viewers are cued into the loneliness that Jim feels as a cop in an inhumane world. This concern for Pop and our newly acquired fondness for Jim are juxtaposed by the next scene where Jim is shown as the lover, a very masculine cop getting information out of the female by any means necessary. Yet this scene, which includes Cleo Moore, illustrates more than just a cop shaking down a gangster's girlfriend. In this scene, the girlfriend of Tucker (played by Richard Irving) coaxes Jim to "squeeze it outta [her] with those big, strong arms," to which he responds, "that's right, sister." What else could he say? He has to remain strong and masculine in the face of the girl who represents the underside of humanity, the very thing that causes his loneliness (Figure 4.1).

It is the very next scene that sets a pattern of transcendence for the remainder of the film. To equalize the softness that has been unveiled in Jim,

FIGURE 4.1 *"Pete, I don't like being alone" in* On Dangerous Ground.

Ray and Lupino bring back the angry, demonic male stereotype of the cop pounding on the criminal yelling, "Why do you do it . . . . I always make you punks talk," in order to get information out of Tucker and to restore Jim to the *über* masculine cop that he must be in order for the film to work in the culture of the day.

At this point in the film, viewers are compelled to humanize the cop-figure that we see in Wilson as he explains that "cops have no friends . . . nobody likes a cop on either side of the law." Jim's statements about the cop persona, coupled with his captain's dress-down of Jim's behavior, "[you're] not a gangster with a badge," highlight the social humanizing that the film attempts to address. We must remember that in 1935 there were restrictions placed on American gangster films, in part due to their violence and their glorification of the criminal lifestyle. The implication that cops could be more directly associated with the kind of criminality gangster characters portray teeters on the line the Production Code marked as "The presentation of crimes against the law is often necessary for the carrying out of the plot. But the presentation must not throw sympathy with the crime as against the law nor with the criminal as against those who punish him."[9] And so it is imperative that the character of Jim Wilson is softened by his true preoccupation with inhumanity and his genuine care for others. When Jim is sent away to *cool his jets* in the cold of the country, we begin to see the transformation that takes place for Jim and we credit this change to meeting Mary Malden (Ida Lupino).

Now the stage is set for the turnaround in the film. We know that Lupino's characters (whether directed by her or played by her) "are progressive in their sympathy for ordinary women and men caught in social dilemmas of various kinds [and] often find comfort in traditional values and relationships."[10] Jim has been sent to the country as a punishment for his brutish behavior in the city to help the country folk solve the murder of a young girl. From the very beginning, we see Jim admire the ways in which these people—rural citizens—survive. For them, the city represents fancy trials and a few cops. Their way of dealing with a murderer is to gather together as a posse and fill the criminal's "belly full of lead." When the posse gets word that the criminal is on the move, everyone, including Jim, takes off in pursuit. Jim and the victim's father Walter Brent (Ward Bond) begin their partnership in the car during a snowstorm while pursuing the murderer. At one point, Jim says to Brent, "I want him just as much as you," showing Jim's moralistic need to apprehend the *punks* that make his world the ugly reality he has come to live in. We see Brent's confusion at Jim's comment, and after a short pause he responds, "what do you care? She wasn't your kid," only solidifying Jim's indisputable care for the welfare of others (Figure 4.2).

The scene in which the two men chase the murderer in the car is noteworthy because it sets the viewer in the car with the father and Jim while in pursuit. The quick jumps between the passenger's view of the icy, snowy road and the side shots of the passengers themselves lend to the immediacy

FIGURE 4.2 *"I Want Him Just as Much as You Do" in* On Dangerous Ground.

of the hunt, but when the car slides out of control trying to avoid a wreck, the tumbling of the camera action to show the rolling of car is masterful for the time. This type of camera work draws the viewer closer to the story line because it places the viewer in the main characters' seat at this point. Because of this intimate camera work, we are significantly invested in the film without even having seen the star (Lupino). We begin to anticipate the meeting of Jim and Mary finding ourselves rooting for Jim to find solace in something, the apprehension of the criminal or the relationship between Jim and the father of the victim or even the obvious love connection that he will walk into in the very next scene. As the scene opens, we follow the two men tracking the murderer through the woods to a house where we are introduced to Mary. We do not see her face, yet we hear her voice for the first few minutes of the scene. Ray and Lupino situate the viewer in the awareness that Mary is in, as a blind woman, by not introducing her facial features to us immediately. We are left out. In fact, we are not introduced to Mary until Brent comes charging in yelling about something being not right in the house. He makes claims of things being hidden and asks, "Why don't you put on a light?" For which she responds, "I'm sorry. I didn't mean to keep you in the dark." This witty exchange between Brent and Mary calls attention to Mary's blindness, along with Jim's future transformation, when his "existential isolation is poignantly overcome by love."[11]

One of the strengths of *On Dangerous Ground* is the way in which the characters of Jim and Mary stand equal to one another in terms of gender characteristics. Jim is strong and solid, a typical man of the times, yet he is plagued by an internal need to rid the world of the criminals that make his world difficult to live within. We view this sensibility as a weakness because he is driven by his anger at injustice and roughs up the criminals that he is trusted to bring in safely, and he is unable to trust (and in turn love) anyone because of his feeling of callousness for humanity. Mary is equally strong in that she must care for her brother Danny, the murderer (played by Sumner Williams), in his state of mental impairment while managing her own blindness. When she reaches down—the act of "reaching downward" seems to indicate power—and touches Jim's hand, mumbling that he is cold, and she immediately assumes the role of caretaker, giving him a cup of tea to warm himself. Viewers know that Jim does not trust anyone, and we know that Mary has to trust people because of her blindness. It is here, with the exchange of a cup of tea, that we see the building of the foundation between Jim and Mary's relationship. She maintains her strength because Jim allows her to make the cup of tea instead of taking the cup and making the tea himself. She observes that "when [he] talks to [her], there is no pity in [his] voice." With this small, unconscious gesture, the character of Jim Wilson elevates to a character with deep empathy for humankind, one who gives the same respect for individual capabilities regardless of blindness (Figure 4.3).

Jim's character continues to grow more empathic in response to his inability to accept "degenerates," especially when we see him assume the caretaker role in his relationship with Brent. He sees that Brent is cold and

FIGURE 4.3 *A cup of tea in* On Dangerous Ground.

wet and immediately says to him that he "better get those boots off and let them dry." Brent begins to unfasten his boots while grumbling that they "really lost him [Danny]." Jim continues to take care of Brent by handing him a bottle of whiskey, covering his shoulders up with a blanket, and taking a place on the floor next to Brent.

At this point in the film, we begin to see Jim's attitude change in terms of his isolation. He cares for his father and he cares for Mary. He wants to bring Danny to a psychiatric ward without hurting him, both for Mary's sake and because this action is the ethical course of action. He wants to apprehend the murderer and put him in a facility so that Brent and his family can find closure. He understands Mary's pain because Danny is her brother, and he recognizes Brent's pain because of the loss of his daughter, but he also distinguishes Danny's crime itself from the traditionally premeditated crimes that have taken place in the city over which Danny has no control. The sadness is that Brent's daughter did not have to die if Danny were able to control his emotions, and this issue is the pinnacle of the sorrow that fills Jim's heart. When the day breaks and the two men begin to chase Danny in a very neorealist scene over rocks laced with ice, Danny slips and falls. When Brent comes upon him and realizes that "he was just a kid," Jim's faith in humanity is, arguably, restored in seeing Brent pick the body up and carry him into the house. If the father of a murdered daughter can find peace with his daughter's killer, then humanity must not be so bad. Jim's faith in humanity is restored but the emptiness in his heart remains because he was rejected by Mary precisely because she feels that he is damaged and hardened. She just wants him to go. And all he wants to do is help Mary, and she feels that he pities her. He leaves. On the drive back to the city he remembers, in a psychological montage, Mary saying, "sometimes people who are never alone are the loneliest" and "most lonely people try to figure it out, about loneliness." Then Pop tells him, "The way you're going, you won't be good to anybody. Not even yourself! . . . To get anything out of this life, you gotta put something in it. From the heart!" Words from people in Jim's life complete his transformation from a hardened cop to a man who opens himself up to love and faith. He returns to Mary, they embrace hands, and kiss.

The use of the handheld camera, the behind-the-eyes camera treatment, and the equality of gender with sexualized scenes are only a few of Lupino's masterful touches that help to create a place in the story line where the viewer may escape reality and become one with the character. Similar to *On Dangerous Ground*, Lupino's breakout film *Never Fear* (*The Young Lovers*) has received little critical appraisal, and, therefore, it has been largely left out of the contemporary film canon. Written for the screen with Collier Young, Lupino's direction of this film clearly places her at the center of the motion picture mainstream, as Annette Kuhn agrees.[12] Lupino, as director, focused on taboo subjects with "the mark of disablement"[13] that the larger studios would not address, as we see in the childhood polio of Carol (played by Sally Forrest) in *Never Fear*. The similarities between this film and *On Dangerous Ground* do not go unnoticed.

The handheld camera work in both films enhances the depth of the disablement so that the viewer is positioned to look through the eyes of the star. We get this behind-the-eyes camera treatment when Mary meets Jim in *On Dangerous Ground* and the viewer can see her struggle to focus on Jim's face, seeing only glimpses of light in the scene where Jim and Brent's car slides off the road and tumbles down a snow bank. The camera follows the car as if the camera were rolling along with it. This camera work positions the audience alongside the two gentlemen as they plummet further into the story line. In *Never Fear*, we are immediately sympathetic to Carol because we are located in a position to see her trauma. We feel her dizzy spells because the camera goes in and out of focus, making the viewer part of the action. From the beginning of this film, the audience is drawn to the couple because of their witty banter and their obvious attraction to one another. The first dance scene is a choreographed sword fight offering violence and sexual undertones throughout the film that cannot be denied. From the beginning of the film, Carol and Guy (Keefe Brasselle) stand as a symbol for gender equity. The dance speaks to this equity that Lupino has worked so hard to honor in her work. In this dance scene, Carol de-swords Guy, establishing herself in a power position. When he counters by grabbing her sword, she grabs the end of the sword, places it on her chest as if to say, "you could kill me but you won't," and pushes the sword tip away. They embrace to show an equal harmony, a yin and yang (interestingly, she is clothed in all black, and he is wearing white and black as if to foreshadow through color symbolism the couple's impending problems and their respective attitudes toward solutions).

William Donati offers excellent insight about *Never Fear* being "lost on the modern viewer," because "the fear of polio no longer exists."[14] However, there are scenes that take place in this film that far surpass the treatment of polio in the 1949 film and reveal an individual struggle to overcome insurmountable odds. The film has been criticized by Barbara Quart as being one that furthers "a sense of female disablement,"[15] because of Carol's self-critical nature, her position as dancer while her lover is her partner and her choreographer, and her submission to him at the end of the seductive sword dance: her head on his shoulder. Quart goes on to say, "once the heroine of *Never Fear* is rendered literally helpless, her regaining of movement and assurance in no way adds up to a tale of empowerment."[16] We can understand why Ida Lupino would have such a problem with feminist labeling based on Quart's argument. To say that Carol is a submissive character is to say that a child who has contracted a life-altering disease is not permitted to feel slightly frightened, that a child facing the loss of her career (everything that she has known) is not allowed to feel some self-pity. The scene that disregards this line of argument is marked by Josie (Rita Lupino) and the story of her and her husband marrying after she contracted the disease. She says to Carol, "Nothing can come between us

[Josie and her husband] now that we are going through this together." Carol is prompted by Josie's strength and her sentiment to begin her fight to walk again. We see the same montage of memories through the peripheral haze here as we did with Jim when he decided to move past his loneliness and pride and return for Mary in *On Dangerous Ground*. The camera focuses on close-ups of Carol's legs and her attempts to walk with the help of the therapy bars while we hear the echo of Josie, "Nothing can come between us now that we are going through this together." We hear the doctor telling her, "You'll be surprised at what you'll do when you've made up your mind to live again." We continue to see her triumph and become stronger through her therapy. Carol continues to be prompted by her memories of Guy, "tough things happen to people every day of the week. You have to have guts enough to face them," and, finally, the montage culminates with words of encouragement, "when people love each other, they don't stop loving when things go wrong." And through this flood of memories, "presented with a mixed voice-over track of pep talks by her coaxing doctor and by memory-echoed reprises of her father, and then of Guy, all crying out their need for her,"[17] Carol loses her self-pity, gains a new positive perspective, and recuperates enough to walk again on her own. Although a contemporary audience may not identify with the fear of losing a loved one to polio, we can certainly view individual and personal problems differently having seen Carol struggle to cope with self-criticism and pity, push them both aside, and triumph over her own physical impairment.

One of the most interesting developments in the film is that Lupino allows Guy to finally leave Carol in order to go back to Las Vegas and show business, and he finds a new partner. Symbolically, the act of taking a new dance partner, for Carol, is worse than his having a new romantic woman in his life. It must be noted that the only time Carol asks for a cigarette throughout the film is after Guy tells her that he has taken a new partner. She is a young girl approaching the age of twenty-one and she is a dancer. She does not accept cigarettes from anyone who tries to give her one. Yet, after hearing that her place on the dance floor has been taken by another, she graduates to a different level in her life, one where the cigarette will not matter. Perhaps she has finally grown up and accepted the fact that she will never regain her life as it once was. She must now become an adult in the real world, and the taking of the cigarette indicates her acceptance of adulthood. The very next scene shows Len lightening a cigarette for Carol and Carol crying as she explains, "It's so funny. It's taken me all this time to feel like a woman. It's the flattest feeling I've ever known. How's that for a laugh?"

In addition to the cigarette as a symbol of adulthood, Carol's actions continue to show her transformation into womanhood. When Carol makes a pass at Len in the hopes that he will tell her that she is not a failure, she is grappling with the thought of being alone. She begs him to love her—"we belong together, we are alike"—and she even tells him that she can make him happy, putting herself into a position to kiss him. She has clearly maintained the seduction and her female strength that we see at the beginning of the film when she and Guy trade sexualized flirtations both before and after their dance number and before Carol becomes ill. When they determine that *the bells didn't ring for them*, Carol collects herself and admits that she is ashamed of her behavior. We know, of course, that Len is "the healthiest man [and] peace of mind gives him a sort of power." We see this power through his conversation with Carol. He is never bothered by her sexualized response to being left behind by Guy. He only wants the best for Carol. In fact, when we learn that "he wouldn't let his bell ring for Carol," we know that he loves her enough to let her be with Guy, the man that she truly loves. She draws strength from Len's honor and learns to become a little more like him in terms of mindset. Thus, we see Carol's full transformation to adulthood taking place.

Ultimately, this shift in frame of mind is what allows Carol to accept her life without Guy positioned at the center. Furthermore, Lupino "integrates [through Carol] an inward, deeply compassionate depiction of a woman who is the victim,"[18] yet one who overcomes her fears by learning to have faith and courage in her transformation to adulthood. We watch as Carol departs the Rehabilitation Center assuring Len that she will "be fine. [She's] going out there on her own." We watch her, frightened, turning back to look at Len twice even after she has displayed her newly acquired confidence, exit the Center's doors looking back over the height of the Center, hugging the walls of the Center as she makes her way down the sidewalk, alone. Just as the viewer comes to accept that Carol will build her life away from dancing and away from Guy, Carol's eyes meet Guy's and they become entranced with one another. They maintain eye contact while Guy provides encouraging commentary: "Come on, darling. Come on. Come on. You can make it. That's my girl," as if to choreograph her steps away from the Center and back into his arms where they embrace and kiss, much as we see in the final scene of *On Dangerous Ground* when Jim returns to Mary.

Anne Morra has written that Ida Lupino's work "remains singular, a vital contribution to the evolution of women in cinema and of American independent film production in general."[19] It would seem neglectful not to mention the influence that Lupino has on the work of two prominent contemporary filmmakers, Martin Scorsese and Sylvester Stallone. Scorsese, in his beautiful memorial tribute to Lupino, shares with her the theme of grit and violence along with character self-awareness. Robert Kolker writes that Scorsese's films are "made self-consciously and are about self-consciousness."[20] We are able to see Kolker's assessment through Travis Bickle (played by Robert DeNiro) and his paranoia in *Taxi Driver* (1976) and with Jake LaMotta (also played by Robert DeNiro) in *Raging Bull* (1980). Scorsese's characters "try to fight the world's imposition on them and impose their own will and spirit back on the world,"[21] much like Lupino's characters do when Jim stands up against humanity's injustices and accepts love into his world when Mary decides to trust Jim and have faith that she will regain her sight in *On Dangerous Ground*, and when Carol chooses to embrace her inner peace and try to walk again in *Never Fear*. In addition, Scorsese uses a handheld camera to capture a more violent sense for a scene where this is indicative of the subject matter.[22] We see Lupino's use of the handheld camera in scenes where violence or tragedy ensues. For example, when Jim and Brent are in the car accident and when we meet Mary and learn she is blind in *On Dangerous Ground* and at the beginning of Carol's plight with polio when she becomes dizzy in *Never Fear*.

Lupino's technique is also echoed by actor/director Sylvester Stallone. Similarly, one scene that takes place in Lupino's *Never Fear* is remarkably similar in content to the training montages in the Rocky films where Rocky Balboa (Sylvester Stallone) is struggling with decisions such as his choice to fight again and, once again, when he listens to an inspirational talk by a sympathetic Adrian (played by Talia Shire) in order to regain his edge and fight for his title. Again, the way in which Lupino directs the scene of triumph for Carol in *Never Fear* is reminiscent to the way in which Stallone directs Rocky to handle his own self-doubt and pity, allowing Rocky to succeed beyond his limitations. Stallone is certainly aware of Lupino's work, and the two types of scenes resemble one another enough to be analyzed alongside each other as specific motivating techniques.

Thus, Ida Lupino is most certainly essential in our film history, and what makes her such is her ability to capture her audience and keep them invested in her characters as they grapple with the unkind reality of humanity. These characters continue to garner our respect as we watch them transform into individuals who are able to come to terms with their predicaments and grow beyond what is expected for the time. Lupino's ability is able to achieve these feats in her work as a director have been recognized by successful, contemporary filmmakers and is a credit to her abilities as a director and should be marked by her entrance into our contemporary film canon.

Notes

1 Martin Scorsese, "Ida Lupino: Behind the Camera, a Feminist," *New York Times Magazine*, December 31, 1995, 43.
2 Robert Kolker, *Film, Form, and Culture* (New York: McGraw Hill, 2006), 101.
3 Ibid., 101.
4 Ibid., 103.
5 Ida Lupino, "Ida Lupino Retains Her Femininity as Director" (feature article in Pressbook of The Hitch-Hiker, 1953), 4. quoted in Wheeler Winston Dixon, "Ida Lupino," *Senses of Cinema* 50 (2009). Available at http://sensesofcinema.com/2009/great-directors/ida-lupino/ (accessed 19 May, 2021).

6 Never Fear aka. *The Young Lovers* (1949) and *On Dangerous Ground* (1952) have been dubbed and presented in a format that is to preserve the aspect ratio of the films' original theatrical exhibition. Both films have sound quality issues and color consistency errors throughout causing the viewer in places to adjust sound and visual balance in order to access the films.
7 Ibid., Kolker, *Film, Form, and Culture*, 103.
8 Ibid., 102.
9 The Motion Picture Production Code of 1930 (Hays Code). artsReformation .com., April 12, 2006. Available at https://en.wikipedia.org/wiki/Motion_Picture_Production_Code.
10 Dan Georgakas, "Ida Lupino: Doing It Her Way," *Cineaste*, 25: 36.
11 Susan Fegley Osmond, "The Resurrection of Ida Lupino," World and I, March 1998:106+ Biography in Context, August 2014.
12 Jackie Byars, Review of "*Queen of the B's*: Ida Lupino Behind the Camera by Annette Kuhn," *Film Quarterly*, 50, no. 4 (Summer 1997): 61.
13 Claire Johnston, "Women's Cinema as Counter-Cinema," in Philip Simpson, Andrew Utterson, Karen J. Shepherdson (eds.), *Film Theory: Critical Concepts in Media and Cultural Studies*, vol. 3 (New York: Routledge 2004), 191.
14 William Donati, *Ida Lupino: A Biography* (Lexington: The University Press of Kentucky, 1996).
15 Barbara Quart, *Women Directors: The Emergence of a New Cinema* (New York: Prager, 1988), 27. Qtd. in Ellen Nerenberg, "Overlooking and Looking Over Ida Lupino," *Voices in Italian Americana: A Literary and Cultural Review*, 7, no. 2 (1996). Available at http://academic.brooklyn.cuny.edu/modlang/carasi/via/ViaVol7_2Nerenberg.htm (accessed 19 May, 2021).
16 Ibid., 27.
17 Ronnie Scheib. *Never Fear* qtd. in Ellen Nerenberg. "Overlooking and Looking Over Ida Lupino," *Voices in Italian Americana: A Literary and Cultural Review*, 7, no. 2 (1996). Available at http://academic.brooklyn.cuny.edu/modlang/carasi/via/ViaVol7_2Nerenberg.htm (accessed 19 May, 2021).
18 Richard Brody, "Ida Lupino's Prescient 'Outrage,'" *The New Yorker*, June 16, 2014. Available at http://www.newyorker.com/culture/richard-brody/ida-lupinos-prescient-outrage (accessed 19 May, 2021).
19 Charles Silver, "Ida Lupino's Never Fear (The Young Lovers)," MoMA. Available at https://www.moma.org/explore/inside_out/page90/P.
20 Kolker, *Film, Form, & Culture*, 89.
21 Ibid., 91.
22 Martin Scorsese Interviews, edited by Peter Brunette, 10.

5

"A Big Family of Little Failures"

Postwar America's Children and Ida Lupino's *Not Wanted*

Julie Grossman

While many critics now recognize Lupino's films as "remarkable for their complexity,"[1] scholars have long dismissed Lupino's style as "technically unsophisticated"[2] and her subject matter and tone as simplistic or conservative.[3] Feminist film critics have often been hard on Lupino, suggesting that she "dealt with feminist questions from an anti-feminist perspective,"[4] or that her films were merely "wounded woman [melodramas]."[5] If the men in Lupino were seen as overly benevolent, Lupino's "first heroines are victims, vulnerable girls struck down."[6] In my view, Lupino's harshest critics have missed the radical nature of Lupino's gender and social critique because they are preoccupied with an understandable though limiting desire to define feminist representation only in terms of positive role modeling. Failure to read Lupino's narrative patterns and mise-en-scène as deeply engaged with social problems and gender trauma does a disservice to the films and to a full understanding of Lupino's unique contribution to film history. An "auteur of social realism,"[7] Ida Lupino captured the brutality of social conformity and the alienation of those who stand apart from mainstream culture. Following the re-evaluation of Lupino's filmmaking ignited by Annette Kuhn's 1995 edited collection *Queen of the 'B's*, and engaging the narrative and mise-en-scène of one of the lesser known of Lupino's films, this chapter engages Lupino's analysis of gender trauma and the failed institution of family, both symptoms of the breakdown of social roles in postwar America.

Ida Lupino began her directing career stepping in to replace Elmer Clifton in 1949 when he had a heart attack very early in the production of *Not Wanted*, a "story," as the initial credits tell us, "told one hundred thousand times each year." A portrait of a young woman, Sally Kelton (Sally Forrest), who has a child out of wedlock, *Not Wanted* is more than simply an *exposé* of a social problem plaguing female American youth. For Lupino, Sally's "problem" is a symptom of large-scale psychosocial dysfunction. That dysfunction is explored in *Not Wanted* through Lupino's use of neo-Romantic notions of the child, through which we see how the film's narrative patterns reflect deep cultural wounds in distinctly anti-Romantic ways. Lupino's first directorial effort, itself characterized by a layered authorial presence (Lupino cowrote the script and coproduced, as well as directed, the film, although she refused to take screen credit for her direction), focuses on a story about social failure that goes well beyond the single issue of unwed mothers.[8] In *Not Wanted*, Lupino establishes what would throughout her career be her authorial stamp: a thoroughgoing critique of imprisoning social and familial roles and a noir representation of the bleak prospects for happiness for men and women in modern America.

In *Not Wanted*, however, Lupino makes particular use of the ideology of childhood, arguing in this film that the neo-Romantic innocence and hope for fulfillment built into the idea of the American Dream are traps for men and women who find themselves making terrible choices that may doom them to a lifetime of unhappiness. The mistakes individuals make are in large part based on a failed romanticism, a childlike insistence that the world is a product of imagination. Lupino's characters, sold a false bill of goods (optimism and fantasies of futurity), are shown bumping up against a recalcitrant, repressive, or hostile social world. While in postwar America the number of families rose and national income increased, the segregation of home and public life with women deified as the modern angel in the house pressured men and women to meet the demands of a rigorously articulated social script. If the 1950s were a time of "outward optimism but inward anxiety and fear,"[9] Lupino's 1949 film *Not Wanted* presages this contradiction, taking a noir look at the American Dream and revealing the powerful streams of restlessness and dissatisfaction that lay beneath it.

Throughout the noir-inflected social problem films Lupino directed, she shows women at risk not only because of predatory men, but also because their inexperience and romanticized views lead to failure. The cycle is a product not only of flawed social institutions but also of having internalized fictions about love and success that, like the "mind-forged manacles" William Blake diagnosed in his *Marriage of Heaven and Hell*, do not survive real experience in a modern social world. Having been programmed by family and social conventions to expect desire to deliver safe and happy rewards,

Lupino's young women are instead confronted with harsh realities and the bitter consequences that follow their naïve choices.

In his sweeping history of childhood in America, Stephen Mintz points to the problematic romanticism that characterized young people's attitudes toward love and sex in postwar America. Popular culture traded on romantic conventions, soaked up by a powerful new teen culture that, according to Mintz, cultivated "unrealistic attitudes toward sex, colored by heavily romanticized notions of true love. In the early 1950s eighty love comics appeared each month, and the song lyrics most popular among girls emphasized wishing, dreaming, and longing for love."[10] Such views of relationships went hand in hand in the late 1940s and 1950s with a rush to early marriage, which was seen as fulfillment and a haven for young men and women. In *Not Wanted*, seen through Lupino's noir lens, the pressures to accede to these models of love and marriage are portrayed as abject and destructive.

While the ostensible subject of *Not Wanted* is babies born outside of marriage, it is less the babies themselves that the film shows to be "not wanted" than individuals who strive to make meaning of their lives when they do not seem to be valued by society at large. Instead of Wordsworth's "father of the man," the child in Lupino's social critique is a figure for the stunted growth of society in general. No longer akin to the "splendor in the grass," Wordsworth's image for a natural conception of childhood innocence, Sally Kelton can be seen as a forerunner to Deanie, William Inge's application in *Splendor in the Grass* of Wordsworth's ideal to the real experience of female adolescence in modern America. Anticipating Deanie and the modern American obsessions with sexual repression in *Splendor in the Grass*, Sally is driven almost to the point of madness by her desire and made to suffer as a result of the repressive social conventions that govern her life. It should be noted that Lupino's bitter portraits of female teenagers contrast markedly with one of the most popular wartime representations of childhood, the novel and film, *A Tree Grows In Brooklyn*. A sentimental view of a young girl's strength against adversity, Betty Smith's novel, published in 1943, and its film adaptation directed by Elia Kazan in 1945, represent a child's suffering absorbed by the "Tree of Heaven" metaphor that insists on resiliency and a fortitude in Francie's coming of age.[11] Lupino carries a wartime focus on youth into an unsentimental postwar context, focusing instead on the brutal consequences of psychosocial repression, especially for girls and women, and the cracked foundations of the family structure in modern America.

In *Not Wanted*, gender and family roles are portrayed as distortions of conventional ideals. Men and fathers are shown as utterly infantilized: Sally's father (Wheaton Chambers) is a henpecked child figure scared of Mrs. Kelton (Dorothy Adams). Sally forgets to bring hardware home to aid her father in fixing a pipe, thus abetting his failure as a competent "man of the house."

Intimidated by his wife, Mr. Kelton says in response, "we'll never hear the end of it." His passivity is meanwhile portrayed by his wife as a lack of thinking, when she says, "You haven't had a thought in your head for the last ten years." The state of "unthinking" represents male escape from the demands of masculine role-playing, a distinct reference to the postwar maladjustment to shifting gender roles. The motif further links Lupino's analysis of postwar gender roles to film noir, which explores the "erosion of confidence in the structuring mechanisms of masculine identity and the masculine role."[12]

Suggesting a kind of panic in not knowing how to fulfill postwar social roles, Mr. Kelton's submissiveness sets the stage for all of the male roles in *Not Wanted*. Like Sally's father, Steve Ryan (Leo Penn) is also characterized in terms of "not thinking." In his first conversation with Sally, she tells him that he "thinks fast." He replies, "I don't think at all, if I can help it." His first number at the piano provides a musical riff on this idea: "Nothing matters," he scats. "Do it. Just you do it." In a postwar sphere when action is no longer defined in unambiguous terms of masculine action, the men in *Not Wanted* are utterly at sea.

As has been widely documented, women in postwar America migrated back into the household after working during the war in positions vacated by the men who were fighting abroad. Women returned to homemaking after experiencing a new kind of independence during the war. Men tried to resume their domestic role as main breadwinner, and women worked instead to bulwark their domestic sphere of influence. Home, as Elaine Tyler May has explored, became an entrenched bastion against "enemies."[13] However, returning veterans of war, as well as other men, in reality found it difficult, if not impossible, to fulfill these roles. Lupino's symbolic intervention in this postwar domestic miasma has men retreating into "childhood," while women become embittered in domestic arrangements.

If Mr. Kelton submits passively to an oppressive domesticity, Steve Ryan (Leo Penn) rejects this world to pursue the equally untenable position of an artist living on the margins of society. His nihilism—"Nothing matters"—is portrayed sympathetically. Steve is another lost child figure in *Not Wanted*. Lupino takes a type, a thoughtless bounder, and imbues the character with pathos. Far from villainous, he is a smirking young man who claims nevertheless to be "tired" and who recognizes himself as a "dime a dozen," moving among other drifting musicians like himself, "just a big family," he says, "of little failures." Interestingly, the Hollywood blacklist haunts the portrayal of Steve Ryan. Leo Penn's acting career ruined by the blacklist, the actor (and father of his more famous son Sean) saw Lupino as "ahead of her time."[14] While later in the film her landlady confirms Sally's worst fears as she futilely tries to reach Steve ("They're all alike, honey. Never call when you want 'em to"), Steve articulates the tragedy of romantic projection Lupino explores in *Not Wanted*, a projection born of unfilled desires. After she chases Steve to "Capital City," and he rejects her, he reminds her, "I never gave you any phony ideas about getting married and growing old together. That's something you've got into your head. If I've hurt you, Sally, I'm sorry. But I never lied to you, now get that straight." While Steve's own desperation is clear in the Capital City sequence (the last shot of him is a grim close-up), he pinpoints a problem of stunted growth linked to frustrated desire (Figure 5.1).

While the men in Not Wanted are represented as childlike (with Drew Baxter [Keefe Brasselle], whom I will return to below, serving as the most prominent example), female independence is likewise stunted. Lupino's signature concern in all of her films is to portray the desire of strong women to have meaningful lives. If male agency is limited, women's actions seem inevitably to lead to trauma. Sally's mother is desperate to keep Sally from having "to slave around a kitchen for the rest of your life the way I have," but Mrs. Kelton is relentlessly negative in her parenting, insisting that Sally find a "respectable" man and that her teenaged antics will doom her. Her mother's advice is limited to punishing lessons on the inevitability of Sally's failure: "You feel fine now cause you're young. In about five years you'll suddenly fall flat on your face one day and don't say I didn't tell you." All of Sally's actions are wrong for Mrs. Kelton, especially any expression of sexuality. When Sally pulls the shirtsleeves of her dress down over her shoulders, her mother is mortified; "Pull it up and keep it up. It's disgusting," says Mrs. Kelton. Chastising Sally and repressing her development, her mother enforces a stifling regimentation within the family.

FIGURE 5.1 *Steve Ryan (Leo Penn) scats, "Do it. Just you do it" in* Not Wanted.

FIGURE 5.2 *Traumatized mother Mrs. Kelton (Dorothy Adams) in* Not Wanted.

Filled with "harried discontent," as Scheib observes,[15] Sally's mother is herself trapped in a generational cycle of female domestic misery. A telling montage reveals Mrs. Kelton's despair when Sally and Steve say goodbye in the woods. Lupino cuts to the river and pans on Steve's cigarette, implying that the couple are having sex, and the film then cuts to a close shot of Sally's mother, lying in bed over a tear-stained pillow, ridden by anxiety. Lupino here renders the postwar American "fear of sexual chaos" Elaine May Tyler describes in *Homeward Bound*.[16] The scene, with a clock ticking in the background as Mrs. Kelton worries about Sally, evokes a cultural setting of female desire, regret, and panic (Figure 5.2).

With female longing and fear foregrounded in the film by Mrs. Kelton's anxiety, resentment, and sexual repressiveness, it is no wonder that Sally escapes into what will turn out to be a failed relationship with bounder Steve Ryan. When Sally listens to Steve's music, his performance and expression attract her, and Lupino not only lingers on his piano-playing to show his talent and passion but gives us shots such as the one below, in which Sally's desire is represented in a noir shadow cast upon her face (Figure 5.3).

When they meet, he says about her listening to his music, "You really like what I was giving out there." She confirms, "It was the best I ever heard," but then adds a comment about the lack of stimulation in her life: "You don't get to hear much of anything good around here." The dearth of outlets for Sally's passion and expression is symbolized by the "broken victrola" at home. Lupino here taps a burgeoning youth culture whose representation culminates most famously six years later in Nicholas Ray's *Rebel Without a Cause* (1955). Anxious to find fulfillment independent from their parents, postwar teens expressed their desire for freedom, as Stephen Mintz observes,

FIGURE 5.3 *Sally (Sally Forrest) watches pianist Steve Ryan "giving [it] out" in* Not Wanted.

"[protesting] the sterility of American life."[17] Resisting the pull to marry young—in large part as social historians note to channel their sexuality into early marriage—many female teens were vulnerable to the guilt or practical consequences of sex, pregnancy, and the "postwar taboos against premarital sexual activity in women."[18]

Lupino shows this threat as developing out of a desire to escape a dysfunctional and unhappy domestic structure at home, though the ideology of motherhood haunts Sally Kelton even more powerfully after she has given up her baby for adoption. In a postwar world in which, as May has observed, women were taught that "motherhood was the ultimate cultural fulfillment of female sexuality and the primary source of a woman's identity," it is no wonder that Sally wanders the streets lost after having given up her baby for adoption.[19]

Sally herself is lost among the shards of a postwar ideology that reinforces the view of single women as an impetus toward moral decay, unbridled sexuality, and destruction (one of the forms of which was said to be venereal disease). Hence, single women who become pregnant need to be shut away in institutions and surrender their babies for adoption. Interestingly, as Sally attempts to avoid suffering the same fate as her mother's, she becomes embroiled in these ideological and institutional structures, a process that leads inexorably to her breakdown.

Lupino shows Sally's affect in her wanderings to border on insanity. The repeated scenes of reality careening out of control for Sally (most notably in the merry-go-round scene) support this view: Lupino's mise-en-scène repeatedly illustrates a distortion continuous with Sally's experience. She is in a kind of fugue state, one of Lupino's many traumatized "sleepwalkers," as Scheib notes,[20] when she picks up another woman's baby on the street to begin the film and is subsequently arrested for kidnapping. In the jail, she is placed with women who all seem insane. Made crazy by contorting real experience into line with personal desire, the women in Not Wanted suffer (Figure 5.4).

Imprisoned among bleak prospects, Sally is seen to escape one trap held out by her mother (marrying a "respectable man" and becoming miserable like herself) to enter another, her short-lived passion with Steve. In one of their early encounters when Sally is looking for work, Drew Baxter tells her excitedly "One of the kids here is getting married next week. That makes us short a girl." Offering Sally a job at the same time as he suggests that it is a dead end (she'll leave when she gets married), Drew's comment alludes to the many women who grew accustomed to working during the war but were then forced back into the home after the war's end.

And, indeed, Sally's desires are met with a lack of real prospects. Surrounded by an angry disappointed mother and a weak sycophantic father, Sally tries to maintain a hopeful disposition. Her first words to her mother in an early scene are about the "beautiful day." On her date with Drew at

FIGURE 5.4 *Crazed women in prison in* Not Wanted.

the merry-go-round, she recalls early childhood experiences. She remembers being happy when she was seven, when "my dad took me to the circus," then in high school when she had the lead in a play about Queen Elizabeth. This was the last time Sally seems to have expressed herself in a healthy way; her reminiscence is followed by Sally sharing with Drew that "Pretty soon after that I left school. I had to go to work to help out at home. I was awfully proud when I got my first paycheck." Drew asks what happened that was "nice" after that: "Nothing much after that. Nothing until today." If William Whyte characterized postwar America as "filiarchal,"[21] and Dr. Spock suggested that "childrearing was easy and that babies' dispositions were naturally pleasant,"[22] Lupino's films seem aimed at puncturing these culturally romantic idylls of childhood, childbirth, and youth.

Literary Romanticism provides an apt context for *Not Wanted* since poets like Blake and Wordsworth in particular explored the corruption of innocence that was seen as a distinct product of modern culture and industry. Indeed, Lupino's Sally, a traumatized female teen *flaneur*, could be seen as a kindred spirit of Wordsworth's little girl in "We Are Seven," a voice insisting on continuity and hopefulness who denies her real experience of loss (her siblings have died) because in her mind and imagination they are still with her. The speaker says:

"But they are dead; those two are dead!
Their spirits are in heaven!"
'Twas throwing words away; for still
The little Maid would have her will,
And said, "Nay, we are seven!"[23]

While Wordsworth's poem foregrounds the narrator's jaded inability to recognize the value of the child's emphasis on continuities rather than disjunctions, girlhood innocence transforms in Sally into dissociation and madness. Sally is, of course, no longer a little girl, although Lupino's point is that she is unprepared for adulthood. Her maturity is overly reliant upon fantasy, and later—as might be said about Wordsworth's girl if she were not a child—she enters a near-insane state of denial and withdrawal. Later in the film, as she walks the street after giving up her baby, the camera tracks her watching the children playing. She sits on the steps next to a young girl, her doll, a boy, and a dog. Before petting the dog, Sally pets the girl, a confused association of feeling and action continuous with the film's expressions of deformed role-playing (Figure 5.5).

In the scene in which she meets Steve, she is drinking through a straw like a kid. Just before she has her baby, she wears pigtails. The film progressively shows her childlike affectation, however, as incongruous. The merry-go-round scene referred to earlier, like Drew's alternate world of electric trains

FIGURE 5.5 *Flaneur Sally, trying to connect in* Not Wanted.

discussed in the following text, is a setting for child's play. Sally and Drew ride the carousel, then sit and eat popcorn. It is notably when Drew asks Sally to marry him that her vision goes awry, and the carousel careens out of control. The scene is a microcosm of the ruination of childhood innocence with Sally's hopefulness and desire shattered as she must confront her pregnancy and new role as a misfit in conventional society.

Like Sally, Drew engages in dreaming, although he continually references his broken life and body. With childlike fervor, he proposes to Sally with an idyll about their proposed future: "We could have lots of little gaseterias, a whole chain of them. Maybe after that a flock of kids to make change, small change at first. You could be superintendent of the railroad and everything." Drew's "skirmish with a mortar shell" and his "plastic leg" establish the war as an important backdrop for failed ideals, but he offsets his bleak past with an idealized view of the future. Although clearly traumatized by his experiences in the war and its aftermath (he is a war-vet with a prosthetic leg), Drew mainly takes pleasure in his elaborate electric train set, a fully realized town with lights that go on and off to create a fictional setting of night or day. The train set is an alternate world for Drew, an imagined place that he can control. When he proposes, Drew tells Sally that she can be "the chief engineer of the railroad." It is worth noting this in Drew's references to Sally's role in the railroad and "lots of little gaseterias," *Not Wanted* imagines female identity at the center of conventionally masculine modern venues. While Erik Dussere recently writes of the "idealized masculinity" figured

FIGURE 5.6 *"Boy meets Girl," Sally and Drew (Keefe Brasselle) in* Not Wanted.

in the modern American gas station—its "image of gritty and masculine authenticity"[24]—Lupino's gaseteria is instead a feminized space that serves, as Scheib notes, as "cosy oases"[25] in Drew's and Sally's fraught lives.

Such destabilization in gender arrangements can also be observed in Lupino's repeated visual association with the couple. Drew leans on Sally's shoulder, comforted by her as if he were her child. The film introduces him with this very image, as he sleeps first under his coat (an image of hiding from life) and finds his way to place his head on her shoulder (Figure 5.6).

The last shot of Drew in the film is also of him nestled in Sally's arms. Like Mr. Kelton and Steve, Drew is unfulfilled. When Sally rejects his first offer to go out on a date, saying, "You understand," he replies, "Story of my life, honey. I always understand."

Most of the adults in *Not Wanted* are figures of abandonment, lost figurative children. Drew tells Sally that his mom died when he was a child and his father three years earlier. His girlfriend left him when he returned after the war because "I wasn't up to her speed anymore." When he asks Sally about her parents, she says with resignation, "Yeah, but I guess they don't want any part of me by now."

In the end, it is Sally's roommate at the home for unwed mothers, Joan (played by Lupino's sister in the film), who captures the plight of modern women for Lupino: Joan grieves over the "rotten deal" she and the other women at the home have gotten. Appropriating childlike affect to survive as the men do, or struggling for opportunities to express themselves beyond the roles of wife or mother as the women do, the figures in *Not Wanted* reflect a modern world upside down, like the image Lupino constructs when Sally watches the merry-go-round careen out of control (anticipating Hitchcock's use of this visual conceit in *Strangers on a Train* two years later). Lupino's stunted individuals are trapped in gender and social roles ill-equipping them to express desire and communicate meaningfully with others. Bus culture and gaseterias symbolize a busy-ness in modern landscapes that only barely disguises a dysfunctional society and its alienated members. Negotiating her own outsider status as a creative woman through her energetic role as a filmmaker, "Mother" (as Lupino was later known on the set) exposed the perverse social arrangements that damage psychosocial development and that constitute some of the truly grim realities of modern America.

Notes

1. Jans Wager, "Ida Lupino," in Alain Silver and James Ursini (eds.), *Film Noir: The Directors* (Milwaukee, WI: Limelight, 2012), 225.
2. Pam Cook, "*Outrage* (1950)," in Annette Kuhn (ed.), *Queen of the 'B's: Ida Lupino Behind the Camera* (Westport, CT: Praeger, 1995), 58.
3. Ronnie Scheib, one of the most insightful readers of Lupino's films, begins her landmark 1980 essay on Lupino's directing work, "Ida Lupino, Auteuress," by quoting Andrew Sarris: "Ida Lupino's directed films express much of the feeling if little of the skill which she has projected so admirably as an actress" (*Film Comment* 16 [January/February 1980]: 54–64, p. 54).
4. Debra Weiner, "Interview with Ida Lupino," in Karyn Kay and Gerald Peary (eds.), *Women in the Cinema: A Critical Anthology* (New York: Dutton, 1977), 170.
5. Barbara Koenig Quart, *Women Directors: The Emergence of a New Cinema* (New York, NY: Praeger, 1988), 27.
6. Ibid., 27.
7. Victoria A. Brownworth and Judith M. Redding, *Film Fatales: Independent Women Directors* (Seattle, WA: Seal Press, 1997), 38.
8. For an excellent analysis of social context and the history of the project *Not Wanted*, see Diane Waldman's "*Not Wanted* (1949)," in Kuhn, 13–39.
9. Stephen Mintz, *Huck's Raft: A History of American Childhood* (Cambridge, MA: Belknap Press of Harvard University Press, 2004), 293.
10. Mintz, *Huck's Raft*, 284.
11. Kristine Butler Karlson suggests as much in her analysis of *A Tree Grows in Brooklyn* ("1945: Movies and the March Home," in Wheeler Winston

Dixon (ed.), *American Cinema of the 1940s: Themes and Variations* [New Brunswick: Rutgers University Press, 2005], 140–61). While the film explores the trauma of Johnny's (the father's) alcoholism as "an illness that endangers the stability of the home" (p. 154), Karlson observes its ameliorative conclusion, "reconfiguring the nuclear family and allowing the American myth of happiness, upward mobility, and prosperity to continue unchallenged by Johnny's exceptional case" (p. 156).

12 Frank Krutnik, *In a Lonely Street* (New York, NY: Routledge, 1991), 64.
13 Elaine Tyler May, *Homeward Bound: American Families in the Cold War Era* (Basic Books, 2008 [revised twentieth-anniversary edition]).
14 In Richard Kelly's *Sean Penn: His Life and Times* (London: Faber and Faber, 2004), Leo Penn is quoted as having said about Lupino that she was "the best director I ever worked with in film. . . . Ida was a considerable person and way ahead of her time. She fell victim, I think . . . to a kind of prevailing chauvinism" (p. 17).
15 Scheib, "Ida Lupino, Auteuress," 56.
16 May, *Homeward Bound*, 92.
17 Mintz, *Huck's Raft*, 299.
18 May, *Homeward Bound*, 115.
19 Ibid., 141–2.
20 Scheib, "Ida Lupino, Auteuress," 54.
21 Doug Owram, *A History of the Baby Boom Generation* (Toronto: University of Toronto Press, 1997), 59.
22 Mintz, *Huck's Raft*, 280.
23 William Wordsworth, *The Complete Poetical Works* (London: Macmillan and Co., 1888; Bartleby.com, 1999). Available at www.bartleby.com/145/ (last accessed 19 May, 2021).
24 Erik Dussere, *America Is Elsewhere: The Noir Tradition in the Age of Consumer Culture* (New York, NY: Oxford University Press, 2013), 51, 52.
25 Scheib, "Ida Lupino, Auteuress," 56.

6

(Not so) "Vicious and Depraved"

Ida Lupino's Portraits of Men

Marlisa Santos

It is well known that Ida Lupino liked to be thought of as a nurturing, "motherly" director. Those familiar with her actress persona, especially in film noir, might find this appellation incongruous with her flair for portraying hard-bitten, no-nonsense women who would sooner shoot you as look at you, especially in films such as *They Drive by Night* and *Road House*. However, Lupino was known to be sensitive and thoughtful behind the camera, very sympathetic to actors' needs and proclivities, even as she piloted feature films and television episodes that leaned toward action, suspense, and crime. She was also keenly aware of her tenuous status as a female director in her time. One could say that her viewpoint on the subject was either maddeningly retrograde or inspiringly savvy.[1] Given her unique status as a female director in that time, many thought that her films and television work would, or should, envision a female-centric universe, and in particular portray empowered women and/or throw light upon their plight. In fact, Lupino's films, while very concerned with social issues and taboos, are quite balanced when it comes to gender, and they do not demonize men or glorify women. Rather, Lupino presents frankly and honestly the challenges of both sexes in an increasingly complicated world.

Having said that, patterns of male character portrayal in Lupino's work do emerge, and even though her level of creative input in character and story vary from project to project (including some scripts that she wrote herself, credited or uncredited), male figures in her films and television programs often suffer from indecision and paralysis, a difficulty or inability to act when faced with complex consequences and shifting social mores. Jans B. Wager argues that "her films do not typically feature strong, resourceful female characters, but her male characters are equally as confused and buffeted by fate . . . her criminals are swept away not by passion but by passivity and engage in almost mindless action spurred by past experiences."[2] This kind of conundrum is seen quite clearly in Edmond O'Brien's portrayal of Harry Graham in *The Bigamist* (1953). Many expected this kind of film, which tells the story of a man torn between two women, both of whom he married, to demonize the insensitive polygamist husband. However, Lupino constructs a complex screen narrative of real people, male and female, with sensitivity, emotions, and weaknesses, caught in various traps of contemporary gender ideology: male husband as provider, female wife as homemaker and mother, and female mistress as seductive siren. His first wife, Eve (Joan Fontaine), cannot have children and emerges as a career woman in the film, but rather than lapse into a stereotypical masculinized shrew, her character is multidimensional, extremely dedicated to the success of her husband's business, her contributions to it, and the loss of a child in their married life a deficit that they both bear. There is a sense that her energies in building the business and succeeding in personality currency where her husband fails is a reaction to her childlessness and a subsequent neglect to Harry as a husband but, for the most part, she is portrayed with all the strengths and weaknesses of a well-defined human being, as is Phyllis Martin (Graham), a cynical and world-weary waitress in Hollywood played by Lupino. Even though her past clearly influences her present attitude, she is not a femme fatale luring Harry into her opportunistic clutches. They meet on a Hollywood star homes tour bus as he is taking the tour to pass his empty hours, while she just wants to get off of her feet. Hard-bitten, Phyllis is hesitantly drawn to him with push-pull overtures, while he pursues her out of desperate loneliness. According to Mary Hurd, "Lupino turns traditional typecasting upside down by showing neither woman as a manipulative, scheming femme fatale; both are good wives— each blissfully ignorant of the existence of the other—whose positions are the result of Harry's emotional and communicative needs."[3] It is difficult to view Harry as a wolfish seducer, bent on establishing a harem of women in various cities, subject to his salesman travels. Critics of Lupino thought that this kind of film would be a prime vehicle to dismantle misogynistic portrayals of women in Hollywood by giving a comeuppance to man in his failings with monogamy. However, the foibles of Harry are also the foibles of Eve and Phyllis, as all of them are culpable in the eventual multi-marriage mess in which they find themselves.

Georgakas comments on Lupino's own description of her films "as being documentary in nature. This assessment means that she preferred straightforward narratives shot on location in the neorealistic, and *film noir* style seen in many low-budget films of the era. In essence, Lupino wanted to make films that would reflect the sensibility and style of the quintessential working-class women she excelled at portraying as an actor."[4] Because Lupino rejected one dimensional portrayals of human beings in her films that would be reductive in the representation of the realities of modern life, she has been seen as squandering an opportunity to effect social change by constructing reversals of existing stereotypes—ironically, even as she was showcasing subjects of social concern that had been considered taboo in film. According to Molly Haskell, Lupino "was more of a feminist in her Raoul Walsh films than she was as a director . . . she probably wanted—as women will do, and for good reason—to make sure that everybody realized she was just a woman, that she didn't want to be threatening."[5] But more to the point is Georgakas' assertion that Lupino "unapologetically believed in romantic love as much as she believed that there was considerable social and gender injustice," adding that the male leads in her films "are evoked with as much care and affection as Lupino's female characters."[6] Lupino was a humanist, rather than merely a feminist, and her films show her efforts to reveal the foibles and challenges of characters in a changing world, regardless of gender.

The conclusion of *The Bigamist* has been seen by critics as the film's chief weakness, perhaps not only for gender concerns, but also for narrative unconventionality. When Harry Graham has been pushed to the limit by the discovery of his double life by adoption agent Mr. Jordan (Edmund Gwenn), Harry is faced with what would seem to the viewer to be a clear decision: Which wife to choose? Should he go back to Eve and face not only the rejection of the adoption, but also the shame of the reason, if he decides to come clean? Or should he stay with the sickly Phyllis and his biological child and face the guilt of rejecting his first wife and their childless state? What Harry does can perhaps be seen as the ultimate weakness: he turns himself in to the police, essentially absolving himself of having to make the choice. Jordan has already told him that, because of pity, he will not report the bigamy: "I can't figure out my feelings towards you. I despise you, and I pity you. I don't even want to shake your hand, and yet I almost wish you luck." This statement encapsulates what Lupino wants to communicate regarding the complexity of a situation that most would consider clear-cut immorality and illegality. But one also senses that it is less Harry's belief in justice and punishment than pure abdication of responsibility. He throws himself on the mercy—and protection—of the justice system to decide his fate. The message in the end, although we never hear the pronouncement of sentence, is that Harry is less a legal criminal than a moral one, and perhaps not even so much that, as his lawyer characterizes him as actually comparatively more moral than the cad who would keep a mistress on the side. Harry, from this perspective, is superior to that type because he did not leave his pregnant girlfriend in the lurch, but took "legal" action to care for her and legitimize the child. In his own defense, Harry states, "How can a man call a woman his wife for eight years—someone who you love, who loves you—how can you call her and tell her that you must have a divorce? Worse than that, you've been unfaithful—you're going to be a father. How can you hurt someone so much?" Mercy and kindness, therefore, are his ostensible motives. The judge's comments at the close of the film are sympathetic, acknowledging these issues and also the fact that any legal punishment would be less than the moral punishment Harry will endure. Interestingly, the narrative does return to the women involved, as the judge states, "When he's once more a free man, it won't be a question of which woman he'll go back to, but rather which woman will take him back. That decision is theirs." In this way, the choice to be made—and the burden of such a choice—falls back on the women involved, rather than Harry. And the film ends with this lack of resolution, no anger or hate on the faces of Eve or Phyllis as they leave the courtroom, and their close-ups reveal only sadness and disappointment. These expressions parallel repeated shots of Harry's face throughout the film, ranging from despair to desperation. Ultimately, the nuanced, rather than polarized representation of such a male character, and the female characters surrounding him, speak to Lupino's desire for *verité* in her filmmaking, along with her refusal to entertain reductive portrayals.

Outrage

These complex portrayals are perhaps no clearer than in another of Lupino's "social problem" films, *Outrage* (1950). The male actors in the film are in supporting roles to Mala Powers, who plays the victimized Ann Walton. She is the focus of the film, but the influence of the men around her, from her protective father and earnest fiancé to the counterman rapist and a preacher friend, force her to undergo a painful and difficult psychological journey. This journey begins with her sexual assault, which is never mentioned as rape and not shown on screen because of production code constraints. In addition to the masterful six-minute assault sequence, Lupino builds the suspense early in her treatment of Ann's interaction with the rapist (played by Albert Mellen) prior to the attack. Significantly, even though he is never named in the film, he does not emerge as a stranger out of the shadows. He runs the lunch counter at the mill where Ann is employed and she seems to interact with him every day, although she finds his overtures unpleasant. He flirts with Ann in a threatening way when she tries to buy cake for her lunch with her fiancé, and he does not give it to her, saying that if he were her boyfriend, he would not make her buy cake for him. Further, he tells her that she should make up her mind about choosing him instead. His threat is further represented the next day, when she is near him having coffee with her friend and discussing that they would work late that night, as his disembodied hands are positioned in the right foreground of the shot, slowly drying cups (Figure 6.1).

In such a subtle way, Lupino manages to capture the ominous nature of his presence. The viewer knows that Ann and her friend are being watched, even before the camera cuts to the reverse shot of him watching them walk away. The fact that Ann knows him underscores the insidious nature of sexual assault that Lupino seems to want to reveal. The character, for the brief time that he is on screen, is not a wholly mysterious, deviant force. He is a man that Ann probably interacts with daily and tolerates, as was the case with gender relations of the time, his consistent, unwanted overtures. His neck is marked with a large scar, suggesting perhaps a violent past, and even though he is not named and is no stranger to criminal activity (as evidenced by his arrest later in the film for armed robbery), the familiar nature of her attacker signifies the unfortunate everyday nature of such crime, the kind of crime later described in the film as "a shameful blot on our towns and cities."

The uncanny pattern of the familiar becoming the strange continues with the actual rape scene. From the moment Ann leaves her office, and the rapist begins to follow her and his male presence darkens, her steps figuratively in the highly shadowed scenes as the menacingly pursuit is shot. The pathways and buildings that were so benign hours ago in daylight now become

FIGURE 6.1 *The rapist's hands in the foreground provide subtle menace amid mundane girlish conversation.*

obstacles of danger and labyrinthine avenues that can only end in capture. When Ann goes beyond the mill property to the streets beyond, high-angle shots highlight her isolation, which culminates in her desperate blaring of a truck horn to gain attention, a jarring sound that shatters the silence but also emphasizes the lack of ears to hear her plight. Finally, the rapist's unseen overtaking of her around a corner is punctuated by the camera's rise to see another impotent male figure leaning out of a high window, too remote to help. This anonymous, helpless man signifies the subsequent failures of the males in the film as social protectors of the female. This idea is borne out in her relationship to and the reactions of both the incidental and the significant men in Ann's life. The attending doctor and the investigating police detective after the rape are at cross-purposes for their respective jobs; one wants Ann to be left alone, and one needs Ann's involvement. Neither one can really help her, however, as they are ill-equipped to heal the most substantive psychological damage that she has suffered and cannot imaginatively place themselves in her violated predicament. Her anguished father, played by Raymond Bond, is searching desperately for answers from the detective, angrily wanting to know how such a thing could happen. The detective responds that the police do not make the laws, that they only enforce them and "are only dogcatchers . . . pick up cases like this every day, slap them in jail. After that, I don't know what happens," suggesting that even if the attacker were apprehended, significant societal problem remains unsolved. Mr. Walton's reaction to Ann's rape is a somewhat selfish disappointment, as he muses, "Is this why you raise a daughter? Is this what you love and sacrifice for? What kind of times are these that such things can happen?" The answers to the first two questions are never addressed—what DO you raise, love, and sacrifice a daughter for? From a paternal (and sympathetic) perspective, for her to be happy, free of care or tragedy. From a paternal (and cynical) perspective, for her to remain unspoiled and delivered safely to a husband of choice to live out a socially acceptable life. Both of these elements coexist in Mr. Walton's reaction, and the frustration he feels as he addresses the detective is punctuated by a cut shot (prior to him asking about the times) to the detective, turned partially away from him, his back to a framed photo of Ann in confirmation attire on the mantel. Ronnie Scheib argues that "the rape produces an instant male-female polarization. . . . Ann's father and the police captain bound in a helpless embarrassed intimacy, glancing uneasily at the bridal-like confirmation photo of Ann, as they discover with a simultaneous shock the sexual otherness of Ann and the sexual otherness of the rapist, and their mitigated innocent-guilty relationship to both."[7] Parallel to the male mutual frustrated paralysis downstairs is the upstairs turmoil of Ann, her mother, and a female detective, whose presence highlights the sexual nature of the crime, as she is presented as necessary to discover the sordid details that a woman could not possibly reveal to a man. Like the male detective, Ann, too, tries to turn away from the event as she tosses and turns on the bed, eventually caught in a shot wherein her face and body are framed within her headboard bars. Ann's victimization has drawn everyone connected to her into a prison of sexual transgression in which the male characters do not emerge as chivalric saviors and are unable to act in any constructive or palliative way.

Ann's fiancé, Jim Owens (Robert Clarke), suffers from a similar inability to bring about healing in Ann. Jim tries to say the right things: that he still wants to marry her and all that matters is them, that he wants to live with her, be happy, have kids, and so forth. He even suggests that they could go away if need be. But she can only respond in anger, saying that everything is "filthy, dirty" and that he would "always be thinking about it." The "it" is the thing that is actually preventing meaningful action on the part of most of the men in the film, the "sexual otherness" to which Scheib refers. Ann herself provides some of this barrier to the male assistance proffered, as she can no longer retain a self-image consistent with the patriarchal mores of her small society. She instinctively knows that, even though Jim probably believes that he could overcome the stigma and his own feelings about the rape, these things would eventually poison their happiness, living as they do in a world that cannot tolerate such transgression—for the perpetrator or the victim. Aside from the physical violation, the uncanniness of the rape event has entered Ann as well. She can no longer even tolerate being in her own skin. Her senses are heightened, as she hears amplified sounds around her and she is unable to feel comfortable in prior familiar surroundings, like her office and her home. She cannot remain in one place for any length of time, on the streets of the town or in her office, and, even in her home, she paces like a caged animal, fingering items in the house as if she has never seen them before. These feelings come to a head when she smashes the aforementioned confirmation photo, in an obvious rejection of her former, "purer" self.

The emergence of the most significant male figure in *Outrage*, Rev. Dr. Bruce Ferguson (Tod Andrews), is involved in the playing out of an almost mythological sub-narrative in the film. Consumed by self-loathing and self-consciousness, Ann goes from wandering around her town to escape the perceived (and likely actual) stares and whispers to taking a bus into the California rural wilderness, where she essentially becomes a missing person. The exiled Ann wanders around in darkness and wind, as the camera captures a low-angle view of her agonizing walk, even to a close-up of her twisted ankle, highlighting her inner impairment that has now taken external physical form. She is rescued by the minister Ferguson, who is not a doctor of medicine but of spirituality. Like her father, he is mild-mannered, smokes a pipe, and is an educated teacher. Although he protects her like a father (or perhaps like her father could not), he is a blank slate without the baggage of history. He responds to Ann as to a wounded animal, seeming to know what she needs in order to reinvent herself, even though he does not know the true nature of her trauma, in which he sees a reflection of his own war trauma that has left him somewhat of an exile as well and deeply scarred. He is perhaps the only male figure that Ann can get close to now—he is kind, but sexless—an emasculated and, therefore safe, male. The war cost him a lung, and who knows what else. But he is able to help her realize that you can be robbed of something and still go on with life.

What Bruce cannot protect Ann from, however, is her damaged psyche that is still unhealed, despite her efforts to erase the past and begin a new life with parallel, but opposite elements of her previous life. Residing with surrogate parents, the Harrisons, she takes a new job at their fruit plant, and spends time with the nonthreatening Bruce. Her encounter with local Frank Marini (Jerry Paris) at a town picnic, however, triggers the dark memories of sexual trauma and of her fear and helplessness. The scene in which his efforts to dance with her and kiss her end with her braining him with a wrench, provides a compelling statement on not only the deep damage of sexual trauma, but also the social forces that, as her father stated earlier, "allowed this to happen." One might read this scene as Ann simply being so traumatized by the rape that any sexual approach, however innocent, becomes a fearsome prospect. But if this point were Lupino's intention, one wonders why she would not have directed Jerry Paris to play the role in a less-threatening manner in order to underscore the idea that the problem is within Ann. Frank's pursuit of Ann does not seem innocent at all, and his efforts to kiss her are quite forceful. Within the rural world of the 1950s, such efforts were likely seen as "innocent" and certainly not dangerous. Following Ann's assault of Frank, Bruce tells her that he knows him, and Frank is "harmless." Frank might be seen as harmless to another man, but he is not portrayed that way in the scene with Ann. One would be hard-pressed not to interpret this scene as Lupino's not-so-subtle indictment of appropriately tolerated patterns of male-female behavior in her time and the dangerous consequences that can result. There is a clear parallel between Frank's "innocent" advances toward Ann and the "joking" advances of the rapist counterman. The fine line between allowable liberties and criminal assault is drawn into sharp relief when Ann sees the face of her rapist instead of Frank Marini's as he comes toward her. The difference between the two is not necessarily a product of Ann's damaged psyche alone, but rather a reflection of a society that tolerates and even normalizes the sexual victimization of women.

More male figures of authority—doctors, policemen, judges—direct Ann's fate further after this encounter, and, even though the psychiatric treatment undoubtedly helps in her healing, it may be that her act of aggressive self-protection against Frank does just as much to heal her. It affirms that she perhaps could be mistress of her own destiny, and not remain a helpless victim. As in other Lupino films, the resolution of the films feels unsatisfying—not because it does not end in a conventionally romantic way, but because the reasons for her returning to her home, family, and suitor are somewhat murky and seem to revolve around Bruce's romantic paralysis. It may be easy to conclude that a future in which Ann does not face her past is no real future at all, and we are left to wonder about the precise nature of Bruce's motives in pushing her away. Does he truly believe her to be too damaged to love? Does he believe that she could not really "belong" to him while her engagement with Jim is pending? Does he believe that he is incapable of being a "true" husband to her, physically or emotionally? The viewer wants an answer, not simply a shot of Bruce glancing wistfully up at the sky after her bus leaves. However, Lupino's desire to show the complexity of human emotion will not be oversimplified. The viewer must acknowledge that Bruce's inability to act, or perhaps taking the most difficult action he ever has, could have been fueled simultaneously by all of those above issues and more.

Directing Television

The problem with men "being men" are also addressed in Lupino's television work, in which she was quite prolific during the 1950s and 1960s. Although she began her television directing with episodes of series like *General Electric Theater*, *The Donna Reed Show*, and others, she would continue to work without contract as a journeywoman director. One can discern a substantive creative stamp on episodes in series like *Have Gun, Will Travel* and *Thriller* in which she directed multiple episodes and formed relationships with the actors and other staff in those shows. In fact, it was Richard Boone's interest in her talent from *The Hitch-Hiker* that prompted her involvement in *Have Gun, Will Travel*, for which she directed nearly ten episodes. Even though Boone was a supporter of hers, he refused to rehearse, and she had to exercise finesse in navigating such an androcentric show. But she was adept at the mastering of suspense in television as well as film, she was able to motivate actors to do her bidding, and she accomplished feats of artistry in the episodes she helmed. The episodes she directed often featured themes of gender-based power that went beyond the unusual series characterization of Paladin as a skilled gunman, while being intimately appreciative of the finer aspects of culture and unusually sensitive to the subtleties of human behavior. For instance, episodes such as "Lady with a Gun" (April 9, 1960) and "The Lady on the Wall" (February 20, 1960) featured female characters exercising power in the face of flummoxed male characters. In "The Lady on the Wall," a saloon waitress steals her own painting, a storied and legendary fixture in the bar, rather than have the saloon owner sell it. It is not until the end of the episode for the truth to be revealed when Paladin, the owner, and the male patrons are at their collective wits' end.

In the "Lady with a Gun," Eve McIntosh (Paula Raymond) terrorizes ex-Union soldier Rudy Rossback (Jack Weston) by stalking him across the country in order to exact revenge on him for killing her brother during the war. The guilt that plagues Rossback makes him appear weak, as she hounds him mercilessly. But their cat-and-mouse machinations are more exercises in stagnation than the actions of hunter and victim. Paladin forces them together at the end, gives McIntosh a gun, and sums up the situation: "You seem to be determined to kill him, and you seem to be determined to let her." When faced with her victim at close range, Eve cannot pull the trigger. As in her films, Lupino's exploration of gender roles lead to larger considerations—here, the inability of people to move on after trauma and the repetition of destructive behavior with no resolution.

Two other Lupino episodes have parallel themes of disempowered men and their routes back to masculinity. Interestingly, both "Day of the Bad Man" (January 9, 1960) and "Charley Red Dog" (December 12, 1959) feature male characters impersonating men of strong authority, and, through this impersonation, they ultimately claim that authority. In "Charley Red Dog," the title character (Scott Marlowe), armed with a correspondence school Marshal diploma, is determined to restore order to the town of Santa Clara. Paladin, summoned there for the same purpose, believes that the town should give Charley a chance. He believes in Charley's determination and he believes that he will not give up until he has had the chance to prove himself. When asked by the justice of the peace how anyone would respect "someone with that name," Paladin replies, "Respect can be as contagious as measles if it's properly spread around." Paladin knows the power of perception, especially in the mob mentality pervasive in small Western towns. Charley's main goal is to make Santa Clara a gunless town in which all residents surrender their guns as the prime peacekeeping method. Such an initiative also places the power of gun, and thus its authority, solely and squarely in the hands of the Marshal. Paladin, who has demonstrated his own fighting power, surrendering his own gun to Marshal Red Dog, and this gesture is enough to begin to shift the perception of power in the eyes of the townsmen. The rest of the episode plays out Charley's uphill battle—one of which shows that he is more than capable of handling—culminating with his gunning down the town's Indian-hating tough guy, and pistol-whipping Paladin in order to let him do it. Reminiscent of *High Noon*'s penultimate badge-in-the-dirt shot, Lupino draws our gaze to a close-up of the torn-up shreds of Charley's "diploma" fluttering on the legs of the dead gunslinger in the street (Figure 6.2).

This image is a sign of Charley's authentic assumption of the Marshal role rather than an abdication of it. His authority is no longer borrowed, and he is no longer handicapped by his youth, race, and inexperience.

Similarly, "Day of the Bad Man" shows the power of group perception on masculine realities. Hired by a cattlewoman to restore the rightful sheriff and general order in Cedar Wells, the town where she sells her cattle, Paladin derives a creative plan that involves her nephew, aspiring gunslinger Travis Perkins. Travis is a schoolteacher whose voracious reading of adventure serials has led him to brandish a gun and call himself "Laredo." Although he enjoys teaching and has innovative ideas, he is adrift, telling Paladin, "I'm

FIGURE 6.2 *The shreds of Charley Red Dog's pseudo-masculine authority flutter atop the result of his hard-won power in* Have Gun, Will Travel, *"Charley Red Dog."*

not man enough to do anything but go back and teach." What he craves is a more overtly masculine identity. He wants, "one day where people would listen to me as if they believed I was somebody." Unschooled in riding a horse, let alone handling a gun, Travis embraces the opportunity to impersonate the fictional "Laredo Perkins," whom Paladin invents as a foil to the real town threat, thereby creating a situation of need to restore the sheriff. All it takes is Paladin pretending to be a liquored-up witness to the power of Laredo Perkins and his gang for the town to fear and respect him before they even lay eyes on him. Tall and imposing, Travis looks the part but not much else, in contrast to the character of Charley Red Dog, who embodies all the qualities and talents of a sheriff, yet appears otherwise. Travis' reticence and lack of action adds to his mystique. But part of the process of Paladin's restoration of order is to set things as they should be, which does not include recognizing Travis as a real gunslinger, but rather to give him the opportunity to know the kind of respect that can be given a man who follows his natural abilities. Travis finds this quality of understanding in Ruth, the town schoolteacher who, appreciative of his help in getting the town to rebuild her schoolhouse and in sharing his novel ideas on pedagogy, exclaims, "Oh, it's terrible...that you should be so vicious and depraved! You would have made a wonderful teacher." Ultimately, Ruth has the pleasure of "reforming" Travis/Laredo into such a position, as he knowingly tells Paladin, "I'm through killin'." The power of Travis' masculinity therefore resides in the potentiality and promise of such power—and others having the confidence in it, similar to

Lupino's evolution as a female director, wielding male authority to navigate the telling of male stories.

Another television series that yielded multiple episodes and Lupino's unique stamp was *Thriller*, hosted by Boris Karloff. Called by Wheeler Winston Dixon "adventurous and individualistic,"[8] Lupino's work on *Thriller* episodes, from 1961 to 1962, one of which she cowrote, focused on darker themes that revealed than *Have Gun, Will Travel*. In the *Thriller* episodes, feminist fans of Lupino may find vindication as there is nary a male character who is portrayed as anything more than a victim or a fool. In both episodes, the disastrous fates of others are fueled by the weaknesses of men. Many episodes are period pieces, such as "Guillotine" (September 26, 1961), adapted by Charles Beaumont from a Cornell Woolrich story, and "The Bride who Died Twice" (March 19, 1962). In the latter, Lupino works again with Mala Powers, who plays a young woman engaged to a young officer in an unnamed Latin American country suffering from civil war and martial tyranny. She is coveted by a sadistic colonel, who bullies her general father into breaking up the engagement and sending the young officer, played by Robert Colbert, on an assignment that will mean his certain death. The decision by her fearful father sets off a chain of events that leads to the faking of her own death to escape the marriage to the colonel and later, when caught, leads to the execution of her fiancé, the murder of her father, and her own suicide. In "The Bride Who Died Twice," General De La Varra (Eduardo Ciannelli), also the governor of this unnamed territory, is threatened by Colonel Sangriento (Joe De Santis) to give him his daughter Consuelo in marriage, even though she is betrothed to Captain Fernandez (Colbert). First he bribes him, telling him that he will allow him to stay on in his governing post, even amid the revolutionary turmoil, and then moves on to threats of torture and death. The acquiescence of General De La Varra is framed in the capitulatory order-following ethic of the military, as he justifies himself to Fernandez: "Soldiers, even old, useless relics like me, forgotten on the shelf, pushed into retirement with empty meaningless titles, must do as they are told." The general is old, tired, and being overrun by a new regime of power, and he is also fearful of pain and death. He had outranked the colonel, but is being usurped since he no longer holds the masculine youth and military credibility that he once had. Lupino mainly captures his anguish in conventional medium shots, but employs impressive use of chiaroscuro in the torture and prison scenes to drive home the very real threat of Sangriento and thereby elicits sympathy for the general. However, the episode makes clear that the real blame should be shouldered by him, and he even indicts himself when the miraculously survived Fernandez is put on "trial" for stealing away Consuelo on the colonel's wedding night. He admits, "It is I who should be on trial. I am guilty—for betraying a father's most sacred trust, of putting my own welfare before that of my child.... This man threatened me ... because I was weak and afraid to die, I did as he requested.... I sold my daughter." Although Sangriento can overturn the trial with violence, he is ultimately shown to be the weakest of the male characters presented, especially by his dogged determination to have Consuelo because he ultimately cannot overpower human will, fueled by love. In a Romeo-and-Juliet denouement, Consuelo poisons herself after the execution of Fernandez, and despite his demonstrations of brute strength, the colonel's defeat is complete and devastating.

Although the male lead in "Guillotine" is far less sympathetic than General De La Varra, his fear of death is equally compelling. The means by which Robert Lamont (Alejandro Rey) seeks to escape this death, however, are less than admirable. He charges his dallying wife, Babette (Danielle De Metz), with keeping the executioner from showing up on his appointed day, because tradition/superstition dictates that a condemned man will be pardoned if the executioner fails to attend. And, in his eyes, she is obligated to do this service, since it was she who caused the unfortunate crime for which he is condemned: the murder of her lover. In the opening prison scenes, Lupino again shows her adeptness at shooting in claustrophobic spaces and emphasizing human, and especially male, frustration, and passivity. These scenes also reveal the less-than-charming aspects of Lamont's character. Rather than accepting his punishment for a crime that his own errant emotions caused him to commit, he blames his wife, manipulates her through guilt to commit a crime of her own (at the least adultery and, at the most, murder) as her punishment, all in order to save him. Her compliance leads her to a man embodying a different kind of plight. Although executioner Monsieur de Paris (Robert Middleton) is wealthy and enjoys material comforts, he is lonely, ostracized by the community because of the stigma associated with his work. He is therefore susceptible to Babette's charms and, by allowing her into his home and trusting her, provides her the opportunity to poison him. The strength of De Paris to carry out his job, for which he has never missed a day, and one in which, despite the stigma, he takes great pride, counteracts his emotional weaknesses and provides an interesting contrast to the calculating Lamont. In true Woolrich fashion, the story shows that no one can outrun his fate, and even though De Paris dies on the scaffold, the jolting of his dead fingers trip the latch that brings down the blade on Lamont's neck. A sudden close-up of this surreal action heightens the already-crushing suspense that Lupino has built. Lamont dies still struggling against the consequences of his own actions, believing in an outside force to deliver him, when it is just such a force that drops the final blow.

The male come-uppances that feminist viewers might have liked to see in her films are pervasive in other Lupino pieces from *Thriller*, such as "The Lethal Ladies" (April 16, 1962), a dual vignette of two women pushed to defeat the men in their lives who would destroy them, either physically or emotionally. The male and female leads in both halves of the episode are played by the same actors, Howard Morris and Rosemary Murphy, giving the viewer a sense of universality that is somewhat disturbing, but very effective. The first vignette features the adulterous husband of an accomplished geologist scheming to kill her to attain the money and power denied him in their marriage. Lavinia Sills is athletic and masculinized, largely because of her profession, but it is clear that she wears the metaphorical as well as the material pants in the family. Myron Sills thinks that he has dispatched her over a cliff, only to be shocked at her ghostlike return, after she saves herself through her swimming prowess. Lupino provides a shockingly effective transition to advance the story: the scene of a triumphant Myron drunkenly cackling in celebration of his freedom cuts to a lazy sweep of the same room, taking in various stuffed animal heads on the fireplace wall and then quickly pans down to Myron's taped-mouth face, with Lavinia's wet and bruised face appearing in close-up to his left (Figure 6.3).

The rugged interior of their living room parallels the mountain cliff to which she returns with the bound and gagged Myron (carrying him, no less). Her plan to end his life the same way he tried to end hers is actually spoiled by his dying before she can finish the job—and in her rage, screaming, "you cheated me!"—she slips off the cliff to her death.

The aggrieved woman in the second vignette is not so cheated. She succeeds in eliminating the scheming male, who is rendering her life obsolete. Librarian Alice Quimby is being forced out of her position by Dr. Wilfred Bliss, a rude and ambitious library director, who wields his advanced education like a weapon. Bliss' character, aside from his cruelty, is a bizarre combination of effete intellectual and predatory wolf. On the one hand, he reveals to Miss

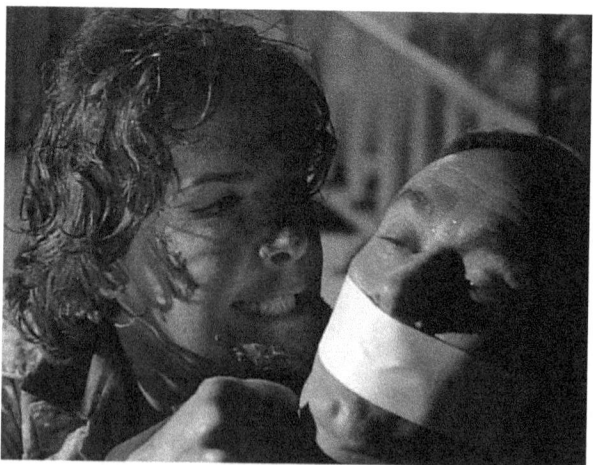

FIGURE 6.3 *Bruised Lavinia is about to exact poetic revenge on the faithless Myron in* Thriller, *"Lethal Ladies."*

Quimby his "one weakness . . . to collect unusual china." On the other hand, part of his staff is house cleaning to replace employees like his engaged secretary, "whose mind is on other things, like marriage," with younger, more available underlings. His intentions are made clear with a leering shot directed at his new secretary's derriere. This odd combination heightens what can be interpreted as a deviant ruthlessness. Although Alice Quimby is not masculinized, she is still desexualized as a female. She is a spinster librarian whose work is her life. She has, by her own admission, "nothing else." Bliss is aware of her subtle threat, dismissing those who support her. His insecurity about maintaining his authority manifests itself in inappropriate aggression, making examples and taking stands. He forces Alice to surrender her key to the library vault, the essential seat of power in the library, as it houses the most valuable books, papers, and documents, and when he cannot intimidate her into retiring, he orchestrates her dismissal. But his underestimation of Quimby proves his undoing as he gives her back the vault key to deposit some letters as her last employee duty, and the metaphorical power of the key becomes actualized: she lures Bliss into the vault and locks him in, cask-of-amontillado style. Once again, one of Lupino's males is contained within a claustrophobic space, a testament to his own psychological entrapment. Bliss is hardly calm or heroic as he realizes his predicament. He immediately panics, crying as a high-angle ceiling cutaway shot of the vault reveals his scurrying around in it like a mouse, and drives home his fear and weakness. Both halves of "The Lethal Ladies" unequivocally show the darker side of male frustration and their immoral efforts to overcome it are punished heartily.

Although other Lupino episodes, such as "What Beckoning Ghost" and "The Last of the Sommervilles" (cowritten by Lupino and her cousin, Richard), also depict men whose weaknesses lead to their undoing, it is ironically Lupino's first episode of *Thriller* that shows the skillful storytelling of such characters to particular effect. "Trio for Terror" (March 14, 1961) is another vignette episode that exposes the fates of men whose hubris leads to their downfalls, and in whom the self-awareness of their own strengths is sorely lacking. They particularly display what William Donati calls Lupino's fascination with the macabre, murder, and mystery. She even pitched her own true-crime murder series to networks, characterized in the following way: "It's about when people love too much. Or hate too much. Or lust too much."[9] Even though this series was never picked up, her work on *Thriller*, especially this first episode, shows her fascination for and enthusiasm with the exploring of dark human—and particularly male—excesses. In the first segment, "The Extra Passenger," Richard Lupino steps in front of the camera to play Simon, who murders his uncle for the inheritance in order to please his *Of-Human-Bondage*-Mildred-type girlfriend. Typical Ida Lupino suspense is evident right away in the murder scene, as the somewhat inept Simon nearly botches the killing in the shadowy study. A shot of the uncle's chair spinning after the murder parallels the wild ride upon which Simon will now embark: unknown to him, his uncle was a warlock, and unleashes his fighting cock to avenge his death. Capitalizing on her noir experience, Lupino's staging of the scene on the train, on which Simon hopes to escape but instead meets his demise, encapsulates the hurtling-towards-doom feeling that so many train noirs evoke. He originally slips off the train to commit the murder and then tries to slip back on for his alibi. The fog that obscures his departure cannot conceal his reckoning back in the compartment, where he believes himself to be safe. A slightly high-angle shot of the confining compartment is just enough to obscure the face of the strange man who has appeared there: the man who displays the face of his uncle but embodies an animal. These shots emphasize the growing suspense, and also the mystery when the train conductors find Simon's body and an otherwise empty compartment. The message is clear: it is only Simon who has caused his death. The second segment, whimsically titled "A Terribly Strange Bed," is less dark, but it tells a similar story of overreaching. Collins (Robin Hughes) has cleaned up at a casino and is invited to spend the night by his gambling house hosts, and he suddenly feels overcome with sleep. He then appears to narrowly escape being crushed by a spiked bed mechanism and flees. What the audience sees at the end is that every aspect of his encounter, even "winning" at the game was an elaborate con by The Hussar, played by Reginald Owen, to make him think that he was being murderously pursued for his winnings and thereby secure all the money, including his own bets, for himself. Collins thinks he has made off with his "fortune," telling his friend that he is about to show him "the surprise of your young life." It is Collins' surprise, however, and the revelation of his hubristic folly when all that is found in the sack is a mound of paper, rather than money.

   The final segment of "Trio for Terror," "The Mask of Medusa," is the most chilling and most revealing regarding male hubris and weakness. Kriss Milo (John Abbott) runs a curious sculpture "museum": he fashions statues in the likenesses of suspected, not convicted, murderers. When Shannen (Michael Pate), who is being pursued by police for murders of his own, finds himself in the storefront to evade police, his refuge becomes his trap. What is most interesting in this segment is the cat-and-mouse game between Milo and Shannen taking place in the crowded, claustrophobic space. It begins to dawn on Shannen that Milo has not only created statues in the image of murder suspects, he has exacted his own justice on them to create statues that are more than mere image, but are the actual suspects themselves. In a bizarre display of ethics coming from a strangler himself, Shannen exclaims, "You took it upon yourself to kill them . . . and petrify them somehow . . . you're a worse murderer than they . . . they wouldn't have killed themselves." It is hard to comprehend the logic of suicide being a worse crime than homicide but, nevertheless, Milo defends himself by asserting that the suspects essentially *did* kill themselves, revealing his pride in his prize possession of the head of Medusa. In his character, too, it is the height of passivity to believe that because a victim is lured into a space and induced to look at a thing that will kill him, and this act does not constitute murder. Medusa's head, even disembodied, consistent with Greek mythology, is still deadly. A disbelieving Shannen compares it to radium, in perhaps the episode's nod to *Kiss Me Deadly* (1955) and its comparison between the radioactive "great whatzit" and Medusa's head. In the postwar world, if Medusa cannot be real, can radium? Milo emphasizes that the murderers killed themselves, simply by looking, by their curiosity. This message is an interesting one when one might be paralyzed by indecision: don't look if you don't want to die; don't seek, don't act, if you don't want to be destroyed. Milo laments, "None of them ever believed me . . . perhaps nobody ever will." He has used lack of belief, faith, as the lure, and it seems to have worked every time, including on Shannen, his thirteenth victim. Ultimately, in each segment of "Trio for Terror," Lupino paints a compelling and noirish picture of the dark consequences of male blind pride and excess.

Because of her worldview, Ida Lupino refused to indulge in depictions of male stereotypes in her film and television directing any more than she would entertain such female stereotypes. What did fascinate her, and is borne out in her work as a director, is the often destructive passivity that particularly plagues men in an unstable, postwar environment. Whether tackling these issues in relation to social issues on the large screen or throwing light on feelings of male entrapment fueled by errant passions on the small screen, Lupino's directing of male characters evokes what is perhaps the legacy of her greatest talent: the creation and maintaining of suspense. She was not called "the female Hitch" for nothing. It is the very passivity and navigation of complex masculinity that perhaps also creates such suspense. We are agonizingly poised to watch men like Harry Graham, Bruce Ferguson, Travis Perkins, and Wilfred Bliss find their way out of mazes and traps of their own creation, and Lupino leaves us there, like Ferguson standing by the side of the road, wondering what lies ahead.

Notes

1 "Keeping a feminine approach is vital; men hate bossy females . . . . You do not tell a man; you suggest to him. 'Darlings, Mother has a problem. I'd love to do this. Can you do it? It sounds kooky, I know. But can you do this for Mother?' And, they do it." Mary Ann Anderson, *Ida Lupino: Beyond the Camera* (Albany, GA: BearManor Media, 2011), 110.
2 Jans B. Wager, "Ida Lupino," in Alain Silver and James Ursini (eds.), *Film Noir: The Directors* (Lanham, MD: Limelight, 2012), 225.
3 Mary Hurd, *Women Directors and Their Films* (Westport, CT: Greenwood Press, 2007), 13.
4 Dan Georgakas, "Ida Lupino: Doing It Her Way," *Cineaste*, 25, no. 3 (2000): 32.

5 Gary Crowdus, "Film Criticism and Feminism: An Interview with Molly Haskell," *Cineaste*, 11, no. 3 (1981): 9.
6 Georgakas, "Ida Lupino: Doing It Her Way," 36.
7 Ronnie Scheib, "Ida Lupino: Auteuress," *Film Comment*, 16, no. 1 (January–February 1980): 60.
8 Wheeler Winston Dixon, "Great Directors: Ida Lupino," *Senses of Cinema*, 50 (April 2009). Available at https://www.sensesofcinema.com/2009/great-directors/ida-lupino/ (accessed 19 May, 2021).
9 William Donati, *Ida Lupino: A Biography* (Lexington: University Press of Kentucky, 1996), 229.

7

Accidental Outlaw

Agency and Genre in *The Bigamist*

Michael L. Shuman

The difference between the dark, tough-talking crime pictures and the more upbeat musical comedies, Westerns, and costume dramas populating movie screens throughout the 1940s and 1950s is not as black and white as the film stock widely used to capture that era's B-movie melodrama. While the French critic Nino Frank may have described the wayward variation on detective movies as early as 1946, the term "film noir" became associated with the more pessimistic, psychologically leaning "black films" only after much critical hand-wringing and more than three decades after Frank's initial observations.[1] Critics, to this day, are hard-pressed to agree on the tropes and conventions of film noir or even to agree on the essential examples of the form. Mark T. Conard identifies the technical cinematic characteristics by pointing out the genre's "constant opposition of light and shadow, its oblique camera angles, and its disruptive compositional balance of frames and scenes." For thematic content, he suggests "the inversion of traditional values and the corresponding moral ambivalence (for example, the protagonist of the story, who traditionally is the good guy, in noir films often makes very questionable moral decisions); the feeling of alienation, paranoia, and cynicism; the presence of crime and violence; and the disorientation of the viewer."[2] In *More than Night: Film Noir in Its Contexts*, James Naremore adds a list of "certain visual and narrative traits, including low-key photography, images of wet city streets, pop-Freudian characterizations, and romantic fascination with femmes fatales."

Ultimately, however, Naremore essentially gives in to the perplexity of the designation and relies, for meaning, on aesthetics and commercialism. Film noir, he maintains, "belongs to the history of ideas as much as to the history of cinema; in other words, it has less to do with a group of artifacts than with a discourse—a loose, evolving system of arguments and readings that helps to shape commercial strategies and aesthetic ideologies."[3]

Ida Lupino, as both actor and director, complicates the noir landscape further by introducing a distinctively feminine perspective into a genre of film otherwise universally dominated by a masculine creative vision. Following her earlier career as an ingénue in such mannered movies as *Search for Beauty* (1934), *One Rainy Afternoon* (1936), and *Artists and Models* (1937), Lupino became the go-to actor for directors needing a tough, chain-smoking feminine foil for their morally ambiguous antiheroes and taciturn loners. When she turned to directing feature films in 1949 with *Not Wanted*, her services uncredited and engaged by necessity only after the original director, Elmer Clifton, suffered a heart attack, Lupino was able to draw from her diverse acting experience and feminine outlook to disrupt Hollywood and box office expectations. Movie audiences, perhaps for the first time, were confronted with women's social issues in the context of the emerging noir form.

Indeed, in *Not Wanted* and the four other films she directed between 1949 and 1951 for Filmakers, the production company that she formed with Collier Young and Marvin Wald to create edgy, socially relevant films on limited budgets, Lupino very nearly flips the conventions of film noir head-over-heels. Rather than masculine concerns expressed almost exclusively through male characters, Lupino courageously employs the female gaze to examine such ostensibly taboo topics as unwanted pregnancy, rape, polio, and the catastrophic effects of a morally compromised parent on a young athlete attempting to find her place in life. These films, for the most part, retain the brooding demeanor and mounting suspense of noir films realized by male directors, but with themes at once more socially conscious and agreeable to the audiences who followed Lupino's early career as an actor. Male characters, more importantly, assume the inert and vacant presence of women in most other noir films, troublesome beings who generally propel the action, when they are active at all, through procrastination and bad decisions. As Richard Koszarski points out in a comment now ubiquitous in studies of her directorial work, "Lupino was able to reduce the male to the same sort of dangerous, irrational force that women represented in most male-directed examples of Hollywood film noir."[4]

Lupino completed directing *The Bigamist*, a film about gender identity, loneliness, and infidelity, immediately following the production of *The Hitch-Hiker*, an exemplary representative of Hollywood film noir. Both films were released in 1953, and Lupino's emersion into the conventions and precepts of film noir while directing *The Hitch-Hiker* has a substantial impact upon *The Bigamist*'s form and content. Based upon the real-life atrocities of killer Billy Cook, who abducted two hunters after murdering a family, *The Hitch-Hiker* includes no prominent female characters and offers little relief from the atmosphere of relentless psychological brutality. "In an all-male film," asks Lauren Rabinovitz, "how does one excavate a pro-feminist auteur when there is no masculine-feminine tension and an absence of male heterosexual desire?"[5] *The Bigamist*, Lupino's on-screen response to that question, once again deals with criminal activity, but here Lupino steps away from the hardened outlaw story typical of film noir and deals with the domestic drama of sexual transgression and moral turpitude. Lupino, while adopting oblique camera angles, brooding sensibility, and a persistent feeling of impending tragedy, imports the style and conventions of film noir into a different context, thus illuminating her "softer" social concerns through techniques already familiar to the movie going audience. "Genres do not consist only of films," Steve Neale maintains in an important work on film and theory. "[T]hey consist also, and equally, of specific systems of expectation and hypothesis that spectators bring with them to the cinema and that interact with films themselves during the course of the viewing process."[6]

Thus, the use of voice-over narratives and flashbacks in *The Bigamist*, common techniques of both film noir and documentaries, serve not only to inform the audience but to establish an emotional distance between the viewer and the protagonist, a separation that the narrator's words alone may not convey. When Harry Graham, the moping male and main offender of *The Bigamist*, tells us that he was merely lonely and did not intend to engage in an extramarital pick-up with Phyllis Martin, the tough cookie (played by Lupino herself), the audience already knows that the credibility of noir narrators is unusually suspect. Joe Gillis, the already-dead narrator of *Sunset Boulevard* (1950), certified the disconnection between audience and narrator two years before tickets went on sale for the Lupino film. Harry's leering and persistent advances to Phyllis far exceed his professed innocence, and the alert audience already is clued in to the deceit.

This idiosyncratic appropriation of film motifs reveals how the introduction of new sources into an established genre disrupts the artistic whole, amplifying and extending past conventions and texts. For Julia Kristeva, a literary critic and theorist whose work in the 1980s revolutionized critical notions of language and expression, such interaction with narrative material emerges as intertextuality, the shaping of one system of expression by another. While the concept of intertextuality primarily remains a function of linguistics and is variously interpreted, even by scholars in the field, contemporary film critics have adopted the term in some very specific ways. Helle Kannik Haastrup, for example, adopts a restrictive approach by defining "storytelling intertextuality" as a narrative process occurring "when a film includes other films or texts explicitly through references and quotes, mainly in dieresis. In other words, intertextuality is understood as a storytelling device."[7] Lupino certainly adheres to this narrow definition of intertextuality by citing, for example, *Miracle on 34th Street*, the 1947 feel-good holiday movie starring Edmund Gwenn, who also plays the *The Bigamist's* fastidious adoption agent, Mr. Jordan. The real-life Gwenn house is one of the notable residences mentioned by the tour bus driver as he winds through other remarkable Hollywood spots, oblivious to the tentative mating game between Phyllis and Harry just one seat away (see Figure 7.1). Contemporary audiences would have chuckled knowingly about Gwenn's earlier role as a very-nearly Santa Claus while, in subtext, Lupino solidifies Mr. Jordan's character as a well-meaning and kindly man perplexed by Harry's deception.

Neale clarifies and perhaps simplifies such critical diversity by emphasizing that iteration of genre, in every individual film, is an evolving process. "Each new genre film," he maintains, "constitutes an addition to an existing generic corpus and involves a selection from the repertoire of generic elements available at any one point in time. Some elements are included; others are excluded."[8] Lupino's transformation of the femme-fatale or, perhaps, the marginalized female characters of noir films, into the male protagonist of *The Bigamist* thus carries all the associations of prior audience perception of gender and agency into a new setting. We see Harry in the light of Ann Miller, the languid female presence in *Out of the Past* (1947), or Katie Bannion in *The Big Heat* (1953), and these associations give form and meaning to our new experience.

FIGURE 7.1 *Harry's leering advances.*

Audience associations also are capitalized upon, literally, by the product placement featured throughout the film. "Quite the style of today's tie-ins and indicative of the financial problems always surrounding a Filmakers' project," Dan Georgakas notes in his extensive *Cineaste* article on Lupino's directorial work, "*The Bigamist* contained paid placements for Coca-Cola, United Airlines, and Cadillac."[9] Modern viewers may be amused by just how prescient this economic move appears, while viewers in the 1950s would have been impressed with the affluent worldliness of it all. In subtext, however, Lupino was emphasizing the class differences between Harry's San Francisco life with Eve, in a well-appointed luxury apartment, and his Los Angeles life with Phyllis, in a cramped cottage surrounded by a rough picket fence and dwarfed by an adjacent high-rise building. Product-as-text disrupts the narrative structure of the film and provides yet another iteration of cultural substance in the process of genre mutation.

Howard Hughes, the enigmatic millionaire and RKO studio boss, suggested the title for *Hard, Fast, and Beautiful* (1951), Filmakers' third release, and the poster-ready title further demonstrates the commercial aspects of both audience associations and the evolution of the film noir genre. Lupino, unhappy with the working title, turned to the enigmatic millionaire and RKO studio boss for help, and Hughes phoned in his suggestion from Arizona. Lupino's groundbreaking film, exposing corruption and under-the-table profits in amateur tennis, went from John Tunis' short story, "Mother of a Champion" and his later book, *American Girl*, to *Loving Cup*, the production title, and on to *The Champion* and *The Money Game* before finding its marque with *Hard, Fast and Beautiful*.[10] The title at once suggests the powerful serve of a tennis ball and the speed and physique of a female competitor, along with the sexual promise of a racy newsstand paperback. Certainly this title, in lights on a marque, would attract viewers anxious to part with their money for some anticipated celluloid thrills. The origin of the film's title also exposes as much about the sources and collaborative nature of film as it does of Hughes's promotional spirit and bawdy sensibilities. Georgakas underscores Lupino's extensive, and often uncredited, work on multiple aspects of the films she developed for Filmakers and its predecessor, Emerald Productions. "Of the twelve films made by the two companies," he writes, "Lupino received formal credit for direction and script for six, acted in three, and had a formal or informal producer's role in all of the others."[11]

Presumably Lupino also participated in designing lobby cards and advertisements for *The Bigamist*, as Filmakers chose to develop their own publicity for that project. The film's pressbook, according to Ellen Seiter, artfully conveys the combination of film noir and "woman's picture," leading the audience to anticipate a level of intrigue and titillation actually missing in the film itself. In addition to establishing audience expectations for this curious mixture of genres, the ads also reveal much about the nature of Harry's crime and the social isolation consuming his life. "Harry appears alone in a head and shoulders shot in some quarter-page advertisements," Seiter notes. "Immediately beside his face is a graphic of the pointing index finger of a gloved hand, encircling the word 'The' in the film's title, and so removing any doubt as to the character's guilt."[12] Naremore's definition of film noir as an evolving construct propelled by commercial incentives as well as aesthetic ambitions appears to reflect Filmakers approach to marketing the movie.

In addition to the directly commercial artifacts such as title and ad campaign content, Lupino also relies upon objects of more indirect signification to support the public's perception as well as the meaning of her film. These cinematic artifacts in Lupino's film demonstrate the intertextuality of *things*, the ability to infuse narrative with a symbolic structure that informs the story and transforms evolving genre conventions. The tin drummer boy fetishized by Eve as a representation of the child she hopes to adopt also connotes the repetitive, mechanical life that Harry so desperately regrets. The department store mannequin, glimpsed by the audience in shop-window reflection as Harry, alone, wanders the Los Angeles streets, evokes the well-dressed presence of Eve lost in her most remotely professional behavior (see Figure 7.2). A fob watch, Eve's gift to Harry following her grandfather's death, symbolizes not only time passing by the infertile couple but the manliness that Harry seeks but will never find.

With his hang-dog voice-over and limp personality, Harry Graham represents the caustic moral inertness of a person incapable of exerting personal agency to affect life outcomes. Graham at times appears indecisive,

FIGURE 7.2 *The mannequin evokes Eve.*

clandestine, deceptive, and emotionally juvenile, unable or unwilling to appreciate the effects of his actions on other people, particularly women. Despite this limpid character, he somehow has established a thriving business selling deep freezers, wholesale, to California appliance merchants, but has developed a suppressed resentment toward his wife's involvement in the company. Eve Graham, portrayed with ravishing spirit by Joan Fontaine, is an energetic and engaging woman with a mind for finances who, at a casual dinner party, is able to sell one of Harry's reluctant clients on the advantages of a specific freezer model, effectively swiping the sale from her husband. She conveys the technical specifications of the product in language normally reserved for male salesmen or engineers while Harry quietly seethes, drinking brandy, at the table. Edmund O'Brien, as Harry, plays the scene with a disassociated scowl, a nearly childish manner of exclusion and resentment that reinforces the audience's sense of Harry's essential wishy-washy nature and, at the same time, supports Eve's dominance as an accomplished and motivated woman (see Figure 7.3).

The overwhelming emotional inertness and paralysis that Harry exhibits is an artifact of his disassociation from everyday life and the role of businessman, an artificial social construct, he is forced to play. "I've been a salesman too long not to recognize sales resistance when I see it," Harry tells Mr. Jordan when approval for adoption appears uncertain. Harry thus imposes his

FIGURE 7.3 *Harry pouts about Eve's success.*

professional experience on an imminently personal event, revealing the intrusion of a socially defined, public identity on private life. When Harry is in action, he apparently is a moneymaking force of the universe, a salesman that one former employer, in his discussion with Mr. Jordan, says he would like to rehire. The narrative alludes to this energy in stock shots of flying planes and telling comments during phone conversations with Eve but, revealingly, never directly in any scene of the film. Harry's engagements with life are obscure and off-camera, accomplishments we accept as a function of his assumed role rather than his demonstrated personality. We witness, instead, Harry in the adoption agency office, preoccupied with his duplicitous life and wary of an inquiry into his personal affairs; Harry's lonely walk through Griffin Park one Sunday afternoon, punctuated by a poignant score by composer Leith Stevens; and Harry in a courtroom at film's end, ostracized not only by society but by every other human being in the room, most prominently his two wives. Ronnie Scheib, in her article on Lupino in *Film Comment*, characterizes this emotional isolation as a consequence of modern expectations:

> Cast out of a familiar, protective environment, torn by conflicting desires or no desire at all, Lupino's characters do not know how to act. Their 'problems' ... have put them beyond the pale, beyond the patterned security of their foreseeable futures. The 'problem' is not how to reintegrate them back in to the mainstream; the 'problem' is the shallowness of the mainstream and the void it projects around them—the essential passivity of ready-made lives.[13]

Just as he is emotionally passive and disassociated from events around him, so does Harry find it impossible to engage with people in anything but superficial conversation. "He's the original Invisible Man," a chatty coworker tells Mr. Jordan when the adoption agent visits Harry's Los Angeles office and finds out very little, indeed, about the man's personal life (see Figure 7.4). The cascading, important events in Harry's existence—the impending adoption of a child with Eve, his impulsive affair with Phyllis—remain not so much consciously secretive but unintentionally suppressed through a failure of will. Communication, for Harry, requires more emotional energy than he is willing to spend. After he first encounters Phyllis in Los Angeles, he attempts to tell Eve about his excursion in a phone conversation that evening. "I cheated on you today," he says in a playful, almost flippant manner that surely conveys how mundane the event appeared at the time. "I thought you should be the first to know....A beautiful brunette, all curves and soft shoulders." Eve, busy in San Francisco and more concerned about managing their business, has no time for Harry's confession, interrupting to let him know about upcoming sales opportunities. She at once appears convinced of Harry's fidelity and unwilling to banter about an inconsequential event (see Figure 7.5). Later in the film, when Harry attempts to reveal Phyllis'

FIGURE 7.4 *Mr. Jordan wonders at Harry's obscurity.*

FIGURE 7.5 *Harry's derailed confession.*

pregnancy, Eve once again interrupts the moment with the gift of her grandfather's watch. As Eve extols, with her typically direct enthusiasm, "Grandfather said that having a watch and chain made a man feel more like a man," thus disarming Harry's intent to reveal the emotional treachery a certain man could commit. Had any of these attempts at communication been successful, Harry's disastrous fate may have been avoided. Yet Harry, emotionally inert by situation and silenced by surprise, is incapable of exerting the agency necessary to confront life-changing events. Ultimately, with a squad car blocking the driveway to his San Francisco apartment, Harry is incapable even of confessing his crime to a distraught Eve, relying instead upon the family attorney, Tom Morgan, to reveal all in a devastating phone call. "In this way," writes Amelie Hastie in her monograph on *The Bigamist*, "the film offers a subtle critique of noir-produced masculinity. The passive male, unable to describe either his emotions or circumstances honestly enough in order to allow women to make their own decisions, defines those around him through his own acts of indecision."[14]

Lupino's self-acknowledged appropriation of a documentary style in her films, in addition to gender-inverted noir conventions, further accentuates Harry's lack of agency and disassociation from society. Mr. Jordon, on his visit to Los Angeles to deliver a paper to his professional society and, as an aside, to investigate Harry's personal life in that city, gazes up at buildings as though he eventually will take us on tour. Harry, in the hospital after the birth of his child with Phyllis, could be a stock actor in any educational film on family and childbirth. The Hollywood tour bus ride, Harry's portentous excursion leading to his downfall, accentuates the separation between wealthy celebrities and the common businessmen and waitresses who engage in such entertainment. The audience has the sense of witnessing important events on celluloid and in the theater, as a news story, rather than participating in the dramatic action themselves. This documentary motif also celebrates the gritty-dirty aspects of the lives of common women and men, a central concern of Lupino's directorial work. "Lupino often referred to her films as being documentary in nature," notes Georgakas. "This meant she preferred straightforward narratives shot on location in the neo-realistic and film noir style seen in many low-budget films of the era. In essence, Lupino wanted to make films that would reflect the sensibility and style of the quintessential working-class women she excelled at portraying as an actor."[15]

Lupino, for all her dedication to honestly depicting women in a modern context, has been accused of an anti-feminist stance in some critical literature.[16] Therese Grisham and Julie Grossman, in their book-length study of Lupino's directorial work, note a prevailing feminist ambivalence toward her films and suggest that Lupino's depiction of gender identity is not consistent with current modes of feminist criticism, including the examination of sexist representations of women and the emphasis upon empowered female images. "Lupino's style and sensibility," the authors maintain, "are feminist in ways that did not make sense to some second-wave feminists. Her films attack conventionality and the social institutions bent on maintaining norms at the expense of individual desire; those on the margins, because of their class or gender, pay most of the price."[17] Certainly the female characters in films she directed during the late 1940s and early 1950s conform to the prevailing notions of gender during that time: women are employed as waitresses or secretaries, they appear subservient to men in social situations, and they generally seek fulfillment in children and family. Representing the current social order accurately, however, effectively accentuates Lupino's documentary style and does not negate the overall agency of her female characters. The modern viewer, especially, comes to understand 1950s gender expectations in the context of an entertaining film, but soon appreciates the skewed sexual dimensions of Lupino's women and men. Phyllis is self-reliant and brusque, and apparently has constructed a psychological barrier between herself, society, and particularly the men she encounters. She consistently tries to brush off Harry's advances when the two first meet on the Hollywood tour bus, then ultimately takes control of the situation by leading him, under the guise of a dinner date, to the seedy Chinese restaurant where she works. Later in the film, as they dance at the upscale club Acapulco and their interest in each other ignites, Phyllis' resolve to remain solitary moves from the situational to the verbal. "Don't you want to know if there is someone in my life?" Harry asks, nearly desperate to make a personal connection with the woman in his arms. "Whether I'm married, divorced, or have six children? Whether I've spent any time in jail?" Phyllis' answer is immediate. "No, what good would it do me if I knew all those things?" she whispers. "I like you as you are. The way we are. I don't want anything from you. And I'm afraid of being in love again" (see Figure 7.6). Harry's already-marginalized identity thus is further obscured even by the one woman who, as he later contends, makes him feel useful. "You may laugh," he tells Mr. Jordon at one point during his flashback confessional, "but for the first time I felt needed. I loved Eve, but I never felt she needed me." With these words Harry assumes the persona of the retail film noir moll, the character trampled due to gender, intelligence, race, or demeanor, the perplexed male in a world filled with accomplished, strong women and perhaps the men who better meet those women's exceptional needs.

Phyllis' emotional barrier is the precise opposite of the intrusive inquest into Harry's personal life undertaken by Mr. Jordan in preparation for the adoption that Harry and Eve have requested. Indeed, intrusion into private space is a recurrent theme throughout the film as, incident by incident, the characters seek access to each other unapologetically. In the opening scene, the portly and pleasant custodian for Mr. Jordan's office knocks on the door for access, only to be soundly rebuked as he closes the window shade with finality. Yet later, as she tidies up his desk, Mr. Jordan apparently sees no problem with dictating personal details about

FIGURE 7.6 *Phyllis demonstrates her independence.*

the Graham's application—including income—into a voice recorder. Phyllis similarly makes an impromptu visit to Harry's hotel room, ignoring his earlier cancellation of a birthday dinner; Mr. Jordan boldly enters Harry's Los Angeles cottage when he hears a baby's cry, the first exposure of Harry's duplicitous life to a person in authority; and Harry bursts into Eve's bedroom while she is packing to visit her ailing father, a commanding scene leading the audience to fear that Eve somehow has discovered Harry's infidelity. Barriers, Lupino suggests, are never secure, whether physical, psychological, or emotional, and the sanctity of personal space is a fabrication we enjoy in an attempt to protect our individuality. As Scheib maintains:

> Space is an emotional entity in a Lupino film. It's not that the space expressionistically reflects the character's emotional state, but that his way of inhabiting it, of sharing or defending it against intrusion, defines his relationship to the world. His desire to fortress or break down his isolation, his fear of or yearning for spatial continuity, his need to protect or avoid enclosure, is felt in every gesture, every movement.[18]

Harry at once appears to embrace the lonely space of his privacy, to protect his isolation, and to reach out to others in an attempt to escape from his mechanical, unfulfilling duties. He ultimately becomes an outlaw through accident and failure of will, an inertness and abdication of individual agency precipitated by social expectations and the restrictive roles he is forced to play in everyday life. "I can't figure out my feelings toward you," Mr. Jordan tells Harry after hearing the story of his deceit. "I despise you and I pity you. I don't even want to shake your hand, and yet I almost wish you luck." Mr. Jordan, a man subject to the same social expectations as Harry and who at one point confesses to making a grave mistake in an adoption case, appears to recognize the moral ambiguity of choices amid conflicting social pressures. During Harry's trial, Tom Morgan points out the hypocrisy of social expectations: "Harry Graham is in no sense a hero, certainly," he maintains, leaning into the judge's bench. "But neither is he a monster. He is an ordinary man that made one terrible mistake. In this case there's a peculiar sense of irony. If Harry Graham had taken Phyllis Martin as his mistress, some people would have winked an eye and turned their head. But because he gave her, and the child she bore him, his name, and an honorable place in the community, he must be utterly destroyed."

The judge appears to agree, calling Harry "basically a decent man" who broke the moral laws of society and therefore will be punished more by the consequences of his acts rather than the laws of the state. Lupino chose to leave important social questions and plot elements unresolved at the conclusion of the film, with Harry's sentence postponed until a later date and both Eve and Phyllis leaving the courtroom to confront unsure futures. This unexpected ending, in a film ostensibly aimed at an audience of women as well as film noir aficionados, invites sympathy for the cad and understanding for the hard choices behind our emotional lives. Decades before today's Lifetime Network movie, where Harry surely would have met an unseemly and tragic end, Lupino's statement seems curiously progressive.

The Bigamist, as a title, is very nearly as ironic as the social punishment facing Harry Graham. Certainly the term "bigamy" does not communicate the complexity of the situation, nor does it explain the moral and ethical choices facing Harry in his essentially lonely existence. Even further, bigamy was a relatively uncommon reason for divorce at the time of Lupino's film, with only 466 incidents of both bigamy and marital fraud recorded by the US Department of Health in 1950.[19] While the prosecuting attorney in Harry's case notes that many bigamist marriages may remain concealed, the subtext of Lupino's argument appears to illuminate more than one isolated and uncommon offense. Social pressures and the necessity of conforming to expectations—the desire to "fit in"—certainly accounts for other crimes including robbery, embezzlement, and manslaughter, all more offensive acts than a duplicitous marriage. The failure of will and the expression of individual agency to prevent unpleasant life outcomes certainly results in the inertness that has led to innumerable tragedies. While not condoning these acts, of course, Lupino appears to assume the role of sociologist to explain how easy it is to become caught up in complex situations without anticipating potentially grave outcomes. Lupino, in a sense, comments upon some of the basic plot conventions of film noir in a way that undermines the common precepts of both the genre and the social and legal condemnation of such acts.

The unresolved ending has been variously criticized and celebrated by contemporary reviewers and later critical studies. Georgakas notes that Lupino earned her most negative reviews ever when the film was released, and points out that "critics chastised the film for being a soap opera with three unhappy endings, none of which were worth a tear or a paid admission." He goes on to provide his own assessment: "The shortcomings of *The Bigamist*," he maintains, "are not due to a changing sexual climate, but to Lupino's inability to provide a resolution to a unique sexual triangle. She may have been justified in believing certain emotional situations go beyond a simple assessment of right and wrong, but she did not push herself to find a means to effectively dramatize her view."[20] Seiter is more positive about Lupino's open-ended wrap-up, suggesting that such an inconclusive finale was mandated by the moral climate of the time. "It is a perfect ending for Lupino," Seiter writes, "in that it resolutely refuses to assign moral culpability. Such a lack of narrative closure, a feature of the made-for television movie, may be a necessary component of narratives that are so potentially subversive of the ideology of the nuclear family."[21] Lupino's decision to let audience members imagine their own resolution to *The Bigamist's* socially hot narrative is further complicated by other inconclusive events in the film, some suggesting important plot considerations and others perhaps a simple matter of technical continuity. The audience is unsure, for example, if Harry spends the entire seven hours with Phyllis at the restaurant when the two first meet; he certainly takes her home when her shift ends, and they mention the lapse of time. When Eve surprises Harry by flying to Los Angeles on their anniversary, meeting him at the office as he finishes his workday, do they spend the night together? It's obviously daylight when Harry comes home to a troubled Phyllis. More importantly, does Eve attempt a subtle wave to Harry at film's end, as the bigamist is led from the courtroom, or is that hand motion, as she leans in the doorway, a meaningless twitch? The two women briefly glance at each other after Harry's trial: Do they connect emotionally in any identifiable way, or do they simply acknowledge the unfortunate situation they share (see Figure 7.7)? Does Phyllis, as she leaves the trial, seem to enjoy her status as a newsworthy wronged-woman, or is her quick pose for photographers an instinctive move for Lupino, no stranger to publicity shoots?

That Lupino, directing herself, could momentarily shed character to assume the stance of movie star reveals the depth and diversity of her Hollywood career. As actor and director, producer and scriptwriter, promoter and manager, Lupino fearlessly defied gender conceptions and excelled in creative areas previously dominated by masculine sensibilities.

FIGURE 7.7 *Eve and Phyllis connect.*

As Hastie maintains, such diversity was as characteristic of the film as it was of Lupino herself:

> Perhaps *The Bigamist* did too much rather than too little; it critiqued masculinity and marriage, it allowed women to have lives outside of marriage, it refused to make a simple moralist argument. In a sense, Lupino also did too much: she directed and acted in the film, she was positioned between fictional and actual roles because of her personal and professional entanglements. The story in this way is less Harry's than it is hers.[22]

Lupino's refusal to provide thematic and narrative closure both emphasizes the moral uncertainties of *The Bigamist's* plot and further defines her status as an outlying filmmaker in a Hollywood predicated on niche markets and proven narrative formulas. Hastie's comparison of the director and her bigamist character is at once insightful and justified. Just as Harry Graham wanders into his fate as an offender through circumstance, so did Lupino assume her duties as a film director out of necessity and chance, disrupting the conventions of film noir by introducing socially conscious themes and thus attracting a wider audience. Both Harry and Lupino become outlaws by accident, Harry tragically through a deficit of moral backbone and personal agency, and Lupino constructively through creative courage and a unique cinematic vision. Lupino's directorial legacy demonstrates how established cinematic genres, infused with innovative content, develop and evolve to be more complex cultural expressions. That she contributed so compellingly as a female director working in a male-dominated Hollywood context says much about her determination, and certainly her legacy supersedes, through accomplishment, any perceived lack of feminist content in the films themselves. "Ida Lupino broke through various glass ceilings for women as directors and producers," Georgakas writes. "In that process she enriched the sensibility and subject matter available in all feature films."[23] Her energy and complex sensibilities as a director influence today's cinema in ways that we do not now, nor may ever, fully appreciate or comprehend.

Notes

1. For further discussion of the origin of "film noir" as a critical term, see, for example, Edward Dimendbert, *Film Noir and the Spaces of Modernity* (Cambridge, MA: Harvard University Press, 2004), 5–6 and James Naremore, *More than Night: Film Noir in Its Contexts* (Berkeley, CA: University of California Press, 2008), 13–18.
2. Mark T. Conard, ed., *The Philosophy of Film Noir* (Lexington, KY: University Press of Kentucky, 2006), 1–2.
3. Naremore, *More than Night*, 9, 11.
4. Richard Koszarski, ed., *Hollywood Directors 1914-1940* (New York, NY: Oxford University Press, 1977), 371.
5. Lauren Rabinovitz, "*The Hitch-Hiker (1953)*," in Annette Kuhn, ed. *Queen of the 'B's: Ida Lupino Behind the Camera* (Westport, CT: Praeger, 1995), 91.
6. Steve Neale, "Questions of Genre," in Robert Stam and Toby Miller, eds., *Film and Theory: An Anthology* (Malden, MA: Blackwell, 2000), 158.
7. Helle Kannik Haastrup, "Storytelling Intertextuality: From *Django Unchained* to *The Matrix*," *Film International* 12, no. 1 (March 2014): 85.
8. Neale, "Questions of Genre," 165.
9. Dan Georgakas, "Ida Lupino: Doing It Her Way," *Cineaste* 25, no. 3 (2000): 35.
10. William Donati, *Ida Lupino: A Biography* (Lexington, KY: University Press of Kentucky, 1996), 176.
11. Georgakas, "Ida Lupino: Doing It Her Way," 32, 34.
12. Ellen Seiter, "*The Bigamist (1953)*," in Kuhn, 113.
13. Ronnie Scheib, "Ida Lupino: Auteuress," *Film Comment* 16 (January–February 1980), 54.
14. Amelie Hastie, *The Bigamist* (Basingstoke, Hampshire: Palgrave Macmillan/British Film Institute, 2009), 37.
15. Georgakas, "Ida Lupino: Doing It Her Way," 33.

16 Julie Grossman provides a useful summary of this criticism in "NOIRNESS and Ida Lupino," *La Furia Umana*. Available at http://www.lafuriaumana.it/index.php/archives/41-lfu-14/103-julie-grossman-noirness-and-ida-lupino (accessed March 1, 2016).
17 Therese Grisham and Julie Grossman, *Ida Lupino, Director: Her Art and Resilience in Times of Transition* (New Brunswick, NJ: Rutgers University Press, 2017), 30.
18 Scheib, "Ida Lupino: Auteuress," 56.
19 US Department of Health, Education, and Welfare—Public Health Service. 100 Years of Marriage and Divorce Statistics United States, 1987-1967. Series 21, Number 24. DHEW Publication No. (HRA) 74-1902. Available at http://www.cdc.gov/nchs/data/series/sr_21/sr21_024.pdf (accessed March 1, 2016).
20 Georgakas, "Ida Lupino: Doing It Her Way," 36.
21 Seiter, *The Bigamist (1953)*," 116.
22 Hastie, *The Bigamist*, 81.
23 Georgakas, "Ida Lupino: Doing It Her Way," 36. Images from *The Bigamist*, © Filmakers.

8

Ida Lupino's Moral Filmmaking

The Bigamist and *The Trouble with Angels*

Ashley M. Donnelly

As I explored the limited catalogue of research related to Ida Lupino's 1953 *The Bigamist*, I found an article that described the film as a conventional film noir with a lackluster cinematic response and interesting but somewhat banal feminine characters. *The Bigamist* is *not* a conventional anything. Lupino's film, influenced heavily by both noir and neorealism, is an intricate, subtle, and well-crafted work of art that exemplifies her stylistic integrity as a director and her unique way of presenting moral subjects through the cinematic lens. As one of the very first female directors (in England and the United States), Lupino received attention and admiration during her time, and the legacy of Ida Lupino continues to grow as theorists and cinemaphiles alike revisit her work, reframing it in new contexts. The 1950s and 1960s saw discussions of her acting, directing, and personal life that reflected the times, similar to the interpretive work of the 1970s. What follows is an attempt to reframe Lupino using a contemporary lens that includes intensive interrogation of her artistic techniques and exploration of how the power of her interest in moral and ethical issues infuses her films with relevance in the new millennium.

In addition to an analysis of *The Bigamist*, I include a brief discussion of Lupino's 1966 film, *The Trouble with Angels*. Filmed more than ten years apart, one a black-and-white independent and the other a color studio picture, there is seemingly little to connect them. But it soon becomes apparent that these films are not nearly as different as they might seem to be. Both films exemplify specific, distinctive stylistic traits of Lupino, and they present moral issues in innovative, intellectual ways. Themes of patriarchy, ideals of womanhood, cultural expectations, and Otherness abound in Lupino's work, and examining these two films in conjunction with one another offers a rare opportunity to analyze her work and dissect her skill in dealing with complex ideas, regardless of genre and constraints that she faced.

The Bigamist

Many would view *The Bigamist*—with its cynicism, low-key lighting, black-and-white visuals emphasizing shadows, and typical unhappy ending—and call it a classic example of film noir. Indeed, the film is heavily influenced by film noir of the 1950s. Filmed in 1953, it contains many of the trademarks of other films of its time. Lupino, who stars in the film, was a well-known noir actress at that time. A Production Code–era piece, *The Bigamist* features twin beds (ironically) and relies on subtle dialogue and innuendo. And, like many noir films, its premise is incredibly risqué: a man has two wives and a child conceived out of wedlock. The way Lupino handles the material, however, is more reminiscent of a close cousin of noir, neorealism. Further, I would identify *The Bigamist* as heavily influenced by Italian neorealism in particular, as will be discussed further. Although many commentators demarcate the film as classic noir with its minimal budget and nonstudio-level production issues, I argue that *The Bigamist* is influenced by the genre, yet is not simply a product of it.

Lupino's vision and visual style are two reasons that I make this argument. Although the tone of *The Bigamist* is dark, the film itself is not. There is significantly more natural and produced lighting in it than in standard film noir. The excessive use of shadow is avoided. There is no femme fatale. Although one weakness of the movie is its poor (and often poorly timed) use of dramatic music, the rest of its cinematic aspects are extremely tight, expertly filmed, and clearly defined.

There are several notable characteristics of Lupino's direction: the use of crossed lines and/or patterned backgrounds, linear narration and linear character motion, and careful control of the actors' proxemics and body language. Unlike someone like Stanley Kubrick, whose parallels and crisp, clear lines of actors, props, and shadows dominate his work, Lupino uses patterns, crossed lines, and abstract space(s). Rather than using the distinct, well-defined scenes favored by Kubrick, Lupino's mise-en-scène is filled with broken lines and visual elements, such as shadows, that distract from precision. This architectural style is most noticeable in *The Bigamist*, with its sparse apartments and offices, coupled with emphatic use of location shooting. *The Trouble with Angels* also features such techniques but, because of the use of color and the cinematic constraints of studio films, they are not as obvious as in her later film. In *The Bigamist*, the Grahams' apartment, for example, is sparse and tidy, yet opulent enough to indicate wealth and security. There are several internal walls that appear to have large squares carved into them. The entire apartment is dominated with Chinese decorations and squares. However, when Lupino films the home, she emphasizes the shadows crossing the squares. The apartment, seemingly geometrically perfect, is filmed in such a way that the lines and squares are consistently in tension. It is a simple technique, but speaks volumes about atmosphere. The perfection of the home is a farce, just as the audience learns the marriage proves to be false as the film progresses. The apartment also reveals a clear parallel: the classy, precise Asian décor in the Graham house mocks the faux Chinese restaurant where Phyllis works, which is full of kitsch and excessive Americanized Chinese décor. It offers a visual representation of the difference between Eve and Phyllis (played by Lupino) and Harry's life.

Lupino often uses this visual technique when Harry is on the phone, emphasizing shadows across his face or cutting the background behind him, which is notable because the scenes in which Harry is on the phone most often represent the times when his two lives intersect; he is in one place talking to his wife or mistress in another or he is attempting to avert some crisis that will lead to the exposure of his two lives. In fact, the entirety of Lupino's use of patterns in filming underscores the narrative of the film: a man caught between two lives, each of which could be structured and clear-cut if not for the other. Lupino's use of mise-en-scène is similar, particularly as she handles her characters' proxemics. In this instance, however, the characters are filmed in a very tidy manner, with tight shots and closed frames, indicating intimacy and stability. The only actual chaos we see is in Mr. Jordan's office: stacks of papers abound, drawers are half opened, and there is a general sense of disorder. This disorder is cleverly designed, as Jordan is the man in the middle of Harry's two lives. The irony of these visuals is that Jordan's dogged determination, focus, and insight lead to Harry's downfall. Despite appearances, Jordan is the most astute character in the film. This juxtaposition fits well within Lupino's customary emphasis on the complexity of humanity, her desire to look beneath the surface of male and female appearances, and to surprise her audiences with unexpected character depth (Figure 8.1).

One of the most complicated aspects of directing is creating the illusion of relationships between actors. For a film to be credible, the characters must create the suspension of disbelief that they are living reality together. Lupino masters this necessity. Eve and Harry, for example, continuously maintain a two-to-three-foot distance from one another, except for a rare hug. The distance is not awkward but offers a sense of domestic expectation—or in the

FIGURE 8.1 *Scenes of Harry on the phone emphasize shadows across his face in The Bigamist.*

Grahams' case, she has the expectation of a businesslike formality. Lupino paints them as a functional couple and, at the beginning of the film, a loving one. Harry's body language is awkward, which Lupino deftly directed. Harry is not hostile or even unloving toward Eve, but his movements and facial expressions are of a man torn which, of course, he is. When Mr. Jordan arrives in Los Angeles at Harry's home and discovers his secret, Harry is not hostile or defensive but quietly resigned. After Harry puts his son to bed, the two men sit next to one another—not across from one another as one would imagine people do at an office or a police station—in a way that shows compassion and tenderness for Harry and his tale even before his complex story begins (Figure 8.2).

Although the narrative begins in the present as Eve and Harry attempting to adopt a child, it very quickly moves to the past with Harry telling the tale of how he became married to two women. The entire film is a linear story of the past until the very end, when the audience watches Harry face the consequences of his double life. Mirroring the linear style of the script, Lupino shoots the film in a linear manner. Although there are two cross flashbacks, both involving Eve, the rest of the film follows the demise of Harry's happiness as he changes from a married businessman and traveling salesman to a man with two separate lives and wives. His time with Phyllis, his lover then wife, is shot in a particularly straightforward manner. Harry even meets her on a bus tour, which places them in a tightly framed shot, sitting

FIGURE 8.2 *Mr. Jordan discovers Harry's secret in* The Bigamist.

next to one another yet moving forward by a force that is not their own. This metaphor underlying the bus scene sets up the entire relationship between the two. It is an effective technique and shows Lupino at her directorial best, navigating a narrow script while including a variety of levels of depth.

Supporting this depth is Lupino's use of found location and low-budget shooting. Reminiscent of Italian neorealism, which depends on location shooting, natural lighting, long shots, use of nonprofessional actors, and scenes emphasizing the ugly side of Italy's glamor after the Second World War, *The Bigamist*, while still employing professionals and light kits, does use long shots to emphasize atmosphere and place. The main driving force of Italian neorealism's was social commentary, exposing the economic, political, and social struggles of the nation after the Second World War. Although Los Angeles by no means faced the same kind of tangible struggles, its inhabitants, like the rest of the world, faced a serious internal struggle in the postwar years. Questions of moral order and insights into the reality of evil after Hitler's regime and persecution of Jews, homosexuals, and a variety of Others, who fell outside of a madman's construct of perfection, left the world reeling, feeling the metaphorical aftershocks of the atomic bomb and a universal loss of innocence. The Production Code limited Lupino's ability to actually film certain images or actions, like the marital bed or someone getting away with murder, the world in which Lupino lived was not naive. Lupino's personal world was not innocent—she herself was a woman married and divorced twice by the time *The Bigamist* was in production—

and she purposefully brought questions of moral order to the forefront of her films. Bigamy is a risqué topic, and the movie could have been a spectacle or a straightforward judgment of a man accused of an illegal act. Instead, Lupino chose to shoot a film with tenderness, understanding, conflicting moral standards, and an emphasis on the gray areas of human life. Her intention is not to shock or upset but to show realistically how complex love and life can be. It is arguably a beautiful, touching movie. Her treatment of both men and women in the film bring forth a world that seems so real, so normal, and so humane that condemnation is lost within the narrative she shoots, and human concern flourishes instead.

The script, written by Collier Young from a story by Larry Marcus and Lou Schor, serves as the backbone for Lupino's film and, like all scripts, serves as a guide for the tone and manner in which the material is treated. Yet even the smallest of changes by the director can shift the way viewers may perceive the film. Lupino set forth with assuredness that her film would deal with Harry and his complex life in a compassionate way, ensuring that the movie seems more like a tale of a man searching for balance and love than one of a man taking advantage of the women in his life. At no point does Harry seem like a man who has everything. Initially, he and his first wife, Eve, have a happy marriage. But when Eve learns she cannot have children, she becomes depressed and distant. To help her out of this darkness and to give her something on which to focus, Harry invites her into his company: she runs the office of his deep freezer sales company. Rather than the housewife and mother Eve had planned on being, she becomes a superb asset to Harry's business: efficient, energized, and happy to be involved. Eventually, however, Harry, who struggles enough with loneliness as he travels often for sales outreach, feels his wife pulling away from him and focusing more on her career than on their marriage. In Eve's mind, the two have merged. She does not seem to disengage intentionally from Harry, as I will discuss below, but her affection and energy turn toward work. So even when Harry returns from sales trips, he feels alone in his own home because Eve wants to discuss work with him rather than their relationship. It is this chasm between them that leads Harry to Phyllis, whom he meets in Los Angeles on a sales trip.

The relationship between Harry and Phyllis, platonic at first, gives him friendship, liveliness, humor, and the female companionship he so sorely lacks. Never one to cheat, Harry is known for being a quiet man on sales trips, not a "take it or leave it" kind of guy. His time with Phyllis, even when it is fairly innocuous, plays on his conscience, and he even tries to tell Eve about it. She rejects this exchange as a tale and teases him. Eventually, when he finds himself alone on his birthday in Los Angeles, Harry and Phyllis become intimate. However, after the one indiscretion guilt consumes Harry, and he does not see Phyllis again. Instead, he pours his energy into making Eve happy, and he suggests that they adopt a child, an idea she embraces.

This plan leads the couple to Mr. Jordan, the adoption agent who discovers Harry's double life. We then learn, as Harry's story unfolds, that he and Phyllis conceived a child during their one night together.

When Harry goes to see Phyllis, although she is alone and weakened by the pregnancy, she remains vibrant and tough, and he asks her, out of a seemingly genuine desire for a life with her, to marry him. He decides to give Eve the child that she has always wanted through adoption, and he then plans to divorce her, in order to maintain his life with Phyllis and their child. Harry wants everyone to be happy. Phyllis, not knowing about Eve, resists his marriage proposal. She refuses to "trap" him and refuses to be a wife for any reason other than love. Yet Harry persists. He does love her—and Lupino's direction makes this clear. His facial expressions, his affection toward her, and his physical engagement with her on screen all show a man genuinely in love. When he is with Eve, as the film progresses, we see a man of dignity, bound by obligation. Harry wants to make Eve happy, and he feels duty bound to ensure that she is. But his demeanor with her is far different than that of his demeanor with Phyllis. Yet neither version of Harry is despicable, and neither version is a man whom the viewer can denounce. He tries to be a good man, regardless of how he got himself into his situation. The manner in which he tells his tale to Mr. Jordan reflects his character and motivation.

In addition to presenting Harry in a sympathetic, problematized way, Lupino offers us two women, neither one of which conforms to the negative stereotypes of the period. They are not frigid, demanding, seductive and destructive, or simple-minded props. Eve Graham, even though she is emotional and struggling, is not a neurotic mess. She has discovered that she cannot fulfill her role as a housewife and mother, as society would stereotypically expect from a woman in 1953. She feels the emptiness of not being able to have the child she (seemingly) had always wanted but, when given the opportunity to focus on something outside of herself, she moves forward. Her work at Harry's company is not simple secretarial work but actual office management. She learns quickly, and, although she is not involved directly in sales, she recruits potential buyers and impresses them with her product knowledge, along with her feminine style and sensibilities. She is a beautiful woman and difficult to ignore. Lupino includes a scene at the Graham apartment where Eve surprises Harry with a sales dinner when he comes home from a sales trip. This scene is complex, and it does not portray Eve as a purposefully emasculating wife, even though this reaction is the effect that the meal seems to have on Harry. Instead, it highlights her intelligence, drive, and insight. The emasculation of Harry is a side effect that perpetuates sympathy for him and the plight he struggles with, rather than a demonization of her. Eve is able to quote nearly the entire workman's manual to her two male clients, all the while maintaining the "if a little woman like me can do this" spiel for effect. She is smart, talented, and benefits everyone around her. That she does not realize the effect this meal has on Harry casts her in a somewhat negative light (she lacks the intimate attention to her husband that might allow her to be more sensitive to his mood), but it does not suggest that she is intentionally trying to demean her husband. It shows. Instead, that the distance in their marriage is not based on animosity, resentment, or spite but is simply the result of a divide that work can create in a family. This scene is very much ahead of its time and well executed in typical Lupino-style: fast, straightforward, and precise.

Phyllis, as Harry's eventual mistress, is not a temptress. She seems bored by the attention of simplistic men and is self-sufficient, funny, street smart, and feisty. She offers Harry fun, the backand-forth joking that he craves, and a simple flirtation that seems more for her benefit than his. She is entertaining herself and not attempting to lure him. In *The Bigamist*, Ida Lupino became the first female director to direct herself in a film. However, she felt some insecurity in her new role according to biographer William Donati.

> It was difficult for her to determine the quality of her performance, so she depended on Collie's [Collier Young's] judgment. She later revealed "I'd always sworn I'd never do this . . . it was a new experience telling myself what to do . . . . I'm one who wants and needs direction but I never in the world expected to be doing it myself. I think it's the toughest thing I've ever attempted in my entire career."[1]

One can understand how even a seasoned performer, like Lupino, would struggle in this situation. She creates a film that relies on subtlety of movement and emotion, exact precision of scene control, and the development of scenes that require expression, without the freedom to speak frankly or openly. But her performance is flawless. The contrast she designs between Eve and Phyllis ensures that there is no female to "blame" in the film, no one to truly demonize, and no female stereotypes on which to rely, leaving her audience, once again, to handle the complex world of the film on their own. She provides no easy answers and no easy way out. To engage with *The Bigamist*, one must engage with ideals of womanhood, masculinity, Otherness, moral rules, and the complexity of human existence (Figure 8.3).

The Bigamist moves quickly, and there is little space in the film for filler as it wastes no time in telling Harry's tale and examines characters' emotional responses at an efficacious pace, an interesting and innovative way of handling such a sensitive subject as bigamy. Lupino is essentially forcing her audience to accept the gray areas of the film as it moves forward, which leaves them to ponder and reflect after the movie is over, an excellent way of presenting a film about complex social issues. The conclusion of *The Bigamist* is perfectly crafted to do just this. As Harry sits before the judge, Eve on one side of the courtroom and Phyllis and his son on the

FIGURE 8.3 *Lupino's Phyllis is self-sufficient, funny, street smart, and feisty in* The Bigamist.

other, the judge rules that Harry has broken the law but offers compassion for his story, noting that Harry is not a monster but a man who has made bad choices. The judge tells Harry after his sentence that Harry will have to support both women and, with pity, says that after Harry has served his time, "It won't be a question of which woman he'll go back to, but rather which woman will take him back." Harry is then led away. Neither woman speaks to him and neither one looks at him with rage or tears. There is a sense of quiet, sad confusion among the characters, Lupino clearly leaving final judgment up to the audience.

A well-crafted, well-shot, and well-acted film, *The Bigamist*, unfortunately, did not receive significant acclaim, largely because it became a Filmakers' production after RKO Pictures pulled out of its production, and Lupino and Collier were forced to deliver the film themselves. Thus, the film's budget, distribution, and publication were smaller than anticipated. Luckily, the disruption of her film did not interfere with Lupino's vision or dedication. Indeed, fiercely independent, Lupino wanted to create cinema without the restraints of studio interference. She always viewed herself as a humanist, working to present the human condition, and she sought stories about "poor, bewildered people."[2] Ironically, the loss of a large portion of the budget, even though it hurt the film on one level, may have bolstered its artistic integrity. Lupino was forced to be more efficient, more direct, and more succinct. The neorealist influences most certainly helped with the realism and visual honesty of film and, arguably, would have been negatively affected by large studio interference.

The Trouble With Angels

After *The Bigamist*, Lupino's directorial work was focused on television. However, in 1966, she was back on the big screen with *The Trouble with Angels*, which starred Rosalind Russell and a new, post-Disney Hayley Mills. Given the film's almost entirely female cast, writer Wheeler Dixon argues that it was "clearly sexism that got her [Lupino] the assignment: hire a woman to deal with a film about women."[3] It is difficult to find any source that offers solid evidence as to why the independent and successful Lupino would return to a studio-based film after such a lengthy absence from directing cinema. Whatever the reason, her return produced an amusing film that "saved Jane Trahey's treacly [sic] novel from being turned into an equally saccharine movie."[4] Lupino was able to turn a written comedy about a Catholic girls school run by nuns into a film that explored ideals of femininity, class, and patriarchy.

There is little scholarship on *The Trouble with Angels*. Unsurprisingly, as it is a mainstream comedy about a school for girls where hijinks take place, and it fits nicely into a niche genre like "girls' comedy," which is often overlooked in film studies. However, in the 1995 essay "Lupino's *The Trouble With Angels* (1966)," Mary Beth Haralovich, Janet Jakobsen, and Susan White tackle the film, arguing that a "queer" approach to the film more adequately explains Lupino's intentions than a "straight" approach, and they explore both the homosocial and the homosexual gazes as they apply them to the young women in the film.[5] The authors argue that *The Trouble with Angels* is about social change and identities in women's communities, and Lupino uses a feminist lens to direct the film. Underneath its fun, quirky exterior, *The Trouble with Angels* offers commentary not just on female relationships and concepts of social change, but also on class, feminine empowerment, patriarchy, and adolescent development.

Lupino directs with a sense of purpose, as always, and her lens aims at the social and moral problems presented in the material that she is given. For Lupino, two precocious high school sophomores sent to St. Francis Academy, an all-girls boarding school run by Dominican nuns, offers an opportunity to explore not only the girls' lives and the setting in which they find themselves, but also the world of women in religious institutions, how relationships are developed and shaped by outside forces, and Catholicism as a metaphor for patriarchy in general.

The introduction to *The Trouble with Angels* is animated, featuring cartoon versions of Mother Superior (Rosalind Russell), Mary Clancy (Hayley Mills), and Rachel Devery (June Harding), with other characters interacting as well. What struck me as most interesting about this particular portion of the film is the giant, cartoon hand of God that interferes directly with the characters, chastising them or striking them with shocking, but nonlethal, bolts of lightning as needed to correct their behavior. It is a silly start but, in a way, also somewhat terrifying. The world of Catholicism (Christianity in general, but Catholicism in this particular film) is presented quite clearly as one in which the giant, masculine hand of God serves to correct, punish, and chastise. The world of the film—the nuns, the emphasis on a girls-only religious school—is set up as one that must be directed and controlled by the ultimate Patriarch, God himself.

As the film opens, Mary and Rachel, both new students headed to the school for different reasons, meet on the train. Mary is a wild child sent to St. Francis in the hopes that the nuns and the Holy Father can somehow sort out her behavior. Rachel is a child of wealthy parents who had been sending her to a progressive school. Her father, tired of his daughter learning what are essentially life skills and ways of understanding the self instead of traditional educational materials, sends her off for a more formal education. The two girls, a pair of misfits, bond quickly and become the bane of Mother Superior's existence upon their arrival.

Lupino's cinemagraphic emphasis on broken lines, obscured blocks, and disrupted parallels is evident throughout *The Trouble with Angels*, as it is in *The Bigamist*. However, this film, in Panthecolor, makes it more difficult to discern shadows or light play. But the physical setup of the academy—part convent, part school—is ideal for Lupino to contrast order and regulation against disorder and chaos. Typically, she accomplishes this comparison by showing the girls running rampant around the carefully designed school with its parallel tables, beds, desks, and lines of students. This carefully constructed world order, much like the early life of Harry Graham, is cast into disarray by the arrival of Rachel and Mary. The film itself, of course, focuses on the relationships of women: how women find strength through their bonds with one another, learn from each other, learn forgiveness, and learn to live in the gray area between the expectations of Catholic school rules and adolescent desires for fun and adventure. The girls also learn to negotiate with Mother Superior, who, in her own way, learns to negotiate with them. Although Mother Superior holds the power, the girls' challenges push her to learn more about herself and more about what the exuberance of youth can offer her calling.

It is a quaint film, and it falls into a repetitive, somewhat boring pattern of hijinks, punishments, and lessons learned. However, Lupino still manages to comment on social issues. She empowers the girls' decision-making skills, using the restrictions of the school to show how bright and creative women can be, and she creates an atmosphere that shows positive relationships between and among women of all ages, a contrast to the overuse of antagonism among women in so much past and current mainstream media. There are allusions to the girls' burgeoning sexuality: Rachel's crush on Mr. Petrie, Mary's jokes about her Uncle George's infidelities, and the girls' crafty acquirement of overtly sexual band uniforms. The band uniform scenes are complex. On the one hand, the girls are using their sexuality at a young age to get what they want, clearly not a feminist message. On the other hand, however, Lupino ramps up the ridiculousness of the situation and the humor, making fun of the overall trope.

As the film progresses, Mary does so as well. Her needs—for a family, for something to which she can be dedicated, for something solid, true, and beautiful—are best seen in the Christmas scene. Mary stays behind at St. Francis while the other girls go home for the holidays, and she sneaks in to watch the sisters celebrate mass. It is a beautiful scene, and Mary, lacking stealth, is seen by Mother Superior but ignored, and is allowed to enjoy the moment of religious engagement that is, for the sisters, full of love, beauty, and honesty. It is here we see the true complexity of Mary. Although it is easy to make fun of the institution and even Catholicism in general as the film plays out, this moment of tenderness is an exemplary example of Lupino asking her audience to reconsider their earlier reactions to the school and to the main characters. Patriarchal it may be, and problematic as it can be, religion is given a shining moment in this scene, and Lupino is forcing her audience to consider all aspects of a complex issue three-quarters of the way deep in a childish comedy.

As graduation approaches and the girls prepare to move beyond St. Francis, Mary surprises everyone by deciding to stay on as a novitiate of the order. She is not forced into the decision, and she did not yield to pressure. She chose (or was "called") to a life not many women would be willing to follow. Rachel is devastated. She fears that she has lost her friend and feels betrayed because Mary did not reveal this before graduation. Eventually, however, with the help of Mother Superior, Rachel recognizes her friend's dedication, and Rachel and Mary part with tears and promises of friendship. It is, in one sense, a trite ending; the troublemaker learns to love her religious order and stays on to dedicate her life to God. But, at the same time, Mary never once yielded under pressure in the rest of the film, and, in a sense, her decision is significantly more difficult and brave than the decisions of those who leave the school for a world of potential opportunities. Although still under the giant hand of the Patriarch, Mary has made a decision to stay and to shape the world around her, a world that she can share with others. It is a selfless act, but it is also one that challenges (and will continue to challenge) the expectations of the characters in Lupino's fictional world as well as the film's audience, asking them to look at religion differently in general. How can women change the world working within undeniable patriarchy? How can they "fix" things without abandoning tradition? These questions are, again, large, and difficult to answer, and they are left to the audience. There is no onscreen discussion and, just as she does in *The Bigamist*, Lupino leaves the onus on the audience to ponder these questions, ideally searching for answers that may help shape the social and moral problems that surround them outside of the theater.

Notes

1 William Donati, *Ida Lupino: A Biography* (Lexington: University Press of Kentucky, 1996), 190–278, quoted p. 202.
2 Ibid., 264.
3 Wheeler W. Dixon, *Disaster and Memory: Celebrity Culture and the Crisis of Hollywood Cinema* (New York: Columbia University Press, 1999), 65–98, quoted p. 74.
4 Ibid., 135.
5 Mary Beth Haralovich, Janet Jakobsen, and Susan White, "Lupino's *The Trouble with Angels*," in Annette Kuhn (ed.), *Queen of the B's: Ida Lupino Behind the Camera* (Santa Barbara: Praeger, 1966), 112–40, quoted p. 127.

9

Ida Lupino's Manipulation of Age Conventions

Valerie Barnes Lipscomb

Most critics of Ida Lupino's work note that her films and her reported off-camera behavior demonstrate that she was consciously reacting to social norms regarding females' roles within the family and society. While some claim that her films and her public statements so steadfastly support postwar female domesticity that they cannot be viewed in any feminist light, Marsha Orgeron posits that Lupino knew how to use feminine stereotypes personally to get what she wanted, to appear nonthreatening in a patriarchal culture while actually adroitly manipulating that situation.[1] I suggest that a similar claim may be made about Lupino's use of age stereotypes. Age-studies scholars have been turning to film as a prime medium for critiquing the performative nature of age construction in Western culture. An examination of Lupino's own reported statements as well as her major films demonstrates that she was acutely aware of the prevailing social norms surrounding age, both on screen and off. Just as she often used the conventions of femininity to her personal advantage rather than openly fight them, in films such as *Outrage*, *The Hitch-Hiker*, *The Bigamist*, and *Hard, Fast and Beautiful*, Lupino does not challenge stereotypical portrayals of age. Rather, these works from the Filmakers years skillfully employ the conventions of age performance to heighten cinematic effect.

Although Ida Lupino had been groomed for a life of performance, her screen career still began relatively early in life, when she was just fourteen, and its launch was directly related to the performance of age. In Mary Ann Anderson's biography, Lupino denies the commonly repeated story that she was first cast for a role that her mother was seeking: "Not at all true, my mum tested for the role!"² Annette Kuhn characterizes Lupino's early film work, "This was to be the first of many similar roles for the young actress, who for some years continued playing women much older than herself." She adds that Paramount originally targeted Lupino for *Alice in Wonderland*, but executives recognized that she did not naturally "play" young and made her an ingénue instead.³ An awareness of age performance and age types was a foundation of her acting career.

Numerous statements that Lupino made during the course of her career show an ongoing awareness of age, particularly of the value of youth in Hollywood. Several of these are collected in William Donati's biography: "Ted Post enjoyed working with Ida but couldn't understand her preoccupation with the lighting. 'Darling, don't shoot me as if I were an eighteen year old,' she pleaded. 'We need some soft lenses. Or maybe a horse blanket,' she would joke. Though only thirty-six years old, Ida was, as always, insecure about her looks."⁴ In this case, Lupino was insecure specifically about how old she looked, that she was past ingénue age, and it showed. In another instance on the set of the *Mr. Adams and Eve* television series, Lupino reportedly asked, "Don't you think the lights should be a little higher for dear old Mum? I'm not twenty-two anymore."⁵ Again, she refers to the traditional age range for ingénue beauty, separating herself as an aged mother, although she was just in her thirties. Her concern revolves around lighting's ability to manipulate the appearance of age for the camera, showing anecdotally her heightened awareness of age-related effects on film.

Some of the more remarkable age-related stories in Lupino's biographies are related to her turbulent years with Howard Duff. Donati tells of a time when a fortune-teller stopped at their nightclub table: "She failed to recognize the famous couple but stared at Ida and said she looked familiar. Ida became uncomfortable. The stranger made the comment a few more times, then [companion Sol] Saks playfully added, 'People tell her she looks like Ida Lupino.' 'Oh, yes,' said the woman, 'but you're much prettier. She's older looking.' Ida's face tightened and the fun vanished."⁶ In the 1960s, as Lupino aged into her forties, she became even more aware of the perceived sex appeal gap between middle-aged men such as Howard Duff and middle-aged women like her: "As she bluntly revealed at the time: 'The other night I said to him, "Darling, so many men are suddenly flipping for twenty-year-olds. Do you think you'll go for some young girl?" He looked at me and saw I was rather serious . . . and then he started to laugh . . . . "What's the matter with you, darling? What a perfectly ridiculous question. Don't you know that old chickens make the best soup?"⁷ Not long after, of course, Duff left her for a young woman.

Lupino's remarks come as no surprise, as actresses are well aware of the commodification of female beauty and its inexorable tie to youth. However, it is notable that Lupino brought up the subject regularly enough to merit inclusion in her biographies, whether she was acting or directing. In fact,

Orgeron reports that in an unpublished interview with Hedda Hopper, Lupino connected aging with her desire to direct: "I might be a star—but without any husband or family and having to worry about my face getting lined, etc. etc. I decided there was something else for me in life other than being a big star."[8] After quitting the studio system, she took acting roles only when she needed to earn money, especially when she wanted to fund her filmmaking, Orgeron asserts.

One final casting story was Lupino playing Steve McQueen's mother in the 1972 film *Junior Bonner*, even though she was only twelve years older than McQueen. Robert Preston as Ace Bonner also was twelve years older than Junior, but Lupino fondly recalled McQueen's frequent, flattering complaints that he just could not see her as his mother figure.[9] At the time of that acting comeback, she was in her fifties, not old enough to be McQueen's mother, but old enough to be the mother of an adult child. Behind the camera, as a director, she had been adopting a maternal role toward other adults for more than twenty years.

As a director, Lupino immediately assumed the stance of an older woman, someone who could mother the cast and crew. Her piece, "Me, Mother Directress" from *Action!* magazine has drawn the attention of scholars who focus on Lupino's embracing traditional feminine roles, but this article is more about age than simply about feminine roles. In her forties, Lupino recalls that the cast and crew bestowed the nickname "years and years ago when I had my own independent company and we made a policy of discovering and using young talent. Some of the kids, like Sally Forrest, who starred in *Not Wanted* for me nearly twenty years ago, were so young, it was natural for them to call me 'mom' or 'mother.'"[10] Lupino distinguishes the new talent as a generation younger, emphasizing the mentor role in a nonthreatening manner. However, Sally Forrest was only ten years younger than Lupino, hardly enough of a gap to be her daughter. As "mother," Lupino could assert generational authority over anyone involved in a production, regardless of their actual age relationship. While the cast and crew could have resented being directed by a thirty-something woman, who could not claim to have earned the wisdom of older age, it is common to acknowledge that one's mother always can assert a level of benevolent authority, regardless of age.

Lupino cared about social age norms and deftly used the conventions of age to her personal advantage to gain cooperation as a director; her films illustrate the same sense of how age stereotypes can reinforce a theme. Lupino was by no means a crusader against agism, but examining her use of age illuminates the cultural norms of mid-century America. As Pamela H. Gravagne observes:

> By seeing the making and viewing of film as part of a cultural struggle over meanings that are never fixed or natural, and as part of contested practices of representation and creation intimately connected to the way

we understand the various texts we encounter and to the way we make ourselves and our relationships, a critical approach to viewing popular film can allow us to recognize and create alternate ways to age.[11]

Often, when age becomes a topic of scrutiny, the assumption is that age must mean old age, just as most identity studies begin with the marked or unprivileged end of a binary. This study will begin with the conventions associated with older ages in Lupino's films but will address younger ages and portrayals of middle age as well, as the films rely on social norms and typical narratives relating to all three of these stages of adulthood.

Older Ages: Appearances of Authority

The Western metanarrative of aging is a downward slope of increasing decline and decay physically and mentally, leading inevitably to death.[12] During the time when Lupino was directing films, that decline tale had marginalized anyone over the socially constructed retirement age of sixty-five. Perhaps the most notable example in mid-century film of the disregard for those who have left the work force is Vittorio De Sica's *Umberto D.* (1952), an Italian neorealist work that follows a pensioner as he struggles to make ends meet. Umberto's outlook is bleak, as he is being evicted from his room and maintains social connection only with a young housemaid and his beloved dog. After he cannot raise the money to continue his meager existence, he considers suicide; the film's ending provides no resolution and little hope for Umberto's future. Postretirement, there would be nothing left of life but to await death.

Life expectancies increased during the second half of the twentieth century, so that scholars now often divide considerations of old age into further categories. Most of the stereotypes now culturally associated with aging actually can be located more specifically among the "oldest old," those over about eighty in the present day, rather than everyone who passes the threshold of sixty-five. While sometimes justifiably seen as arbitrary and limiting, categories of age also can be useful when discussing stages of the life course. Scholars debate whether the onset of what is known as the "Third Age" is around retirement or earlier, and the "Fourth Age" is the category of the oldest citizens, when incidence of frailty and impairment rises.[13] This division is more recent, as life spans have increased, so it is necessary to keep in mind the decline associated with reaching retirement age during much of the history of film.

Unlike *Umberto D.*, which confronts the alienation of the poverty-stricken retiree as a social problem, the majority of Western films have not focused on characters of Third or Fourth Age, preferring to center on youthful protagonists. Rather, older characters tend to fill supporting roles at best, while the dramatic action revolves around young adults, those who are just entering the Second Age of "independence, maturity, and responsibility."[14] Although Lupino's films work within these conventions, a few choices are worth noting: first, hardly any characters beyond retirement age appear in her most-respected films, which is not entirely uncommon in mainstream cinema. Lupino earns recognition as a director of social-problem films, but they are not the problems of old age. More interesting is that her plots are likely to be pinned to characters who are firmly established in the Second Age, who are shouldering the daily responsibilities of raising a family, rather than to those who have just crossed the threshold into adulthood. In Lupino's films, characters who are nearing the end of middle age often represent authority and stability, contrasting with the younger adults who serve as protagonists. This air of solidity not only reflects the voice of society, but also brings into stark relief the conflicts with which the protagonists struggle.

Lupino's characters encounter traditional cultural authority figures, particularly in the more melodramatic films *Outrage* (1950) and *The Bigamist* (1953). In the former film, which focuses more firmly on a young protagonist, older characters fill the roles of the doctor who examines Ann Walton after she has been raped, and the judge who decides her fate when she assaults a man after reliving her own attack. *The Bigamist* includes an older doctor who cares for Phyllis during her pregnancy and a judge who has the last say regarding the legality and morality of Harry Graham's bigamy. Some critics do take note of this appearance of social authority, such as Orgeron's commenting about the doctor in *The Bigamist*, "The authoritative voice of the medical establishment enters the film to motivate, perhaps even to legitimate Harry's proposal to Phyllis."[15] These characters sport graying hair and/or glasses, being portrayed as a generation older than those in the conflict. To the societal authority conferred upon figures such as doctors and judges, Lupino adds the authority of age. In these instances, authority is associated with males at the height of their professional and earning power, which typically occurs toward the end of middle age.

By the same token, the San Francisco adoption agency official in *The Bigamist*, Mr. Jordan, appears to be nearing the Third Age retirement threshold and certainly wields power over the lives of the thirty-something Grahams, who submit to a background check as part of the process of adopting a baby. Jordan functions in a detective role, investigating the couple until he discovers Harry's double life: a second wife, Phyllis, and baby in Los Angeles, where he travels often for business. The audience's horizon of expectations may shift during the course of the narrative, as the plot at first seems to be set up to climax with the inevitable discovery of Harry's bigamy. However, relatively early in the film, Jordan tracks down Harry at his second home, caring for his child while Phyllis sleeps, and the structure adjusts to being Harry's explanation to Jordan of how the bigamy came to pass.

This narrative structure calls for an age-casting approach that differs from the doctors and judges who are simply the voices of authority and social convention in Lupino's films. Jordan must first appear competent enough to discover the truth, old enough to be well established in his career and represent a real threat to Harry. If Jordan were meant only to discover and expose bigamy as a blow to social stability, casting him in the same distinguished manner as the doctors and judges—a generation older than the protagonists, a polished professional in his fifties, perhaps gray hair and glasses—would suffice.

Jordan represents more, though, as he has been established as the moral center of *The Bigamist* in an exposition scene with an older cleaning woman.[16] Jordan tells her that he must be very careful about placing babies in the right families, because he had made a mistake once. His character quickly is drawn as truly caring as well as righteous. He then is thrust into an ambiguous moral situation, sharing the viewer's stance of listening to Harry's story, which is told in voice-over of scenes from the past. He may be expressing the viewer's ambivalence in responding to Harry's narrative: "I admire you, and yet I pity you," he says. "I don't even want to shake your hand, and yet I almost wish you luck." The character must be both authoritative and approachable. Casting Edmund Gwenn met both criteria. Already a successful character actor, Gwenn had won lasting fame as Santa Claus in *Miracle on 34th Street* (1947), associating him forever with a jolly old elf. He stood at about 5'5" and was in his mid-seventies, more than a decade beyond the expected age for a character participating in the working world. The press coverage of the film noted that this was the first time in Gwenn's fifty-eight-year career that he was directed by a woman, emphasizing his longevity.[17] Film dialogue portrays Jordan on the oldest end of Second Age, also, as the cleaning woman calls him "an old fussbudget" and Harry calls him "an old codger."

Moreover, this much-older casting occurred during the same era when stars such as Bette Davis, Joan Crawford, and Gloria Swanson were relegated to playing "has-beens" when they were only in their fifties. As critic Sally Chivers notes, in mid-century films such as *Sunset Boulevard* (1950) and *Whatever Happened to Baby Jane* (1962), "the spectacle of aging film stars replicates and dictates the very cultural attitudes that make acting old in public risky, even when the characters are middle-aged (i.e., by no means old)."[18] Of course, women are "aged by culture"[19] more harshly and at earlier ages than men, as evidenced by Lupino's playing an "aging" star when she was just forty-one years old in a 1959 *Twilight Zone* episode. However, Gwenn's well-known advanced age affects audience reaction to this purportedly middle-aged character. While it is important to recognize that chronological age can differ significantly from apparent or performed age (of which Lupino was aware from personal experience), Gwenn hardly cuts a forbidding figure; confessing one's transgressions to an elderly Kris

Kringle is relatively easy. Lupino thus uses the stereotypes of age to construct the necessary element of lawful authority in *The Bigamist*, but also builds audience sentiment favoring Harry by giving him a confessor who may be able to sympathize.

This nonthreatening stance also serves Jordan in his detective role. When he seeks details about Harry at the Los Angeles office, Jordan meets a younger businessman and a younger secretary, which indicates a youthful business culture that contrasts starkly with Jordan's age. The pair obviously perceive Jordan as harmless, allowing him to discover what a young man may not have. Rather than posing a real danger, Jordan displays traces of the classic senex blocking figure, an older man who stands in the way of the protagonist's happiness. The type is comic and soon defeated, which adds to the sense that Harry should be able to maneuver around Jordan and somehow find happiness. Nevertheless, the standard comic plot ultimately affirms the social order, which Harry has violated. Casting Gwenn adds to the uncertainty of the plot's outcome, heightening the effect that Lupino claimed she wanted, to allow the viewers to make up their own minds about the fate that the bigamist deserves (Figure 9.1).

Not surprising for this time in American culture, the representatives of older-middle-aged authority in Lupino's films tend to be male. Older female characters include the aforementioned cleaning woman as well as Phyllis' landlady in *The Bigamist* and an onlooker in *Outrage*. The cleaning

FIGURE 9.1 *Mr. Jordan strikes a balance between Santa Claus approachability and an elder's authority over middle-aged characters.*

woman offers a convenient mode of exposition without involving another character in Jordan's investigation; she can relate to Jordan as a peer in age (actress Jane Darwell was only two years younger than Gwenn) but not pose any interference with his course of action. The landlady (played by Lilian Fontaine, mother of Joan Fontaine, who portrayed wife Eve) provides a modicum of maternal care for Phyllis when she is portrayed as weak-but-tough in pregnancy, as well as additional social pressure for Harry to take the proper action and marry her. The onlooker in *Outrage* also has a brief appearance, an entertaining bit in which she eavesdrops on Jim's proposal to Ann, at first disapproving when she is not positive that Jim is proposing, then smiling when he takes that leap. While the moment is brief, the social constraints that the woman represents are memorable; Richard Brody's recommendation of the film claims "that glare casts a cold shadow on the rest of the movie."[20] Each older woman, while on the fringe of the action, fulfills the type by acting as a voice of propriety.

Ida Lupino's most-respected films break no new ground in the portrayal of older people; the Third and Fourth ages are nearly invisible, and the end of Second Age is associated with upholding cultural norms. The films do skillfully employ the stereotypes of aging to support other themes and emphases, showing a consciousness of age-related social constructs. That awareness is just as evident in portrayals of the other end of the age continuum that often is a focus in film narrative: entrance into the Second Age, the cusp of adulthood.

Younger Ages: Voices of Innocence

Among *Outrage*, *The Bigamist*, *The Hitch-Hiker*, and *Hard, Fast and Beautiful*, two main characters are the appropriate age to experience the trials of entering adulthood. At twenty, Ann Walton is becoming engaged, indicating that *Outrage* could ultimately follow the arc of a traditional female Bildungsroman, ending in marriage. Similarly, Florence Farley is just out of high school and meets an eligible young man early in *Hard, Fast and Beautiful* (1951), so that the audience could expect another female coming-of-age plot. Few critics have addressed Lupino's handling of the coming-of-age story. Ronnie Scheib asserts:

> If Lupino made films about adolescent coming-to-consciousness, the emphasis was less on the shock of discovery of a world which is different from expectations than on her sleepwalker-heroines' complete inability to read their place in the world--an inability compounded, one supposes, by the limitations imposed on them by both their gender and their class.[21]

I would agree that each film focuses on a young woman's innocence at the beginning, but that it contrasts with increased maturity by the plot's end, even if the woman has not demonstrated full assimilation into adult society. In each case, young womanhood appears girlish, vulnerable, and impressionable through a majority of the film, a state accentuated by costuming choices as well as dialogue and camera angles.

Following the course of maturation in *Outrage* begins with Ann as a working young woman who plans to marry Jim; as the couple informs her parents of the engagement, they overtly separate the two generations, designating specifically the "young" people and the father as an "older" educator. The father disapproves at first and condescends to them, saying particularly that they are young for marriage. The beginning scenes thus establish Ann as young and not exceptionally mature. This stance continues when Ann flees and takes refuge on the Harrisons' ranch, as Mala Powers performs youth relative to the older ages of most of the characters. The Harrisons are old enough to substitute as parental figures, as Ann stays in their grown daughter's room, and the males on and around the ranch appear older than Ann. There is age contrast even in the brief appearances of men who could help her along the way, such as the older man who hears the horn during the attack and shuts his window, and the older man working at the diner counter. One consequence of the rape is to remove Ann literally from characters in her peer age group, while the older generation appears unable or unwilling to assist her.

Critic Pam Cook points out not only the "male authoritarianism" that Ann encounters, but also a pursuit/flight motif that extends far beyond the initial attack, "and her journey can be seen in terms of a wish to discover forms of male identity more hospitable to female subjectivity."[22] I would add that Ann's flight demonstrates a childlike response to trauma as well. Ann says that she ran away from home, just as a child would, and slowly the minister Bruce paternalistically guides her to return home and face her situation, which is a mature response. This temporary escapism, an interlude movement from town to country, fits the pattern of countless coming-of-age stories.

Outrage traces Ann's progress on the life course not only through action, but also through her costuming. She initially wears a bow and her hair is youthfully long, which magnifies the evidence of trauma after the rape scene, when she arrives home looking dirtied and disheveled with the bow untied, symbolic of the innocence that has been stolen from her. When Ann returns to work after the attack, she wears a scarf at her throat, less juvenile than the initial bow, but her dress when she works at the ranch is decorated with another childlike bow. Ann's harvest dance dress appears quite juvenile: it is peasant style with ruffles and a laced bodice, complementing her hairstyle of girlish pigtails. Not until the end of *Outrage* does the audience see Ann in an adult-looking dress, reflecting that she now has recovered enough from her attack to return to the traditional life course that awaits her. At that point, she still sits girlishly at Bruce's feet, while the camera accentuates her position in reverse shots looking down at her and up at him, but, despite her reluctance, she appears marginally ready to resume her life (Figure 9.2).

Similarly, Florence Farley at the opening of *Hard, Fast and Beautiful* wears a letter sweater, associating her with adolescence rather than young adulthood. While the sweater serves as a point of connection with Gordon, who attended the same high school, it also separates his adult sphere from her teenage world. These markers continue as she wears hair bows during early scenes; her innocence is apparent as she begins tennis competition. As Mandy Merck notes, "Florence Farley enters this world as the classic ingénue—eager, unsophisticated, guileless" and lacking a good backhand, both literally and figuratively, of course.[23] The occasional high-angle shot underscores her status, showing Florence looking up at the adult who addresses her. As she gains success, the hair bow disappears and she dons more sophisticated evening wear to celebrate victory, but at times appears to be playing dress-up, particularly when she rebels against her mother by drinking and smoking.

More than in *Outrage*, the dialogue in *Hard, Fast and Beautiful* infantilizes Florence, clarifying that her parents do not view her as being on the cusp of independence. Her first interactions with her parents include her father calling her "baby," and when Mr. Carpenter approaches the family to offer Florence

FIGURE 9.2 *Ann's costume still features a juvenile bow and ruffles, emphasizing that she has not recovered full adult capabilities.*

complementary tennis club membership and tournament backing, he tells the parents that the businessmen of the town are eager to support "your little girl." Florence's father also calls her "little one"; the terms of endearment that the older generation uses consistently categorize Florence as a child. When she first wins the national championship, Florence cements that assumption of immaturity by deferring to her mother to speak for her, as a child would.

The typical coming-of-age progression is evident by the time Florence defends her national tennis title. She looks older, just as mature and hardened as her mother, no more girlish attitude or hair bow. When Florence makes the sudden decision to fly home and see her ailing father, she still looks quite mature and wears a hat rather than a hair bow, but calls her father "daddy" as he reiterates that she is his "little one." Such alternating maturity and regression are standard in the Bildungsroman structure, and Lupino trains the spotlight on characters' perceptions of age.

Florence's mother never allows her to progress beyond this infantilization; Milly calls Florence "baby" when Florence loses, when she wins, and when she rebels against her mother's control. At the film's end, when Milly is rooting for her daughter to defend the title, she still calls her "baby." When Milly tries to discourage Florence from marrying Gordon, her first reasoning is, "You're so young." Florence replies, "You were even younger when you married Dad." While Milly does recognize the similarities between her daughter's wishes and her own life course, she claims to want to save Florence from making a major mistake. The age-oriented dialogue underscores that Milly never trusts her daughter to make adult decisions.

Although Gordon, too, sometimes labels their age group as juveniles, suggesting that they play doubles because some of the local "kids" need to be defeated, and eventually asking her to be his "girl," in the colloquialism of the time period, his interaction with Florence most often acknowledges her adult status. The necklace that he gives her says, "I love you, champ," rather than using a diminutive term of endearment, and he calls Florence "champ" when she defends her title, a clear contrast with Milly's calling her "baby." Florence can distance herself from childhood when she is with Gordon; when she apologizes after a quarrel, she says she "acted like a silly kid," which positions her as an adult experiencing a momentary lapse of maturity. An age-studies approach to *Hard, Fast and Beautiful* foregrounds a different aspect of Florence's abandoning a promising career in the public sphere to embrace traditional female domesticity. The age-related diction in the film supports Florence's choice, in that marrying Gordon is a step toward the Second Age, while obeying her parents constrains her in childhood.

Although Ann in *Outrage* and Florence in *Hard, Fast and Beautiful* face very different personal trials and obstacles to demonstrating their maturity, they eventually follow the course of the female Bildungsroman. Lupino uses age conventions to illustrate how the characters progress toward the Second Age. The films may not end with wedding gowns and church bells, but both women appear to be on the trajectory toward traditional marriage and domesticity. The audience is allowed to envision a typical mid-century happy ending, even though the films themselves do not provide that neatly tied denouement.

Youth equates with innocence in other Lupino films as well, and is particularly used to great effect in *The Hitch-Hiker* (1953), which contrasts the cold-blooded evil of Emmett Myers with youth and children who are real or potential victims. The screenplay is based on the real case of William Cook Jr., twenty-two years old, who was characterized by the media as a "young man with a gun."[24] Interestingly, Lupino's film raises the age of the killer to twenty-eight, taking him past the traditional age range for a Bildungsroman, as he is not to be viewed as a young character. Instead, youth represents vulnerability from the beginning of the film, when fragments from Myers's crime appear on screen. The film substitutes the murder of a young couple for the real-life killing of a family of five.[25] The scream heard is evidently that of a young woman, and the viewer glimpses the victim's youthful dress before her purse drops to the ground, all tying vulnerability to female youthfulness. The opening portrays that the killer has no qualms about murdering a young, innocent woman, so he must be evil indeed.

Female youth accentuates defenselessness later in the film as well, in a scene showing Myers entering a store with the two main characters whom he has taken captive, Gilbert Bowen and Roy Collins. The presence of the shopkeeper's young daughter heightens the suspense regarding whether the trio will get their supplies and leave without hurting anyone. When it appears that the girl may be in harm's way, Gil runs to her, desperate to protect this innocent youth, and tells her, "Go you with God, little one." Even on this small scale, Lupino's portrayals of young characters often follow a pattern of a female naïf encountering danger and being protected by an older male. Ronnie Scheib observes that Lupino creates characters that are the ultimate in passivity, "a self as pure subjectivity" that therein asserts its own force.[26] The youthful characters in her films may embody innocence, but they are by no means left powerless throughout the action.

Mid Ages: The Locus of Conflict

As Ida Lupino's films tend to polarize the ends of an age continuum into innocence and authority, the midpoint of full adulthood becomes the most contested site. Rather than addressing the issues of becoming an adult, Lupino's films are more likely to focus on conflicts affecting characters who already are entrenched in professional obligations and family life. In films such as *The Bigamist* and *The Hitch-Hiker*, the plot revolves around characters in the "prime" of life, from late twenties to thirties, while *Outrage* and *Hard, Fast and Beautiful* require that the young women who are coming of age share the spotlight with characters in their thirties. Each film shows self-conscious construction of age through dialogue and/or casting choices.

The most evident self-consciousness in manipulation of age is in *The Hitch-Hiker*, as it was based on a true story, with Lupino's film making Emmett Myers twenty-eight, firmly placing the killer among adults. The character foregrounds his full adult status by telling the two men he kidnaps that he had an unhappy childhood and has been a criminal for more than a decade, since he was seventeen. However abused Myers may have been as a child, the film resists building sympathy for the character, as he is well past the point of taking adult responsibility for his own actions.

Casting for the serial killer role underscores this undeniable adulthood; William Talman was born in 1915, so he was past thirty-five when the film was shot, certainly not twenty-eight in chronological age or apparent age. The killer was in the same chronological age range as the actors cast as his two captives: Roy was played by Edmond O'Brien, also born in 1915, and Gilbert by Frank Lovejoy, born in 1912.[27] The parallels in age establish the blatant contrast between the two average family men, who seek a carefree weekend escape from their routine and the psychopath whose life course has taken a horrifically evil trajectory. Critics commonly note that *The Hitch-Hiker* is a wholly male film, but it is important also to realize that the men Myers encounters are overwhelmingly responsible ones rooted in the Second Age. Even minor characters of the store owner and the boat owner in Mexico demonstrate concern for their wives and children. All of them starkly contrast with Myers, the criminal social outcast (Figure 9.3).

This is not to say that the captives' adult status is so firm that it goes unthreatened in the film. At one point in the desert, Roy breaks down emotionally and weeps, which Marsha Orgeron sees as feminization in response to Myers's constantly barking orders.[28] However, Lauren Rabinovitz observes of Roy, "Exhausted and overwrought, he collapses crying on the ground, and the high-angle overhead view of him reduces him physically to the state of a small, frustrated child."[29] This reading of infantilization carries more weight than one of feminization, as boys do regularly cry when parents exert authority, especially the stereotypically harsh father figure authority that Myers channels as he gives orders. Unlike most scholars, Rabinovitz at least identifies such age-related issues, but still she does not pursue the line of inquiry. She observes that during the ordeal Gil is rational and protects Roy and that "Roy's repeated empty challenges to Myers appear immature."[30] Despite noting that Myers proceeds to "bully" Roy, and Roy acts "impulsively," both juvenile traits, the critic tends to analyze all the behavior as machismo instead.[31]

Gil appears to pass this captivity-based test of manhood. When the saga ends, he paternally comforts Roy, putting an arm around him to say, "It's all right now," as they walk off at the close of the film. Rabinovitz also explains

FIGURE 9.3 *The three men were born between 1912 and 1915, which underlines the stark moral contrast between the life choices of a criminal and his victims.*

that the final RKO screenplay for the film offers a different ending, in which the men's wives come to meet them. The character of Forrest (who later evolved into Bowen) is called "an older and wiser man than the husband who went away eight days ago," an acknowledgment that even though he is fully adult, the experience ages him.[32] Characters in the Second Age may already be meeting adult responsibilities, but continue to face trials and encounter new opportunities, however harrowing, to gain wisdom.

Taking advantage of that opportunity varies from film to film, however, as is evident in *Hard, Fast and Beautiful*. Milly, Florence's mother, fails at her chance to develop maternal wisdom and to grow closer to her husband, Will. The strain in her family is long-standing and the second scene establishes Will's wistfulness over the distant past as well as Milly's bitterness over her youthful choices: "What did I know? I was 17 then and everything looked great." Regardless of Florence's increasingly mature actions, Milly never progresses beyond this essentialist view equating youth with folly. She continues to take control of the family to advance Florence's career; as scholars have observed, Milly usurps the prescribed paternal role by buying a car and negotiating Florence's tennis arrangements.[33] Milly's voice-over reveals that she actually is trying to recover the lost opportunities of her youth vicariously through her daughter, which inevitably backfires in the effect on her family relationships.

The plot follows a traditional patriarchal pattern of punishing the woman who transgresses the boundaries of her domestic role, as Milly loses the affection of both her husband and daughter. She has not accumulated wisdom or even the sympathy of the viewer. By the end of the film, Will must be cared for, which, Orgeron points out, is typically the woman's fate in melodrama.[34] The need for constant care has not only feminized but also infantilized Will, who accepts nurturing from a newly adult Florence while rejecting it from his wife. The parents fail to successfully navigate this Second Age trial, leaving Will in childlike incapacity and Milly stripped of the conventional fixtures of female adulthood: a loving husband and children.

Conversely, Eve in *The Bigamist* attempts to strip herself of adulthood when she cannot help outshining her husband in the business world. Downplaying her abilities, she calls herself "an efficient little white-collared girl"; according to Orgeron, Eve's being a girl "instead of a 'woman' or a 'wife' is emblematic of her 'failure' to be a proper homemaker."[35] She tries again to elevate her husband during a sales dinner, calling herself "Harry's little secretary," which is immediately exposed as a performance when she shows considerable technical expertise about the freezer that their company sells. Like Milly, Eve transgresses the domestic boundary and succeeds notably in the adult male public sphere. However, Eve attempts to devalue her substantial Second Age achievements because they are considered inappropriate for her gender, while she is unable to assume the maternal role that society considers her ultimate fulfillment. She has truly achieved the "independence, maturity, and responsibility" of the Second Age, but as this achievement is threatening to Harry; she covers it with a veneer of girlishness. *The Bigamist* and *Hard, Fast and Beautiful* are viewed as traditional cautionary tales against adult females' counter-normative behavior in the public sphere; both women's actions result in unhappy families. Lupino herself, of course, was navigating the treacherous Second Age waters of succeeding in a male-dominated occupation, and, as Orgeron asserts, these films show "Lupino's awareness of her own precarious position."[36]

Perhaps Lupino's most interesting take on gaining Second Age wisdom is in *Outrage*, as the reverend who helps the victim recover, Dr. Bruce Ferguson, is thirty-five. Little has been written about the fifteen years' difference between him and Ann; he is well into the Second Age that Ann is only just entering. Moreover, the casting of the roles was true to chronological age, with Tod Andrews at about thirty-six and Mala Powers at about nineteen when the film was released.[37] As an attractive, empathetic character that is situated between Ann's generation and the film's authority and parental figures, Bruce is uniquely qualified to aid Ann as she deals with the trauma of rape. Pam Cook reads Bruce as feminized and nurturing, his asexuality symbolized by his sucking on an empty pipe. He is not threatening to Ann because he does not approach her sexually.[38] Cook repeatedly calls Bruce "young," though, as if he were in the same age group with Ann. I maintain that Bruce speaks for Ann not only because he is the "healer" authority that Cook notes, but also because he is significantly older, the voice of experience, who has overcome his own crisis of identity and faith during wartime, demonstrating maturation.

Bruce's age also can be seen as a factor of the melodramatic resolution of the film. While it is common for women to marry men who are older than they, a gap of more than about a decade begins to be suspect, and the twenty years that represents a different generation long has been considered outside the norm for a companionate marriage. This fifteen-year gap casts doubt on Bruce as a suitable match for Ann and supports his more-paternal treatment of her. Despite Ann's finally claiming the ability to voice her own desires by telling Bruce that she prefers to stay with him, Bruce asserts authority to send her back to her parents and fiancé. His age and experience add weight to this insistence, and the age gap between the pair reinforces that Ann's return to her previous life is the proper choice. Cook points out the ambiguous, "anxious ending" that does not assure the viewer that Ann will find happiness. Instead, the concluding shots focus on Bruce as Ann's bus departs.[39]

Although *Outrage* has been Ann's story, the character who is firmly ensconced in Second Age is the final center of attention. The audience is left to realize that because Bruce was at war during the years when most men marry, he may not ever find a mate, that perhaps this aspect of the traditional life course has passed him by permanently. Ronnie Scheib has argued that Lupino's films portray postwar characters going through rites of passage while alienated from an uncaring society.[40] Bruce remains alienated from the traditional life course of marriage and family; he appears to have sacrificed his own attraction to Ann for what he deems will be her ultimate mental health. Whether or not his conclusion is accurate, the experience has developed his Second Age maturity.

Perhaps Lupino's focus on conflicts of "prime" adulthood relates to the issues of censorship and television's encroachment on the film industry that Seiter details in her analysis of *The Bigamist*. Promotional materials touted the film as targeted to adult audiences: "Yes, the screen is more than ever free for grown-up entertainment."[41] This contrasts with television programs that had to appease family-oriented censors. Seiter remarks on the film's lack of typical notions that romantic love will save all, which I read as a more mature approach to romantic conflict, one more suitable for audiences who are well established in the Second Age.

It is fitting that Lupino's last film directing role was for the mainstream *The Trouble with Angels*, as it starred Hayley Mills, whose acting career echoes Lupino's in portrayals of age. Mills was twenty when Lupino directed her, but she was used to playing younger, a teen, as she did in this film. According to Haralovich, Jakobsen, and White, Mills was portrayed in the press as "looking forward to playing older characters (that is, girls her own age)."[42] While those critics link Mills's perpetual performance of youth to questions of gender and sexual tension, Lupino could relate to being a youth cast against one's chronological age, even though she played older. This last film reminds us that Lupino understood from the beginning of her career how to manipulate the conventions of performing age, whether they serve to alter the audience's perception of an actor's age or to underscore major themes.

Unfortunately, Lupino's films make use of all the stereotypes of age across the continuum from younger to older, rather than challenging those perceptions. Young women start as naïfs who need shepherding, often by paternally oriented men, while older men are authority figures who represent social norms. Critics tend to overlook or silently accept such portrayals, as age has been the last of the "identity" categories to garner critical attention in the humanities. As Margaret Morganroth Gullette observes, "Ageism is often quiet, factoidal, unheated."[43] Although age or aging is not the stated focus of Lupino's films, these conventions consistently support her central themes while upholding mid-century Hollywood's received notions of what it means to be young or old.

Notes

1. Marsha Orgeron, *Hollywood Ambitions: Celebrity in the Movie Age* (Middletown, CT: Wesleyan University Press, 2008), 172.
2. Mary Ann Anderson, *Ida Lupino: Beyond the Camera* (Albany, GA: Bear Manor Media, 2011), 26.
3. Annette Kuhn, ed., *Queen of the 'B's: Ida Lupino Behind the Camera* (West Port, CT: Praeger, 1995), 1.
4. William Donati, *Ida Lupino: A Biography* (Lexington: University Press of Kentucky, 1996), 205.
5. Ibid., 216.
6. Ibid., 218.
7. Ibid., 235.
8. Orgeron, *Hollywood Ambitions*, 176–7.
9. Anderson, *Ida Lupino*.
10. Richard Koszarski, ed., "Me, Mother, Directress," in *Hollywood Directors: 1941-1976* (New York: Oxford University Press, 1971), 372.
11. Pamela H. Gravagne, *The Becoming of Age: Cinematic Visions of Mind, Body and Identity in Later Life* (Jefferson, NC: McFarland, 2013), 36.
12. This has been detailed by numerous age-studies critics, but notably described by Margaret Morganroth Gullette. See, for example, *Aged by Culture* (Chicago: University of Chicago Press, 2004).

13 See Peter Laslett, *A Fresh Map of Life: The Emergence of the Third Age* (London: Weidenfeld and Nicolson, 1989).
14 Ibid., 4.
15 Orgeron, *Hollywood Ambitions*, 187.
16 Critics tend to agree on this; see, for example, Orgeron, *Hollywood Ambitions*, 187.
17 Ellen Seiter, "The Bigamist," in *Queen of the 'B's: Ida Lupino Behind the Camera*, ed. Annette Kuhn (West Port, CT: Praeger, 1995), 115.
18 Sally Chivers, *The Silvering Screen: Old Age and Disability in Cinema* (Toronto: University of Toronto Press, 2011), 35.
19 Gullette, *Aged by Culture*.
20 Richard Brody, "Ida Lupino's Prescient *Outrage*," *The New Yorker*, June 16, 2014. Available at http://www.newyorker.com/culture/richard-brody/ida-lupinos-prescient-outrage (accessed 19 May, 2021).
21 Ronnie Scheib, "Never Fear," in Annette Kuhn (ed.), *Queen of the 'B's: Ida Lupino Behind the Camera* (West Port, CT: Praeger, 1995), 45.
22 Pam Cook, "Outrage," in Annette Kuhn (ed.), *Queen of the 'B's: Ida Lupino Behind the Camera* (West Port, CT: Praeger, 1995), 62.
23 Mandy Merck, "Hard, Fast and Beautiful," in Annette Kuhn (ed.), *Queen of the 'B's: Ida Lupino Behind the Camera* (West Port, CT: Praeger, 1995), 80.
24 Lauren Rabinovitz, "*The Hitch-Hiker*," in Annette Kuhn (ed.), *Queen of the 'B's: Ida Lupino Behind the Camera* (West Port, CT: Praeger, 1995), 93.
25 Ibid., 94.
26 Scheib, "Never Fear," 48.
27 According to IMDB.com.
28 Orgeron, *Hollywood Ambitions*, 199.
29 Rabinovitz, "The Hitch-Hiker," 100.
30 Ibid.
31 Ibid., 96, 99.
32 Cited in Orgeron, *Hollywood Ambitions*, 200.
33 See, for example, Merck, "Hard, Fast and Beautiful"; Orgeron, *Hollywood Ambitions*.
34 Orgeron, *Hollywood Ambitions*, 190.
35 Ibid., 183.
36 Ibid., 195.
37 According to IMDB.com.
38 Cook, "Outrage," 67.
39 Ibid., 63.
40 Discussed in Cook, "Outrage," 59.

41 Seiter, "The Bigamist," 114.
42 Mary Beth Haralovich, Janet Jakobsen, and Susan White, "The Trouble with Angels," in Annette Kuhn (ed.), *Queen of the 'B's: Ida Lupino Behind the Camera* (West Port, CT: Praeger, 1995), 121.
43 Margaret Morganroth Gullette, *Agewise: Fighting the New Ageism in America* (Chicago: University of Chicago Press, 2011), 36.

10

Ida Lupino and Acting

Situating Performance in Cinematic Context(s)

Curtis LeVan

Writers and critics of film can often easily articulate and describe many of its elements, including lighting, editing, and composition. These parts have clear, observable structures and, more importantly, the consistency in appearance required for accurate and meaningful definitions. Acting, however, proves too mercurial to be defined as precisely as these other elements. The parameters of a performance reside mostly within the actor, albeit often under the sway of a director. As such, directors seem to have the least amount of control when it comes to acting compared to the other components of a film. Nonetheless, actors arguably draw audiences to the cinema more so than any other component.

This chapter examines the acting of Ida Lupino, placing her work as an actor within relevant cultural and historical contexts. These patterns emerge through not only examining performance, but by also considering their execution within contexts. In particular, this chapter will look at three roles played by Lupino, each in a different decade, and will attempt to analyze her acting in relation to the circumstances contextualizing production. These conditions cover many dimensions of cinema, including acts of law, studio practices, and theory. While acting may prove more difficult to analyze than other fundamentals of cinema, looking into the cultural values and milieus surrounding films from different times serves as a strategic point of departure in investigating and evaluating an actor's skill. First, Lupino's early work in English film provides the grounds for understanding her later work in America. Then there is the Golden Age of Hollywood, during which the procedures of studios prove essential for situating Lupino's stance within American cinema. From there, performances were informed by the rise of method acting and its influence on presentation.

"Quota Quickies": *The Ghost Camera* (1933)

The Cinematographic Films Act of 1927 required British cinemas to show a certain number, or proportion, of British films. Enacted by Parliament, this act hoped to revive a declining industry in Britain. H. Mark Glancy offers the numbers to illustrate this dire situation: "The British film industry was facing oblivion in the mid-1920s. In 1926, there were just 36 British films made, and these comprised only 5 percent of all films released in British cinemas. By comparison, 620 American films were released in Britain that year, and these accounted for 84 per cent of releases."[1] The act was to last for ten years, and, over this course, the term *quota quickie* appeared. Essentially, movie theaters needed British films to show to audiences in order to meet the quota demanded by the act. In response, studios made *quick* films to meet the number, including such American studios as MGM. Film historians have debated whether American studios purposefully damaged the reputation of Britain's film industry or, if the parameters of the act could produce no other response than fast, often cheap, products. Historians also debate, aside from American influence, the overall outcome of "quota quickies." Such films helped directors and actors establish careers that they may not have otherwise been able to achieve. Yet some critics argue that the films of this era were grossly inferior, if not worthless. This section of the chapter does not intend to enter this issue, but rather will explore Lupino's role in one of these *quickies*, the lucrative film, *The Ghost Camera*.[2]

The plot follows John Gray, played by Henry Kendall, and Mary Elton, played by Lupino, as they search for Mary's missing brother. A camera happens to be in Gray's vehicle while he was returning home to London, and he subsequently develops the film in hopes of discovering the owner. Much to his surprise, he finds a picture of a man being slain with a knife. The negative and camera are presumably stolen shortly thereafter, prompting John to develop the remaining negatives. One of the prints depicts Mary by a street sign, and John sets off to find this woman in order to unravel the mystery.

Lawrence Napper recounts that the film did not receive much praise at its first viewing; however, it eventually became an immensely popular film. Napper suggests that its initial unpopularity could be due to its being "unashamedly publicized as a British film with 'English scenes and English humour.'"[3] Certainly the film depicts London life and the British countryside, as well as brimming British railroads, inns, and even Norman ruins. Further, the film's comedy rests mostly on English stereotypes: John's exceptional manners and elevated diction, a dunce of a maid, and a cockney assistant (Figure 10.1).

We find, therefore, two dominant narratives of British films: one that states films were made cheaply and quickly, and a second that argues that films had the freedom to be British, (or at the least English). *The Ghost Camera* fits both narratives. It film was shot quickly and clearly exhibits English life and popular tastes in comedy. Additionally, the film is remarkably self-aware, with characters commenting routinely on melodrama (or genre in general), filmmaking, tastes in film, and even "haste." Viewers today cannot help but recognize "meta" tendencies in *The Ghost Camera*. For example, while John and his assistant Sims are developing the remaining film found in the camera, John speculates as to what the emerging female figure might look like: "oh golden hair and large lustrous eyes—a ravishing creature, my dear Sims. The heroine of a mystery drama is always a ravishing creature." His conjecture proves accurate.

These combined components point to a film that must make use of character roles, a practice not uncommon in 1930s England, and the role of Mary is certainly no exception. She first appears on the screen (other than in a photograph) entering her home as John is about to depart. He recognizes her from the photograph and stops her. She appears young and vibrant, as John had

FIGURE 10.1 *John and Mary search for clues in the countryside in* The Ghost Camera.

speculated about heroines of mysteries. Lupino has her eyes exceedingly open and speaks only in the upper register of her voice. Lupino is young in this film, but her character demands a particularly overt depiction of innocence. She is courteous, proper, and not without an immediate appearance of sensuality. After seeing the photo of herself, she invites John into her brother's room, as to avoid being too sexual, and sits on the bed. John, a dashing Englishman, becomes uncomfortable and her sexuality paired with his propriety makes for a comical interaction, a dynamic the film employs throughout. Later in the film, Mary hides her brother's handkerchief in her hand as to avoid his implication in a crime. When John attempts to grasp it, she quickly places it down her dress, near her breasts, to which John wittily replies, "Well, that was very unfair of you." Mary asks, "Why unfair?" And he responds, "Well, you're taking advantage of your sex to put me in a very embarrassing position."

Mary plays in an ensemble of English characters that unifies the film, and not only does her character affect comic overtones and sexual tension, but it also accentuates the elements of melodrama. The opening sequence clearly suggests melodrama, with dramatic music and sounds, a nighttime setting, and the ruins of a castle. Because of Lupino's portrayal of Mary, several scenes project a heightened sense of the melodramatic, particularly of horror and danger, toward which other characters seem oblivious. First, when John and Mary arrive at an inn depicted in one of the photographs, the innkeeper emerges from the shadows. Gruff, curt, and stiff, he resembles an assistant from a science fiction or horror novel. The inn is lit with candles and lanterns only, thereby adding to the suspense. John appears unaffected, even stating that a good night's rest is possible in such a place. Mary appears clearly suspicious as she walks timidly behind John. In the dead of night, an intruder enters her room and attempts to muzzle her with his hand, but she escapes to give a large scream, waking up the inn. Upon John's entrance, the scene quickly turns comedic, again through sexual innuendo and the unseemliness of a man entering a woman's room at night. Eventually, the innkeeper comes on screen, and, as expected, is unmoved by the situation, keeping in character.

In the climax of the film, Lupino has another chance to turn the film toward the melodramatic with her acting, this time in the ruins where the murder occurred. Like the setting of the inn, we find dim lighting and many shadows. Mary walks with extreme caution, while John appears excited to be experiencing a real-life mystery. After assuring her that she is safe, he walks off into the dark. Mary wanders about amid extreme contrasts in lighting, trips on an unseen object, and then screams as the camera quickly zooms in on her face. When her companion inquires as to what is wrong, Mary replies in her calm, innocent voice, "I don't know, John." This extreme change in demeanor and voice is obviously awkward, but it does allow for John to influence the momentum of the scene. A limp hand falls into the light, affecting no scream, and John composedly lights a match to see if it is her brother's body. John recognizes the body and scenery from the first photograph he developed, and the film quickly turns to a montage of law officials and radio announcers repeating "murder," creating a sense of hysteria.

Interestingly, the role of Mary diminishes after the climax. Once her brother is found and the accusation of murder is made, the film transforms into a courtroom drama. While the comedy continues, it does so without Mary, having her displaced by comedic witnesses, such as John's assistant and Mary's maid. Mary's ability to incite horror into the film is no longer necessary, and "sex-comedy" seems unfitting once the focus has shifted to her brother's trial (and presumed guilt). However, Mary does appear in the courtroom as her usual innocent self, engendering pity and anxiety, but she is never the focus of a scene. The film ends after John has successfully solved the murder mystery and the suspect is set free. However, Mary emerges as none other than John's bride, while the film ends in a similar montage as with *murder*, only this time, with *wedding*.

Lupino's character helps the film conclude with the common trope of "the good guy gets the girl," despite the film's primary focus on murder and mystery. Taking a step back, we find that Lupino's acting works in this film mostly to develop a consistent character type that emphasizes common figures found in the films of its day. Given the contexts of filmmaking, paired with the screenplay's tendency to lean toward the meta-dramatic, her performance works brilliantly. Producing films in such rapid succession often required that plots be filled with character types in order to facilitate acting and overall production, especially production pace. Interestingly, many of these quota-quickies were well aware of their situations, and they made the most of it. *The Ghost Camera* clearly establishes itself, through its meta-dramatic tendencies and capitalization of comedy through stereotyped characters, as a film well aware of its contexts as it turns the cinematic conditions of its time into becoming an integral part of the film's aesthetic. Lupino's acting, although not particularly dynamic, substantially contributes to the overall artistry and disposition of the film.

American Studio Acting: *High Sierra* (1941)

American studio acting is important to Lupino's acting career since her major films came forth within the Golden Age of Hollywood, widely considered to last from the 1930s to the 1950s. Within these two decades, we find what is perhaps her most major role, Marie, in *High Sierra* (1941), starring Humphrey Bogart.[4] During this time frame two systems existed, the studio system and the star system, and these two paradigms worked together in generating movie stars. A studio would hire an actor, provide basic acting lessons and coaching in voice and movement and yet, most important, would create an image for a movie star, both on screen and in the media. As Robert C. Allen and Douglas Gomery argue, "the [movie] star's private life has little if anything to do with his or her 'job' of acting in movies, yet a large portion of a star's image is constructed on the basis of 'private' matters: romance, marriage, tastes in fashion, and home life."[5] In other words, the studio created an image for an actor in real life that parallels the types of roles an actor receives. In sum, an actor would embody the social and cultural values and mores of a time—both on screen and off. Image was all.

To illustrate, Bogart's image was of significant concern for Warner Brother Studios. Throughout the 1930s, he had character roles, usually consisting of gangsters and cold-blooded killers. In fact, Bogart saw *High Sierra* as a way to break away from such roles and image because of lead character Roy Earle's emotional depth. The studio had well-founded fears that his on-screen persona would affect his overall image. In order to massage this apprehension, Warner Brothers changed his birthday from January 23, 1900, to December 25, 1899. According to Clifford McCarthy, this alteration was mostly done "to foster the view that a man born on Christmas couldn't really be as villainous as he appeared on the screen."[6] Such a fabrication of personal information was permitted under studio contracts.

Under such contracts, acting often came after image and profit.[7] Charles Affron recalls that the "almost total absence of analytical approaches to screen acting reflects the belief that screen acting is nothing more than the beautiful projection of a filmic self, an arrangement of features and body, the disposition of superficial elements."[8] Stars, under this approach to acting, were to be known by their looks, voices, and consistent mannerisms of bodily movement. Whether it were appearance, athleticism, or talent in acting, a studio would capitalize on the distinguishing characteristic or characteristics of an actor in order to create an aura or image that would captivate an audience in wonder, and sometimes even awe. Such is the environment Lupino entered when she joined Warner Brothers Studio. As an Anglo-American actor, Lupino had a different background from most movie stars of the American Studio tradition. Coming from a family well versed in stage performance (on both her father's and mother's side) and attending the Royal Academy of Dramatic Art, she already had experience in British cinema in the 1930s. These factors combined surely influenced her craft, as we see in *High Sierra*. Lupino pays close attention to gesture and facial expressions, even when she is not the focus of the shot, and her character shows depth and elasticity, despite the American studio tendency for consistency. In a film intended to be a typical caper drama, based on pulp fiction of the day and full of stock characters, Lupino delivers her cultivated and diverse talent and charms to the screen.

The first scene in which she appears, Roy Earle (Bogart) drives up to a campground to meet his counterparts for a heist in a nearby resort. After receiving directions to the cabin, Roy approaches Marie (Lupino). In this shot, we see her seated on an elevated porch with her feet on the dirt. Her feet are rotated inward, and her hand lackadaisically swings a stick around on the dirt. A large tree blocks her face, with Roy exiting his car appearing in the foreground. Viewers may not particularly note Marie's presence on screen, but close examination suggests that the character is bored or uninterested. When Roy approaches her, the camera turns to Marie's feet and does a slow sweep up her body, showing her face pointed toward the ground, peering intently at the stick swinging in the dirt. We see Marie with her shoulders slumped downward. Upon hearing Roy's steps, she slowly tilts her head up finally revealing her face, which gives little expression of awe. On the whole, it is not a dramatic reveal of her face, nor is it even a close-up. However, seeing Marie's face prompts Roy to turn away and grab some needles from a nearby pine tree, suggesting unease, discomfort. Marie only sits upright in order to call for Red, whom Roy intends to meet, after which she resumes her initial posture. Her lines are short, if not curt, and they are very direct, suggesting a disdain for the monotony of life in the mountains. We later find out that she was a dance hall girl in LA who followed Babe and Red to the mountains (Figure 10.2).

Lupino continues this tendency to project ennui over the first couple of scenes. As Marie, she has her body retracted, as though in some form of restraint, minimizing both gestures and her stature. It is important to note,

FIGURE 10.2 *Marie plays with a stick while turning her gaze to Roy in* High Sierra.

however, that she does not remain still. With the men talking on the cabin porch, she resumes her play with the stick in the dirt. Red is starstruck by Roy's presence, but Marie remains unimpressed. Babe stands by, not interacting, but later reveals his envy of Roy's reputation. Marie, however, only looks up when she is introduced to Roy, with a slight high-angled close up, again prompting Roy to turn his gaze quickly. In both shots that center on Lupino's face, her look suggests an emphatic lack of concern. Shortly after this introduction, Roy takes Red aside and says that Marie has to go, holding that women often mess up such heists. Somewhat ironically, the men in these shots appear eager and juvenile in their movements and voice, in direct contrast to Marie's disposition. Right from the start, she introduces her character as collected and somewhat aloof. However, her facial expressions show no anger, disdain, or conceit—just boredom, probably from being surrounded by men whom she thought were adventurous, worldly, and perhaps criminal—but in reality, were basically childish and inexperienced.

Marie's character, therefore, remains difficult to place in light of usual studio acting, which suggests that certain actors fill specific roles. Roy is easy to recognize as a troubled, if not hardened, criminal. Red and Babe are inexperienced protégés, probably doomed because of their obvious inexperience. To compound Marie's place in the film, Roy had met his apparent love interest, Velma, before Marie comes on the screen. Played by Joan Leslie, Velma appears as an innocent, sympathetic, and club-footed young lady who appears to be the perfect remedy for Roy's harshness. While her face is seen within a car, it becomes apparent that she is the classically beautiful woman of the film. When Roy stops for gas, Velma and her mid-Western grandparents stop as well, allowing a chance for Roy and Velma to interact. Unlike Marie, Velma consistently smiles, sits upright, and shows attentiveness and eagerness in her gaze. Moreover, right before her grandfather introduces her, she emphasizes herself by dramatically, if not aggressively, brushing her hair. Leslie's voice consistently remains airy and elevated in tone. In fact, she often asks questions, thereby raising her intonation. At first glance, audiences may be tempted to see her as purely a foil. If Velma is Roy's savior, perhaps Marie is his downfall.

Such a black-and-white understanding of Marie never comes to fruition, however. Rather than being easily understood, Marie's character gradually reveals itself throughout the film enhanced, of course, by Lupino's subtle and effective acting. Eventually, Marie does fit the mold of a studio-acting character, but not before gradually shifting.

The first sign of emotional life in Marie comes when Red returns to the cabin to inform Babe and Marie that Roy wants her to return to Los Angeles. Babe has just finished his tantrum in which he doubts Roy's capability, and, upon Marie's defense of Roy, Babe threatens her with violence. Marie, however, remains calm in her chair, responding in fast-paced sentences. Upon hearing that Roy wants Marie gone, Babe immediately storms to the door. Yet Marie remains steady in stature, and her voice carries the tone of earlier gangster films: short, curt, and slightly elevated in pitch. She changes her tone as though to taunt Babe, knowing fully well that he is mostly hot air and she is actually tougher. As the two men decide on what to do with Marie, we see her seated in the forefront of the shot, with her body again retracted. The focus of the action is in background with the two men shouting and standing tall, shoulders spread, in clear juxtaposition with Marie's stance. During this dialogue, we see Marie's arm hang over the chair, beginning in a relaxed position. Throughout the yelling match, she gradually tightens her arm, grasping the chair firmly but subtly as the action between the men continues. Such movements imply that Marie is willful, yet restrained. Once again, Lupino makes herself integral to the scene, even when she is not the focus of the scene. Marie is fully upright for the first time as she resolves to talk to Roy herself, but only to be checked by Babe, causing her to return to her retracted stance, shoulders slumped and with her arms crossed, caressing her arms. Through Red's intervention, Marie does leave the cabin to speak to Roy, again displaying a cool expression of face. She enters Roy's cabin and approaches him in her reserved posture and adopts a softer voice. Once she begins to list the reasons why she should stay, Lupino employs the faster voice used to affect Babe in the previous scene. Gaining confidence, her body opens up to firmly grab a chair, and she explains to Roy that he must be concerned about the "inside man" at the hotel named Mendoza. Roy listens and then admits that he does not have a problem with her and she can stay, at least for a couple of days more. This scene proves interesting because the power dynamic is unclear. Viewers are left to wonder if Marie successfully changed Roy's mind because she demonstrates her keen eye for detail, or if Roy always wanted her there, but was concerned for her safety because of the two "jitterbugs," as he calls them. We are left to wonder if Marie is a potential love interest, a downfall, or a victim overcoming adversity, reminiscent of the "woman's film" genre.[9]

Over the course of the narrative, we see Marie consistently develop. Viewers readily recognize that she is a woman who looks for love and respect, but has not been able to find it until Roy comes along. However, Roy's interests are clearly in Velma early on in the film. Perhaps the two most influential scenes that demonstrate Lupino's skill appear in the scenes in which she must cry. In his biography on Lupino, William Donati recounts her difficulty with crying scenes, due in part to their overall complexity.[10] Donati explains that Lupino obtained positive reviews for her portrayal of Marie, due in part to the complexity of this character. Surrounded by studio actors with their fitting roles, Marie does prove more complex. We might see her as a newcomer, or an outsider, coming from Britain and new to Warner Brothers and their practices. Lupino certainly appears to take her circumstances to her advantage.

In the first (emotional) deep scene up for analysis about midway through the film, we see Roy's courtship with Velma more fully developed when Roy strongly affirms that Marie must leave the camp since Babe had beaten her earlier. Marie first tries to reason with Roy, stating that she is like him: both know the desire to escape or "crash out." She wants to escape a cycle of abuse, ranging from her past with her drunken father to Babe. Roy wanted to break away from prison, and he also wants to break away from his criminal lifestyle, as seen by his tenderness to Velma and this perspective is revealed by his paying for Velma's surgery to correct her club foot. Lupino's lines are direct and cool, delivered with her typical retracted stance, shoulders slumped and head pointed down, despite being seated. Her appeal to reason does not work, so she leaves the room to collect her things. Out of sight, she buries her head in her bed and cries. It is not clear if Roy can hear her, and he appears to follow Pard, a stray dog who roams around the camp, to Marie. Her cry is subtle, with her sound muffled and face hidden. Audiences at this point now may understand Marie's past and why she wants to stay: Roy provides a way for her to retreat from her current life. Yet Marie does not open her movements or accentuate her crying. She consistently refrains from being too open, a somewhat atypical approach to a crying scene for studio acting, through which women's crying is often hyperbolized to produce affective responses both on screen and in the audience.

This nuanced scene helps portray why Marie stays, and her second crying scene further demonstrates Lupino's acting ability. In the closing scene, we find Roy's dead body, shot by a sniper after Roy has been found out and pursued by the police. Donati writes that the scene "is powerfully moving. Marie's tears of sadness are transformed into tears of elation as she realizes that the tortured soul of Roy Earle is finally free."[11] The film is clearly effective in encouraging viewers to sympathize with Roy, hoping that he and Marie can escape a life of crime and live happily ever after. However, there was a wrinkle. In 1934, the Production Code was adopted by studios in order to promote morality. This code means that films must avoid profanity, overt violence and, perhaps most important of all, sexual representation. Applied to *High Sierra*, the code meant that Roy could not use a machine gun and his romantic intrigues with Velma and Marie must be subdued. Moreover, Roy and Marie could not escape punishment for their crimes. Roy is shot, of course, and falls down a mountain. As for Marie, the film strongly implies that she is going to prison as an accomplice.

If the film had ended with Marie crying over the body of her lover, the film would have lost all its hope of escape, a dominant, recurring theme. However, Marie's shift of tears suggests that Roy had performed the ultimate getaway, an escape from a life in which he never strayed from the hardened criminal. As before, Marie initially hides her face, burying it in Roy's unmoving chest, later covered by his limp hand. As she sobs, an unsympathetic copper states, "Ain't much now, is he?" while lighting a cigarette. This line prompts Marie to ask what it officially means to "crash out." The officer states that it means to be free. From there, Marie rises, looks up and stands, but not in her usual

FIGURE 10.3 *Marie shifts from despair to hope over Roy's body in* High Sierra.

withdrawn posture. With hair tangled from the elements, Marie repeats the word *free* as she triumphantly walks away, Pard in her hands, but with her face unobstructed. With the Production Code, death is necessary, if not on the mountain, then in the gas chamber, but it takes extreme talent to defy the code's necessity of retribution and end with a message of hope (Figure 10.3).

Method Acting: *Private Hell 36* (1954)

Yet another context by which to analyze acting consists of understanding method acting, its general inception, the adoption by American theater, and its application for film. Unlike studio acting, which varied from actor to actor (or studio-fabricated image to image), we find a greater amount of consistency in recognizing method acting. However, like studio acting, investigating the context or circumstances of a film, actor, and studio enriches considerably the understanding of an actor's approach to performing in front of the camera. Therefore, this section looks to the principles and manifestations of method acting, paired with the conditions of Lupino's film *Private Hell 36*.[12]

Method acting, as it is called in the United States, is based on the theory of acting created by Konstantin Stanislavsky, who started the Moscow Art Theater in 1897. His approach required actors to look into the psychology of characters, acknowledging the histories of characters and allowing such awareness to inform and influence the actors' portrayals on stage. Simply stated, actors must "become" the character before even trying to "play" the character. Critics of acting, both of stage and screen, often refer to this idea as playing a character from the "inside out." Rather than pairing a character with a conventional stock character or archetype, each with its own conventional movements and voices, an actor learns about the character as a person, an individual, with a mind that recalls its past and is, therefore, a product of its past experiences. While intended for the stage, Stanislavsky's theory appeared in film as well, particularly in Russian silent films by a range of directors in the 1920s.

One such director influenced by Stanislavsky, Vsevolod I. Pudovkin, modified this approach in the 1930s in his book, *Film Acting*.[13] In this text, Pudovkin argues that acting on the stage relies on continuity of action and collaborative acting. In other words, actors on the stage carry the momentum of the narrative plot from one scene to the next, carrying also energy from the ensemble of actors. Films, consisting of shots that are often out of chronological order, do not have this luxury. Thus, he writes the following of film actors:

> [T]hey lose every possibility of feeling the unity of the image, every possibility of preserving during the process of shooting a sense of live continuous individuality, owing to the fact that they act the end of their role today, the beginning to-morrow, and the middle the day after. The various bits are tangled, they are terribly short; from time to time somebody photographs a glance that relates to something the actor will be doing a month hence when somebody else has photographed a hand movement that has to do with the glance. The image created by the actor is split into minutest particles, only later to be gathered together, and *horribile dictu*, this gathering is effected not by him but by the director, who, in the majority of cases, does not allow the actor to come anywhere near to or observe the process of even have the remotest connection with it.[14]

Therefore, film acting must displace the collaborative nature of the stage, and, in its place, actors and directors steadily discuss the action of a scene, thereby requiring actors to spend much time in preparing and rehearsing individual scenes.

The principles taught by Pudovkin made its way to Hollywood through the theater. In the 1940s and 1950s, actors, writers, and directors such as Stella Adler, Elia Kazan, Arthur Miller, and Marlon Brando helped shape Stanislavsky's ideas into method acting. Drawing from Stanislavsky's and Pudovkin's ideas, method acting calls for a more "natural" use of movement and voice. Actors were not to move and speak in the same manner as they do on stage, but rather as they do in their private lives. Method acting also requires performers to call upon their own life experiences in order to channel the emotion(s) needed to create a convincing portrayal of human behavior. While the internal thought processes of actors may be impossible to discern from merely looking at a screen, the overall effect of shifting from studio acting to method acting reveals perceptible differences.

In the movement toward realism, new approaches to acting became apparent in the 1950s. Richard Barsam and Dave Monahan list a number of "major characteristics of method acting: intense concentration and internalization (sometimes mistaken for discomfort) on the actor's part; low-key, almost laid-back delivery of lines (sometimes described as mumbling); and an edginess (sometimes highly neurotic) that suggests dissatisfaction, unhappiness, and alienation."[15] In sum, acting for the stage sought to make gestures and voice clear and direct for audiences. Yet often, these movements and sounds did not accurately portray the ways people actually move and speak. The same can be said of studio acting—creating and maintaining an easily recognized image is paramount, yet not a commitment to "reality." Stanislavsky's method, refined for the cinematic medium by Pudovkin and then modified by American directors, wanted performance with subtly, nuance, and a sharp sense of realism.

Examining *Private Hell 36*, one can see that the circumstances surrounding its production, as well as Lupino's character, suggest that this film offers an excellent illustration in method acting during the 1950s. First, Lupino and Collier Young (her second husband) cowrote the screenplay. Lupino starred in the film along with her soon-to-be third husband, Howard Duff (playing Jack, a police sergeant). The film also featured Steve Cochran (playing Cal, Jack's partner). Lupino's character, Lili Marlowe, is a nightclub entertainer, which parallels nicely with Lupino's career of both singing and acting. Duff and Cochran portray cops in search of counterfeit money, and they enlist Lili to help them locate the criminal(s). A contemporary film critic, Bosley Crowther, wrote of Lupino's character, "A critic might note that attention is sharply divided between the main theme and the incidental character that Miss Lupino plays. This is somewhat understandable, since Miss Lupino happens to be one of the partners in Filmakers and a coauthor of the script." Not only does Lili's profession as an entertainer allow Lupino to draw upon her personal experience, Lili must also "perform" in order to help catch the perpetrator during stakeouts. Once more, while it is difficult to ascertain internality of an actor, the situation surrounding this film points to keen interest on the part of Lupino. Nonetheless, method acting is more than an actor's internal approach. There are certainly physical, perceptible expressions that viewers may analyze in light of method acting. With this thought in mind, this section will examine two important scenes from the film.

The first scene in which we see Lili demonstrate this shift toward realism, Jack and Cal are interviewing a bartender regarding a counterfeit $50 bill.

The bartender informs the officers that he received the note from a woman who works at the club, singing and running a hat check. Then Lili walks in. Lupino's gait is quick and nonchalant. As she walks toward the bar, she quickly takes off her jacket and tosses it on the piano. Then she greets the bartender with a quick "Hello, Sam." The camera has no opportunity to zoom in for a close-up: Lupino is constantly moving, eventually taking a seat at the bar and mistaking Cal and Jack as customers. These first few shots move quickly, not allowing for a "movie-star introduction." Instead, the scene seems to be more concerned with establishing Lili as an employee of a nightclub. Her voice is quick and a vocal fry near the end of her short sentences. This approach to voice may be a gesture toward establishing realism, since the vocal fry is a sign of natural speech and not an issue for clarity. Once the officer's purpose become clear, Lili renders a slight pause and, somewhat nervously approaches the men. Lili's hesitation is neither exaggerated nor prolonged, and nothing in the soundtrack suggests fear or concern. However, her mannerisms in the next few shots imply reservation.

Both Jack and Cal begin questioning Lili, with mundane questions, such as name and address. She tries to carry on with small talk and even tautly cracks jokes in a seeming attempt to establish levity. She fumbles around in her clutch, looking for something to occupy her hands, probably a cigarette holder that she cannot find. The owner of the club bursts in, angry that the workplace has been disrupted, but Jack takes him off screen, leaving Cal alone with Lili, and the interchange between them reveals the noticeable influence of method acting.

First, Cal's stature is "lazy" with slumped shoulders and head facing down. He asks her where she got the counterfeit money with a weak, airy voice, ending in a sigh. It seems that either he does not want to question Lili, or that this exchange is just a formality. At times, his voice sounds so "low-key" that lines sound mumbled. At first, Lili continues with her jokes, but she eventually interprets Cal's mannerisms and tone, responding in light of her perceptions of his intentions. And she continues to joke with him at first, stating that she has witnessed his routine on *Dragnet*. Cal looks at her bracelet and ring. Lili notes his questioning eye and immediately responds by offering a monetary explanation, suggesting that she wears costume jewelry and has not used counterfeit money for expensive jewelry. Cal continues questioning her about the money with his airy voice, giving sighs mid-sentence, and Lily interrupts with "Eh, just put this down in your little book. Ready? 'Not what you're thinking.'" Again, Lili responds to the subtext or undertones of the scene, rather than surface dialogue.

As Barsam and Monahan note, a mark of method acting is "the importance of creating an ensemble and expressing the subtext."[16] Lili's voice, throughout the start of this conversation, is direct and well enunciated. However, the quality of sound and pronunciation declines, as though she begins to emulate Cal. Her voice takes on more air, and her vocal fry returns:

syllables at the end of sentences becoming split with a cracking of her voice. This does not suggest a frightful crack, but rather a typical, realistic way of speech. She takes on this voice as she recounts how she obtained the bill, as a tip from a "loaded man," one whom she knows nothing about other than he likes to go to horse races (Figure 10.4).

Later on, in the horse track scenes, we see once again a clear illustration of naturalistic expression. The sequence begins with a shot of Lili, restless, probably from boredom but just as likely as concern for her safety. There is no dialogue and the ambient sounds of horses, crowds, announcers, and horns dominate the soundtrack. As they search for the man who gave Lili the bill, there is little dialogue, resulting in long silences in many of the shots. Oftentimes, the actors rely on body language to communicate. In one scene, Cal approaches Lili as she nervously drinks from a large paper cup, obscuring her face as though in hiding. They engage in conversation, and again their voices are subdued, with *uhs* and sighs prevalent throughout. Moreover, the ambient sounds of the crowd compete with the dialogue, limiting clarity but aiding the "depiction of reality." Once again, much of the dialogue is left unsaid.

Lili and Cal share a cup, suggesting intimacy, and when they look over to Jack in the distance, he waves a ticket, showing that he has placed a bet. Lili and Cal smile at his presumed innocence. However, Lili continues to show signs of agitation. As she alters the direction of her gaze, she catches a glimpse of a woman's diamonds, and Lili sighs that she, herself, would like such diamonds. Cal grunts this off, reminding her that they are not looking for diamonds. Rising up and down on her toes, Lili responds

FIGURE 10.4 *Cal takes Lili's statement on the counterfeit money in* Private Hell.

with an elongated and lifting intonation, "I am." On the whole, Lupino's performance in this scene suggests discomfort, internalization of fear, boredom, and perhaps even desire. Among her actions include nervously grabbing a program for the races, shifting the weight on her feet, averting her gaze, and abruptly turning her neck. She consistently portrays unease and is engaged in something other than the mere delivery of lines.

Private Hell 36, as a crime drama, a film that relies on hidden motives and overall secrecy for its narrative trajectory. The tenets of method acting accentuate this theme, largely in part by Lupino's performance. Like a police officer truly engaging in detection, she construes meaning in other characters' words and motions, responding appropriately as dictated by the immediate circumstances. Moreover, she internalizes the complexity of the human psyche involved in a crime to produce a nightclub singer who, despite her "incidental" presence, adds to the humanity and realism of the film.

Notes

1. H. Mark Glancy, "Hollywood and Britain: MGM and the British 'Quota Legislation,'" in Jeffrey Richards (ed.), *The Unknown 1930s: An Alternative History of British Cinema, 1929-1939* (London: I.B. Tauris, 1998), 57–75, quoted p. 59.
2. Bernard Vorhaus (dir.), *The Ghost Camera* (RKO Radio Pictures, 1933).
3. Lawrence Napper, "A Despicable Tradition? Quota Quickies in the 1930s," in Robert Murphy (ed.), *The British Cinema Book* (London: BFI Publishing, 2001), 37–47, quoted p. 42.
4. Raoul Walsh (dir.), *High Sierra* (Warner Bros., 1941).
5. Robert C. Allen and Douglas Gomery, *Film History: Theory and Practice* (New York: Knopf, 1985), quoted p. 174.
6. Clifford McCarthy, *The Films of Humphrey Bogart* (Secaucus: Citadel, 1994), quoted p. 7.
7. Studio acting operated under option contracts, meaning that the studio would review an actor's ability to draw in sales approximately every six months, and, if profits were not good, changes could be made to the actor's image—or the actor would not have a contract renewed. This situation meant that actors could not make movies with other studios and that the studio holding the contract determined the films and roles of actors. Also in these agreements were restrictive clauses that permitted the studio to handle an actor's image, which even included changes in name or, as in the case of Bogart, date of birth. Following this system, studios produced movie stars known to the public for their off-screen lives but, of greater importance, known for their relatively unchanging on-screen characters. Bogart, therefore, consistently appeared as a troubled man, often on the wrong side of the law. In film after film, audiences

expected the same of Bogart, and the studio obliged, as long as the box office continued to deliver acceptable profits.

8   Charles Affron, *Star Acting: Gish, Garbo, Davis* (New York: Dutton, 1977), quoted p. 3.
9   The "woman's film" genre, reaching its height in the 1930s and 1940s with actors such as Joan Crawford and Bette Davis, centered on stereotypic "women's concerns," usually consisting of domestic life, motherhood, and romance, and the protagonist was a female who had to overcome various contretemps within such spheres. Hollywood studios intended for such a trajectory to reach a female audience, but critics have noted that the "woman's film" was technically not a specific genre, but more of a narrative mode since the films can be codified under other genres such as melodrama, film noir, and even horror. See Rick Altman, "Reusable Packaging: Generic Products and the Recycling Process," in Nick Browne (ed.), *Refiguring Film Genres: History and Theory* (Berkeley: University of California Press, 1998), 1–41.
10 William Donati, *Ida Lupino: A Biography* (Lexington: University Press of Kentucky, 1996), 66–8.
11 Ibid., 68.
12 Don Siegel (dir.), *Private Hell 36* (The Filmmakers, 1954).
13 Vsevolod I. Pudovkin, *Film Acting: A Course of Lectures Delivered at the State Institute of Cinematography, Moscow*. Trans. Ivor G. S. Montagu (London: G. Newnes, 1935).
14 Ibid., 33.
15 Richard Barsam and Dave Monahan, "Acting," in Richard Barsam and Dave Monahan (eds.), *Looking at Movies: An Introduction to Film* (New York: Norton, 2015), 271–316, quoted p. 287.
16 Ibid., 286.

11

Against the Grain, Within the Frame

The Double Consciousness of Ida Lupino

Mary Lynn Navarro

In the 1940s, Ida Lupino formed her own production company, The Filmakers, and she became identified on her own creative terms. English-born to a prestigious theatrical family, Lupino emerged in Hollywood in the 1930s as a prepubescent starlet but the trajectory of her multifaceted career spanned decades. An exceptional innovator, she developed and starred in her own TV show, was the first and only woman to have directed an episode of *The Twilight Zone* series, the first to direct her own acting, and the second woman to be recognized by the DGA. In addition to her cutting-edge independent films, her creative contributions include TV classics as *Alfred Hitchcock Presents*, *The Fugitive*, *Bewitched*, and highly popular Westerns.[1] In spite of these accomplishments, Lupino's body of work has been generally ignored and underrated, with the exception of Therese Grisham and Julie Grossman's volume, *Ida Lupino, Director: Her Art and Resilience in Times of Transition* (Rutgers University Press, 2017).

Her fans, however, have lauded Lupino for revealing controversial real life struggles of women, and Lupino is much more than a director who focuses on women's issues. I will examine *The Bigamist* and refer to *The Hitch-Hiker* and "The Masks."[2] Contextually, Lupino is situated in an

America swiftly moving past postwar angst to a new consumer-driven angst. I suggest that the concept of "double-consciousness" as a critical analytical method. Lupino's scope of direction reveals duality and duplicity, radical shifts in character and plot, as well as the transformative nature of American culture. I use the metaphorical terms "within the frame" and "against the grain" to illustrate double consciousness. Even though the term "historically" indicates race representation, it certainly is applicable to other social contexts.[3] No two films better display double consciousness than *The Hitch-Hiker* and *The Bigamist*.[4] But first, let us address the question of Lupino's role as a woman director and unaffiliated feminist.

Lupino herself used double consciousness to survive in a patriarchal studio system. In challenging the production code by subversively using objectionable material, Lupino is a disruptive figure who, in her words, "never smashed" into a man's world. She used her feminine wiles and that spells double consciousness.[5] Often labeled a "women's pictures" director for her early work, Lupino transcends being pigeonholed into a category of feminist or female director to emerge as a strong and significant director, bar none.[6] Born before women could vote, successfully working before, during, and after the second wave of women's liberation, perhaps she missed the feminist boat. More likely, though, feminists missed her.[7] Feminist film critics who embrace Lacanian theory in critiquing the alpha male directors would be doing an injustice to fit Lupino into their new critical paradigm. Laura Mulvey's seminal text, *Visual Pleasure and Narrative Cinema* (1975) that led to de facto analysis of the male gaze and a new film grammar (inserted subject positions, suture, scopophilia, for example) in effect eliminated Lupino from the discussion.[8] In *The Subject of Semiotics*, Kaja Silverman (1982) dissects Hollywood's golden age films as representing the symbolic and social order (Freud and Lacan) and the reproduction of culture (Althusser). Silverman asserts that "standard format of classic cinematic text duplicates within the fiction as a whole the paradigm of the shot/reverse/ shot disrupting the existing symbolic order . . . only in order to subsequently re-affirm that order, those positions and those ideals."[9] Lupino's films do not fit this critical paradigm, in part because she never reaffirms positions and ideals; she instead breaks them.

Possibly even dismissive of her, feminists ironically reified the system they critique and castigate. Clearly, Lupino was capable of making Hollywood movies. With Lupino's own deep experience in the studio system, she participated in the male club on both sides of the camera. And yet she chose to deliver unique films that cannot be deemed as either feminist filmmaking or standard Hollywood fare.

I further emphasize this point: if feminists want to adopt Lupino as one of theirs, I would imagine that Lupino would retort with her own "not wanted," not because she was anti-female but mostly because she defies categorization. From a prestigious theatrical family dating back to the

Renaissance, and as an English-born nationalized American citizen, Lupino is clearly unique. Yet her personal dismissal of feminism presents us with inconsistencies. Audrey Gwendolyn Foster, in "The Narcissistic Sociopathology of Gender, Part 2," analyzes Lupino in the context of postwar anxiety: "women, too are in a phase of a return to the home from wartime jobs, coaxed into conformity and a hyper-feminine roles." As "wildly ahead of her time and progressive," Lupino contrasts the 1950s idealization of women with "hard-boiled experience."[10]

Lupino's personal life often blended with the professional. Lupino continued to work with ex-husband and business partner Collier Young and his wife Joan Fontaine, who costarred in *The Bigamist*. She reveled in her progressive attitude on marriage and business, and she may have encouraged gossip, perhaps for the publicity it garnered, but more so as an aspect of her direct, "in your face" attitude. Starring in her television show, "Mr. Adams and Eve," with her future husband Howard Duff, indicates a curious perspective of her wifely status and turns on its head the progressive attitude that she had flaunted in the making of *The Bigamist*. Although she conspicuously places herself second, she is not your average wife. For example, in one episode of "Mr. Adams and Eve," Star Lupino enters center stage, waving her red fingernails, name-dropping other Hollywood stars, including her husband, are in the scene. Contrast this performance with Lupino, plain-faced in dungarees and baseball cap, bullhorn in hand, directing one of her pictures—the same woman battling the movie bosses and knocking at J. Edgar Hoover's door to attempt to glean FBI information on a serial killer. Always bold, Lupino refused to adhere to Hollywood's unspoken policy of nondiverse casting, bravely employing a blacklisted writer, Daniel Mainwaring (uncredited), and consistently resisted studio executives—and that took guts.

Lupino sidesteps a feminist stance by actually constructing her life around her professionalism. And, therefore, one might also argue that those actions place her squarely in the center of feminism. Rather, I would suggest, her work is her very self. To pigeonhole her into any category is misguided, but considering a double consciousness does give insight and means to articulate her work.

Lupino takes advantage of all she learned about movie-making and then adds her own intuitions. She exploits social convention that dictates marriage and children for woman, and for men their patriarchal role to be providers for upward mobility. At the same time, her films go "against the grain" of the very American values system that honors home, community, and nation building. In *The Bigamist*, unexamined consumerism is an unstated, destructive presence—but worse—a married childless woman is a waste while a woman with an out-of-wedlock child is a social outcast. In *The Hitch-Hiker*, common decency and civility emerge all shattered and Lupino exposes the ugly side of postwar America. By masking and then revealing motifs as sleight-of-hand, appearances are deceptive. Inflected with masterful interweave of narrative and composition, Lupino contributes to an American brand of new realism paving the way for 1970s directors like Coppola, for example, in *The Conversation*, or Scorsese in his early work, *Mean Streets*. Yet in this scope of realism is poeticism/drama that breaks boundaries and features characters embroiled in fantastic circumstances. Lupino has always insisted on stark realism, yet her formalistic sense emerges in her artistry,[11] for example *The Twilight Zone* episode "The Masks"[12] (Figure 11.1).

In this episode, a greedy family anticipates the demise of the family head, the wealthy patriarch who is on his death bed, alone in his massive mansion, save for a kind servant. In New Orleans during Mardi Gras, the family gathers together for the last time and pretends to show loving concern for the dying man. In order to bequest their inheritance, he orders them to wear hideous masks until midnight. At midnight he dies, and each family member becomes transformed into the grotesque mask that mirrors his or her true personality.

Lupino's direction is stark, concise, beset with contrasts, and expressionistic. The opulent mansion, at first a safe haven from the outside disorder of the Mardi Gras, becomes a claustrophobic prison. The motif of alienation resonates with Lupino's other work. In *The Bigamist*, the main character Harry Graham's antiseptic apartment lays bare while his secret home reeks of an illicit marriage. Even the tourist bus that journeys past houses of Hollywood stars is a lonely ride for the two main characters.

FIGURE 11.1 *The Mardi Gras masks of fate in* Twilight Zone, *"The Masks."*

In *The Hitch-Hiker*, alienation is displayed as the hijacked car, an isolated road, and a vast desert, alienating and condemning.

In "The Masks," the Mardi Gras masks contrast the destiny of entitlement that the family thought was theirs with a reality that strips them of all but money. It is a satire on society, a horror story, an irony of true *Twilight Zone* order, and, personally, my favorite episode. The reasons are clear: in the expressionistic interior world into which Lupino draws us, we become characters compelled to feel and/or resist a sudden display of "sins."

Lupino never discussed her work in artistic terms, nor did she put herself in the camp of other auteurs like Hitchcock or Welles. (Maybe she never cared or felt that she belonged there?) Yet her films do have a working-class edge, perhaps because of her identification with prior acting roles, her grit, and the anomaly of style of The Filmakers. *The Hitch-Hiker*, a noir cast in the blinding light of day, is just as unsettling and ranks with any standard noir, and, yet, Lupino has been branded as a director of women's issues.

One director we can compare her to, Sam Fuller, wrote, produced, and directed the 1964 exploitation film, *The Naked Kiss*. The opening sequence thrusts the viewer inside a seedy front where prostitute Kelly beats down her chiseling pimp who manages to pull off her wig revealing a stark, bald head. The effect was achieved with Fuller having Kelly (Constance Towers) actually hit the camera, captured by cinematographer, Stanley Cortez. Although the title refers to sexual perversity, *The Naked Kiss* is a spirited attack on middle-class values, mores, and social decorum. This film clearly addresses social issues but no one would dare accuse Fuller of doing women's pictures, even though Kelly is one of the fiercest females ever. After labeling herself as a "broken down piece of machinery," she embarks on a new life in small town Grantville to work with handicapped children in a racially integrated hospital. She becomes engaged to the town's rich philanthropist, no other than Grant himself but—alas—she discovers he is a pedophile, and she kills him. Watching this film is like having cold water, with ice cubes, flung in your face.[13]

Lupino's opening sequence in *The Hitch-Hiker* is a lead up of several shots, images that announce "victim," creating a meta-narrative around violence. Film critic Michael Atkinson describes it as follows:

> *The Hitch-Hiker* is a bullet-spray of noir haikus, with one of the most evocative and protracted title sequences of the period: a man standing on a receding highway (just his body, with his head loped off at the frame edge), like a partial figure in a Tanguy painting, a car, feet, a scream, a gunshot, all the while the camera pointed down, identifying nobody but also averting its gaze like a witness who's been told not to look up.[14] *The Bigamist*, I would argue, is hardly a "weepy" or even a "women's picture," just as *The Hitch-Hiker* is no road buddy film. Lupino exposes gender stereotypes to the core. Beyond the realm of relationships is the shaky

ground upon which our hallowed institutions and social values hinge. The foundation of American society can collapse at any moment and then appear to be put back together again, all in broken pieces. And we will see just how Lupino does this.

The Bigamist (1953)

Double consciousness is registered in the film's title, and the protagonist Harry/Harrison Graham is already a marked man.[15] The flashback narration reveals the conflicted and morally indecisive Harry/Harrison Graham, who has a secret life, another wife, and a child. When Harry and Eve Graham enter into an adoption screening process, a highly moral Mr. Jordan (Edmund Gwenn) decides to delve into Graham's life. The viewer's entry point into the discourse of negotiating states of consciousness is thus established. Unlike a standard noir that charts the ill-fated steady downfall of a main character, this film defies categorization: one conceptual lens frames a weak man and, in another lens, a caring husband. Tethered to Eve, Harry looks to be better suited for Phyllis, but he does not want to hurt either one and, in the final analysis, does he even want either woman? After Jordan has tracked down and learned that Graham has fathered a child and married, Graham's conflicted character is exposed, along with Jordan's inherent prejudices.

Early in the film, Jordan finds Harry in Los Angeles in a modest home, where Harry answers the door to a curious Jordan and nearly puts him off. Jordan, hearing the cries of a baby, practically barges into Graham's open door and abruptly walks into the child's bedroom. But right before Jordan's outburst, the lens follows Harry into the baby's bedroom, and, in atypical 1950s fashion, he cradles the child. The close-up shot of the baby in his crib, pacified and smiling, is humanizing and looks like a family photograph. As Harry tends to his son, the scene shifts to another contrasting frame of Jordan observing the other (and "othered") home, messy but brimming with the life of a family, in contrast to the meticulous sterility of Graham's San Francisco residence. Jordan's face is startled. These frames layer double consciousness throughout, from the shifting of Harry tenderly caring for the baby, to the shock and moral outrage of Jordan, and then to the double consciousness of what home represents to American family: A home without a child is not a home, but an illicit home, even lovingly bestowed with a child, is morally wrong and unacceptable. Note the following dialogue between Jordan and Graham:

Jordan: How long has this double life of yours being going on?
Graham: About eight months.

Jordan: And you were trying to adopt a child?
Graham: What are you going to do?
Jordan: Call the police.
Graham: You can't . . . not now. Not at a time like this. Let me try to make you understand. Please.
Jordan: I can't believe it. How . . . how could a man like you . . . successful, admired get into a position as . . . vile as this?

The position may be vile, but is his life? While Jordan gives his blessing to Eve's white, antiseptic house, which he compliments Eve for ("really pleasant," he says), he is blind to the comfort of this home. Lupino offers us a set of critical lenses, one to examine morality and the other to question it, while at base what remains unquestioned is social class and the illusion of the American Dream. Jordan's approval of Eve's house further elucidates the class difference between Phyllis and Eve and his marked preference for ultra-whiteness, affluence, and consumption shown in new appliances and the chic design of Eve's apartment, which posits upward mobility as a moral imperative. Eve and Harry Graham's wealth, however, steadily increases at the expense of their marriage. Material success as a moral obligation, a sign of one's values and decency, are hidden in the trappings of affluence. In Graham's parallel world, they are a struggling married couple, fraught with challenges of parenting and materializing their dreams.

Jordan sanctions that appearance of the American Dream fulfilled. Harry, in his vile life, has let him down. But is Jordan the hypocrite? Let's further imagine one Harry as the victim of too much success, and the other Harry as the victim of obligation. Yet before we are able to pass our own judgment, Harry must explain. After Harry pleas for more time to tell his story, his voice-over compositions further reveal double consciousness. Harry's insistence that his loneliness has driven him to despair and ultimately Phyllis would play out as a shabby excuse. One scene that captures his isolation, an empty street in Los Angeles along MacArthur Park, opens with Harry turned from view. In a long take, the camera then follows his full-body profile: Harry walks aimlessly past a park empty of people, with plasticized trees, and he slouches along as if he were dragging the weight of his artificial, unfulfilled life.

The shot ends in front of the glass showcase of a high-end department store. The camera pans to the front of a window and stops at mannequin that looks like a replica of Eve. Behind the glass window is like a block of ice, and the effect is of a frozen woman (Figure 11.2).

This shot encapsulates Harry's opening dialogue: "I felt a distance between us which was more than miles." The store and mannequin showcase a model life of materialism that has not worked to bring any happiness to Harry. Yet the shot is a momentary stop. In another long take, Harry continues his solitary walk on the wide street until he reaches the end of the road to

FIGURE 11.2 *The mannequin who resembles Eve in* The Bigamist.

the tour bus, which is angled and exaggerated in length, emphasizing an emptiness within Harry.

Enter Eve Graham within the frame/against the grain. Eve Graham is a full business partner in their Deep Freeze company, a title that ironically speaks to their marriage. The poised, elegant Eve, who stands remarkably above her husband's station, is a striking contrast to Harry's lack of refinement. A catch for a self-made man, Eve exudes charm while serving a roast and doing the hard sell to potential clients, all men. We see her framed among the men, in elegant attire, pearls, a coiffed chignon, not a hair out of place. And yet, she is a marked woman—bitter—as stated by Harry. In the parlance of the 1950s, barren is a semantic marker that castes a woman, and even though the word is never explicitly stated, this film is pregnant with "barren." Eve's ability to assist her husband is therefore "justified," and she even exceeds him, but this does not offset her misfortune as a woman not to be a mother. Rather, it amplifies what she lacks rather than her talents.

The presence of the 1950s functions like another character. The postwar economic boom is a hegemonic force that needs a growing consumer class: children! We learn of Eve's unfortunate diagnosis as Jordan records into his Dictaphone the medical confirmation further stigmatizing Eve. His words pathologize childless women and conspicuously magnify what they lack. Lupino appears to maintain a woman's place until she disrupts the status quo. Eve always outperforms her husband, and it is he who always defers to her "perfection," and he seems to not fully accept her superior business acumen. She is absorbed in her "executive, career moods." Harry explains the situation as if female ambition is a type of affliction, like her desire for a child, and it is an attempt to gain sympathy from Jordan, who also stands for the status quo. In an exchange of gender roles Eve, in the dominant role of the household and business, emasculates Harry. Her status is illustrated later in the film when Harry admits to Jordan that Eve does not need him, but Phyllis does. Harry Graham suffers from what women traditionally complained about—husbands abandoning them for their careers. The 1950s heteronormative male is thereby, feminized.

At the film's midway point Harry, desperately guilty, intends to talk Eve into taking a vacation break in order to save their marriage. Consider this bedroom scene: lying on her separate bed (within the production code but perfect for this scene) and with her classic chignon finally undone, Eve is framed as a vibrant woman. And then she turns her back to Harry, receding into sexual indifference. Her coldness garners sympathy for Harry. However, her response to Harry, before she slips into sleep after a hard day of work is: "I love our marriage." This statement jolts this scene and promotes sympathy for Eve and she completely trusts Harry. Her unrelenting and desperate desire for the child is a narcissistic solution. The medicalization of Eve, nakedly exposing the status of the unfulfilled childless mother, is further ramified by Hollywood mainstream movies, both in past and in this decade, in which single, childless women are seen as rejects but, more precisely, threats to society.

Hitchcock's stigmatized femme fatales underscore the tensions of childless women. Protagonists like Eve Kendall (Eva Marie Saint in *North By Northwest*) are sophisticated and dangerous; Frances Stevens (Grace Kelly in *To Catch a Thief*) is a beautiful and spoiled thrill-seeker who seduces a charming burglar; Kim Novak's imposter Madeleine/Judy (*Vertigo*) drives a man to the brink of insanity; and the sexually latent serial thief Marnie (Alfred Hitchcock, *Marnie* (1964)) endures a forced marriage with a husband (Sean Connery) who rapes as a cure for her deep neurosis. And if a woman is beyond repair, as in Judy's case, she must die. The Hitchcock female, driven by wild desires or cold calculation, vacillates outside of the stable, nuclear patriarchal family.

Eve Graham is not a single woman but she might as well be. She functions as an independent, smart, successful woman. And her major flaw, located in the womb, is a material reality and not a degradation of character. Or is it? Lupino makes us wonder whether this portrait invites feminist commentary or is a postwar reality check, or perhaps all or none of the above? Perhaps Eve really just wants to be a mother. (In her own life, Lupino admitted to neither enjoying motherhood nor being good at it, with which her daughter agreed.) Eve describes Jordan as "Santa Claus, a man who likes to give babies away." (This inside joke is only one of several in the film.) However, this characterization also fits Eve. Accumulating wealth, the first step, led them onto adoption, as if she were acquiring a bright shiny new object, a Christmas gift, like the little toy she dangles in front of a disaffected Harry, who matches her sexual indifference with his own ambivalence of fatherhood.

Harry had planned to stay with Eve long enough for her to get a child (the ultimate gift) and then he would leave. But then what? That question is unanswered. Eve is possibly just a clueless, self-absorbed woman, but she is also a wife who sincerely loves her husband and believes that her marriage is stable. Still, we wonder about her true talents. Is she the more talented head of the household or a woman who failed to keep her man? Does she even need a man? In any case, no marriage is safe sums up the message against the grain. This film presages the disruption of the nuclear family and the heterosexual norm of the fifties. As we enter the latter part of the twentieth century, the solution of marriage and family to provide lasting fulfillment is a totalizing concept. Yet the baby boom and nuclear family will eventually bust.

Enter Phyllis Within the Frame

Inside the Hollywood tour bus, Phyllis is seated with her head tilted back. Harry eyes her, sits on the opposite side of the aisle and, in his feeble advances, lights her many cigarettes, joking, "You just want me for my lighter," to which Phyllis, in Lupino trademark rasp, says, "I could give up smoking." While Eve compliments Harry, yet Harry and Phyllis are fellow travelers on the lonely road, and the composition levels them equally (Figure 11.3).

The long take of the road augments Harry and Phyllis' isolation and shared destiny. They connect as the bus rolls into the road of privilege to where the rich and famous live royally. Or—do these Hollywood homes, too, reveal double-consciousness? (We *could* be on "Boulevard.") Harry asks Phyllis, "Haven't you ever wanted to see how the other half lives?" "Not particularly." Afterward, she takes Harry to the restaurant, "Early American Chinese restaurant," where he is led to believe that they are on a date. "What is this, charades?" he asks, after she has changed into her work outfit, a silly costume. Phyllis is clearly self-deprecating. She was hired to spike business and she calls herself a "howling success."

Phyllis' Life: Against the Grain

To enhance the sense of deliberate strangeness and the "not normal environment," director Lupino stages a very brief scene that could easily be missed. A man (Collier Young) siting at the bar smiles at Harry; a chagrined Harry slouches and turns his back. Aside from the covert homophobia, as if Lupino is poking fun at it, this moment adds to the "not-normalness" of Phyllis' life in comparison to Eve who, beyond normal, is polyurethane, like their deep

FIGURE 11.3 *The Hollywood tour bus and the road of alienation in* The Bigamist.

freeze refrigerator. Lupino's male heterosexual dominance, so apparent in *The Hitch-Hiker* as well, is met with advancing impotence. Conformity, the Cold War, fear of homosexuals in the State Department, Reds in show business (among other unseen places), and the reassurance of heterosexual normality all play into a larger pathology symbolized in Eve's childless state and in Phyllis' status. The restaurant scene situates Phyllis' character within social class and among outsiders of society, without a secure place or position. The weird little restaurant could be a low-rent version or alternate world of the famous and opulent Grauman's Chinese theater. The lack of people, Phyllis' corny uniform, bad food, and kitschy décor embody the totality of Phyllis. Although disconnected and sad, Phyllis does not entirely quit life. Note how Harry's phone conversation to Eve about Phyllis is double consciousness revealed: "I met a little mouse," which he abruptly spins to say, "all shoulders and curves." Intended to ignite some jealousy, "I cheated," he says (even though at that point he had not cheated), and his contradictory description reveals the presence of double consciousness as a dubious connection to another person.

Phyllis and Harry: Against the Grain

After Phyllis and Harry's night on the town culminates in a one-night stand, Harry returns to San Francisco. Months later, he tracks Phyllis down at another downtrodden establishment, a rooming house for unwed mothers.

Guilt-ridden, he makes a preposterous marriage proposal that she falls for, even though she has doubts. This moment would have been the time for him to let Phyllis know about his other life. Instead, he forces himself in deeper trouble, but he genuinely wants to do right by Phyllis. Yet Edmond O'Brien effectively portrays a believable character.

Phyllis declares her love Lupino-style, dressed down and unsentimental: "You kill me," her signature line and the hardboiled shell that hides a soft core lends authenticity to her character. (How could she not suspect something was terribly wrong with Harry?) Phyllis warms up far more than the icy-cold blonde Eve ever could. As Bogart's Dixon Steele said of Gloria's Graham's Laurel in *In a Lonely Place*: "She isn't corny or coy or sweet. She's a good guy." Similarly, Phyllis becomes "Phil," as Harry calls her, and proves to be a "good guy" too, even when perceiving that she trapped him into marriage, and allows his indiscretion with Eve. Phyllis, clearly stronger in character than Harry, is among a sector of women on their own, unsupported, pregnant, not socially accepted. And by marrying an *already-*married man, she, too is a marked woman.

The Moral Compass/Going Against the Grain, Within the Frame

As the court case proceeds, Mr. Jordan declares to Harry, "I don't know whether to despise you or pity you. I don't want to shake your hand. On the other hand . . . . I almost wish you luck," and that signifies double consciousness as Harry Graham's bigamy case enters the legal arena. But as he represents the world as it is changing so, too, does his adjudication as the judge delivers a speech on how people would have "looked the other way" had Harry Graham kept Phyllis as a mistress instead of a wife. These two streams of consciousness unravel right up to the film's climax, and the judge suspends Harry's sentence. The two wives, present in the courtroom, exchange sympathetic glances. A shamed Harry is led out by a police officer and Harry shuffles his feet in his characteristic heavy way.

In 1953, *Peter Pan*, directed by Clyde Gironimi and Wilfred Jackson, was the number one box office hit. And then along comes Ida Lupino. No popular film other than *The Bigamist* examined sexuality as human connection, and in characters not traditionally Hollywood sexy. In mainstream movie screwball comedies (*My Favorite Wife* comes to mind), the theme of bigamy was an excuse to write funny dialogue and characters.

Lupino accomplishes that which would garner disbelief (a sincere and kindhearted bigamist?) and delivers a convincing set of life's possibilities.

Double consciousness masks and reveals. The desire for and, at the same time, failure of marriage to provide lasting security, commitment, and love raises a more complex question. What happens if the individual breaks conventional rules? If an individual is allowed to become stronger than the institution, what does this mean for all institutions? For civility? Like the suspended sentence that the judge renders, this written sentence could suspend the answer as well. Lupino would have you decide.

Notes

1. This partial list includes television episodes that Lupino directed: *The Ghost & Mrs. Muir* (one episode) 1968; *The Virginian* (one episode) 1966; *Gilligan's Island* (four episodes) 1964–8; *Bob Hope Presents the Chrysler Theatre* (one episode); *Honey West* (one episode) 1966; *Bewitched* (one episode) 1965; *Dr. Kildare* (one episode) 1964; *The Untouchables* (three episodes) 1962–3; *Have Gun—Will Travel* (eight episodes) 1959–61; *Alfred Hitchcock Presents* (two episodes) 1960–1; *Screen Directors Playhouse* (one episode), 1958. A partial list of the films she directed: *The Trouble with Angels* 1966; *On Dangerous Ground* (uncredited) 1951; *Hard, Fast and Beautiful* 1951; *Outrage* 1950; *Never Fear* 1949; *Not Wanted* 1949. She claims eight writing credits, contributing to the films she directed and produced and for television. Available at http://www.imdb.com/name/nm0526946/?ref_=nv_sr_1 (accessed on April 5, 2015).
2. A *Twilight Zone* episode (1964).
3. W. E. B. DuBois in his classic work *The Souls of Black Folk* (1903) defines double consciousness as the "sense of always looking at one's self through the eyes of others, of measuring one's soul by the tape of a world that looks on in amused contempt and pity." DuBois also uses the metaphor of the veil as both a "blessing and a curse." The use of double consciousness in this chapter is not intended to co-opt the original concept, but more recently double consciousness has been extended to other social contexts. Lupino's work resonates with "veiling" and "unveiling," or masking and revealing.
4. *The Hitch-Hiker* (1953), directed by Ida Lupino. Collier Young and Ida Lupino, screenplay; Robert Joseph, adaptation; Daniel Mainwaring (uncredited). Other credits include: Nicolas Masuraca, director of photography; Collier Young, producer; Christian Nyby, associate producer. Principal cast in credits order: Edmond O'Brien, Frank Lovejoy, William Talman. *The Bigamist* (1953), directed by Ida Lupino. Collier Young, screenplay; Larry Marcus and Lou Shor, story. Other credits include: Diskant, director of photography; Collier Young, producer; Robert Eggenweiler, associate producer. Principal cast in credits order: Joan Fontaine, Ida Lupino, Edmund Gwenn, Edmond O'Brien.
5. Ida Lupino with Mary Ann Anderson, *Ida Lupino Beyond the Camera* (BearManor Media, 2001). In this autobiographical account (written with Anderson), Lupino states, "I didn't see myself as any advance-guard or feminist, I had to do something to fill up my time" (109). Throughout her career, Lupino often made irreverent comments about her abilities. She very famously said, "Any woman who wishes to smash into the world of men

isn't very feminine" (116). She inadvertently distinguishes what is deemed as feminine from what is strong. She stated, "I held my own in the toughest kind of man's world" (83).

6 *Queen of the 'B's: Ida Lupino Behind the Camera* (Greenwood Press, 1995), edited by Annette Kuhn, attempts to find Lupino's place in film history as a "first" of female directors. But since then, no critical assessment furthered the inquiry into Lupino's weighty contribution. Moreover, to argue and either prove or disprove Lupino's feminism is either dated or historically situated, as feminism cultural theory of that era was calcified by a singular construction, overshadowed by the discussions of the male gaze.

7 Joan Braverman, a feminist filmmaker, discusses the early years of the second-wave feminist movement upon women filmmakers during the 1960s and 1970s. She mentions Ida Lupino as a woman director who made films about "bigamy and rape." This nod to Lupino shows the awareness of her work but to brand her as part of a "feminine aesthetic," I believe, misrepresents the totality of Lupino. This might be attributed to feminism and film criticism's own genesis. "Feminism and Video: A View from the Village," *Camera Obscura* 64, 22, no. 1. Duke University Press.

8 Laura Mulvey, "Visual Pleasure and Narrative Cinema," written in 1973, was originally published in *Screen* in 1975. A great deal of criticism has followed but one additional point I would like to make is that Mulvey's own later critique of spectatorship employs double consciousness in her 1981 article "Afterthoughts on 'Visual Pleasure and Narrative Cinema,' inspired by King Vidor's Duel in the Sun (1946)," in which she uses the term "transvestism" as code-switching between identification with male and female cinematic characters.

9 Kaja Silverman, *The Subject of Semiotics* (Oxford: Oxford University Press, 1983), 220–2, quoted 221.

10 Audrey Gwendolyn Foster, "The Narcissistic Socio-pathology of Gender, Part 2," *Film International*, March 9, 2014. Available at http://filmint.nu (accessed March 14, 2014).

11 Robert Stam, *Film Theory, An Introduction* (Oxford: Blackwell Publishers Ltd. 2000), 75–9, quoted p. 75. "Both formalist and realist featured their own brand of 'progressive' teleology technique," a comment I have applied to Lupino's style.

12 Rod Serling, "The Masks," *The Twilight Zone*, Season 5, Episode 25, directed by Lupino.

13 *The Naked Kiss* (1964) directed by Sam Fuller. Produced by Fuller, Sam Firks, and Leon Fromkess. Screenplay by Fuller. Cinematography by Stanley Cortez. Principal cast includes Constance Towers, Anthony Eisley, Michael Dante.

14 Michael Atkkinson, "A Noir Journey into No-Woman's Land: Ida Lupino's The Hitch-Hiker," January 21, 2011. Available at https://web.archive.org/web/20170114062203/http:/www.fandor.com/keyframe/a-noir-journey-into-no-womans-land-ida-lupinos-the-hitch-hiker (accessed February 13, 2014).

15 In the 1940s and throughout the 1950s, mainstream films had already given us spinsters such as Bette Davis's Charlotte in *Now, Voyager*, whose sex act consisted of sharing a cigarette with Paul Henreid. (Her previous spinster, also named Charlotte, was *The Old Maid*, 1939). Then several spinster-themed Katherine Hepburn movies include *The African Queen*, *The Rainmaker*, and *Summertime*. Her comedies also show a married unmothered woman as selfish, spoiled, or psychologically stilted in, for example, *Adam's Rib* or *Woman of the Year*. But the worst yet is *Leave Her to Heaven*, in which Gene Tierney plays a sinister depiction of the unmothered married woman whose psychotic controlling love of her husband leads to self-abort her baby, murder her disabled brother-in-law, and commit suicide to frame her husband.

12

Outrage and Trauma

A Reconsideration and Reevaluation

Kathleen "Kat" Robinson

The common perception is that Jonathan Kaplan's *The Accused* (1988) is the first feature-length film centered on the act of rape and the related, corresponding reactions to the effect of rape as trauma. *The Accused* is a probing film that captures the sense of rape as a trauma. In this film, the act of rape both disrupts and creates a narrative structure by employing a traumatic event as both catalyst and anchor for the visual telling and retelling of the trauma. However, Jonathan Kaplan's film is by far not the first or only voice that attempts to use rape as the place and space for a film narrative. Yet the 1988 film garnered so much discussion and exploration that it actually helped to provide a base to generate discourse that has, finally, led to the discovery of Ida Lupino's relatively unknown film about rape and the effects of rape. In 1950, Ida Lupino directed her second film, *Outrage*, which places a rape at its film noir center. Lupino's film is much different, more controlled—both by the times and the rules of the Production Code—than *The Accused*. However, Lupino's film still attempts to speak from and to and for the breach of the trauma of rape.

Many decades before the culture and times were ready for a film about rape, Ida Lupino exposes that extreme risk that she made to direct such a film. In the face of production codes, cultural insecurities, and gendered thoughts on feminine roles, Lupino asserts a stance in her film that provides a basis for conversation and discussion. William Donati, one of Lupino's biographers, observes that "bringing to the screen such a socially sensitive subject as rape brought Ida into numerous conferences with Jeffrey Shurlock of the Production Code Administration."[1] Lupino was aware of the tension in her decision to use certain subjects as the foundation for her work as a director, and it is for this reason and so many other reasons that her *Outrage* should be viewed in a new, informed light. That *Outrage* focuses on a rape in Lupino's second film is and should be seen as groundbreaking for not only the time that it was written but also for our contemporary time.

The representations and portrayals in *Outrage* attempt to capture and to portray a sense of trauma's effect on narrative structure of the film. Further, the film also captures and presents a commentary on trauma and rape. However, one of the more salient observations connected to the film is the impulse to examine how this narrative functions cinematically from the feminine perspective provided by Lupino, rather than a more traditional masculine perspective, often privileged, crafted, and presented in narrative world of film. Relatively few films—especially where rape is central to the work—have been directed by women. (Recent exceptions include Catherine Breillat *Fat Girl* (2001) and Virginie Despente *Baise Moi/Rape Me* (2000).) Most films with rape at the center of cinematic action are directed by and from a masculine prospective. These films include *The Crow* (1994), *Black Snake Moan* (2007), *The Girl with the Dragon Tattoo* (2011), and *Last House on the Left* (1979 and 2009), and they were often meant to reflect serious social messages—most pointed toward a female-heavy audience—such as avoiding rape by being "proper and good" in a postwar context. This privileging of message is yet another illustration of the dominant male narrative that structures and reinforces a misguided understanding of rape. However, Lupino's work refuses to justify this gendered presupposition.

Lupino's often categorized film noir or melodramatic treatment of rape in *Outrage* shapes representations of the notions of trauma, narrative structure, and integrity in such a unique but accessible manner that the film truly deserves more recognition and study. Lupino's film presents the act of rape as trauma, as a violent break between subjectivity and objectivity and intimates the Freudian sense of trauma. In this understanding, Cathy Caruth asserts, in *Trauma: Explorations in Memory*, that trauma "is an experience that is not fully assimilated as it occurs."[2] Caruth argues that texts that use trauma propose a question that focuses on "what it means to transmit and to theorize around a crisis that is marked, not by a simple knowledge, but by the ways it simultaneously defies and demands our witness."[3] Lupino's film occupies Caruth's space of inquiry in the face of the trauma of rape. The film narrative forces, yet simultaneously denies, an accurate understanding of the cataclysmic event.

Lupino's 1950 film is sadly often overlooked due to its branding as simple melodrama or an attempt at a film noir. Yet, the film examines not only a violent rape but also the subsequent wrestling with the trauma of that rape by the main character, Ann Walton. The placement of rape as the central crime or focus in the Lupino's film references the idea, expressed by Lynn Higgins, that rape is a perfect crime for representation in film. Higgins argues:

> [S]ince rape leaves no concrete, inter-subjectively veritable evidence to prevent the construction of multiple and contradictory narratives . . . the specific difficulties of proving that what occurred was a rape, framed within the possibilities and limitations of filmic representation, add up to stage (even invite) the discursive disappearance of a crime.[4]

Lupino's second film selects an attack, rape, and subsequent aftermath as her main focus. This approach, as Higgins explores, creates a tension in the representation of the crime and the aftermath. The narrative projected and represented in *Outrage* clearly invites both an awareness of the act *and* an acknowledgment of the disappearance of that rape onto the screen.

In the film, twenty-year-old bookkeeper Ann Walton is stalked and attacked following a late-night shift in an industrial setting. The attack occurs fairly early in the film, and the majority of the film focuses on the immediate aftermath and the tangential effects of the traumatic attack on Ann's life. Further, the film hints at the effects of the rape on her family and fiancée (briefly), and, most important, the film exposes and attempts to give voice to a narrative speaking from the space and discord of rape trauma. The film captures the sense of discomfiture that occurs during and following a traumatic event like rape. As such, Ann is not able to ameliorate issues in her narrative; her days, her experiences, and even her job all begin to operate as something of an attack to her, following the horrific sexual assault. *Outrage* centers on her need to escape both the experience and aftermath connected to the rape and to create a new or different mode of subjectivity and agency. In a sense, the film ultimately focuses on her attempts to repair the structure of her understanding and to create a space for healing in relation to the trauma experienced.

Outrage remained in relative obscurity for some time, save for the rare readings and retrospections of Lupino's works, both as an actress and as a director. *Outrage* was routinely dismissed as a simple melodrama. Many critics—including early feminist literary and film and culture critics—refused to see the film as anything more than another example of Lupino's relentless pursuit of work and productivity. Pam Cook, in her essay on the film in *Queen of the Bs: Ida Lupino Behind the Camera*, counters these positions, while opening a space that helped to contribute to rereading *Outrage* from a different yet similar perspective. Cook asserts that the film defies one set method of interpretation, whether feminist or anti-feminist, and she further proposes that the engagement with the film "offers the opportunity to explore the limits of feminist enquiry by testing it against a text which refuses to conform easily to political or ideological categories that readers and viewers might wish to impose."[5] *Outrage* refuses to conform to societal expectations or norms. Instead, the story line attempts to use a very fractured point of view to establish the sense of trauma's effect on the narrative subjectivity of Ann. The representation of the rape cannot be distilled into a single binary or even multiple points of view. On the contrary, the representation of the act of rape is split and refracted into a layered and tensioned presentation of subjectivity and objectivity. As Cook argues, "Ann's flight and her search for subjectivity are a rejection of traditional femininity. Her victim status and 'neurosis' are the direct result of social forces, yet they exceed that too-neat explanation."[6] As such, similar to other rape and trauma-effected narratives, the center of the structure that holds the film together is not so much the actual trauma, but rather it is focused on the tensioned search or the fight to regain one's subjectivity that was breached and ruptured during the attack.

Ann's departure from her existing life and order following the attack also references a societal reaction to rape: a reaction that contemporary society has now deemed *rape culture*. In Lupino's film, Ann's mere existence forces her small-town society to not only react but to define rape: an act and series of reactions that Ann can neither control nor accept. Her character and the traumatic act of rape are a breach in the simple narrative of her social world and surrounding culture. Therefore, she must escape in order to craft a definition that is not placed or forced upon her; in a sense she must escape the double rape that has occurred with her experience and society's awareness of the act. Carine M. Mardorosssian explains that no matter if rape is represented as metaphor or reality, the central question of the analysis is to question the agency of the victim. Mardorosssian states, "agency and victimization are conceptualized in opposition to one another, and the presence of one automatically implies the absence of the other."[7] Similarly, Ann's existence in the film confounds and confronts an existing narrative that cannot handle the rupture and rapture caused by the act of rape, anymore than it can handle the agency or victimization that will disrupt the societal, ontological network in the film.

These observations emphasize the value of rereading and reengaging the narrative of the film. In an essay in *The New Yorker*, *Outrage* received significant respect as Richard Brody draws attention to important narrative contexts:

> Lupino approaches the subject of rape with a wide view of the societal tributaries that it involves. She integrates an inward, deeply compassionate depiction of a woman who is the victim of rape with an incisive view of the many societal failures that contribute to the crime, including legal failure to face the prevalence of rape, and the over-all prudishness and sexual censoriousness that make the crime unspeakable in the literal

sense and end up shaming the victim. Above all, she reveals a profound understanding of the widespread and unquestioned male aggression that women face in ordinary and ostensibly non-violent and consensual courtship. Her movie is about the experiences of one young woman and, yes, about the experience of all women.[8]

As Brody observes, the notion of shame, regret, and fear connected to the act of rape pervade the film. Brody claims that Ann's experience is a kind of "every woman's" story of rape, and, thus, Lupino's portrayal of Ann's reactions to the trauma of rape captures an understanding that can inform all discussions of rape.

Following her rape, Ann feels as if she is no longer the woman she was; she feels that everyone is looking at her and toward her. Ultimately, she appears as a spectacle. In the act and the acknowledgment of her rape, she has been made the object of view and act while being forced to assume a subjectivity in relation, solely, to the act of rape. Lupino focuses on how Ann is made to be cast out by being cast upon. The only option for Ann to escape and to reclaim her body and her narrative and her story is to leave and/ or depart the one that has been written or crafted for her. In this fashion, the film could be seen as operating as a metaphor for Lupino's career and life. As Brody intimated, Ann's experiences are represented as all woman's experiences, and, furthermore, the film appears to express the hope that her experiences can speak for all victims who have faced the breach of agency and victimization as a result of a sexual attack.

In order for Ann to reclaim order in her life, she must choose to become independent of the act not simply because she has survived the attack, but because she is able to transcend the traumatic bind she was thrust into as a result of the rape, and thus, in this bind, she is caught between being both subject and object. She is trapped in the breach of trauma. To understand the power of this breach and bind, Caruth builds on Sigmund Freud's understanding of trauma as she observes that trauma "is not simply . . . the literal threatening of bodily life, but the fact that the threat is recognized as such by the mind one moment too late."[9] To capture trauma in a narrative like *Outrage* requires the structure to capture the literality of the threat along with the corresponding textual presentation of the delayed recognition of the threat of that traumatic event. Lupino's visual representation references an attempt to project an understanding of the complexity *and* difficulty of capturing visually a truth about rape trauma. Further, the film attempts to reference and illustrate the difficulty of creating a narrative that captures the literality of the traumatic event along with the delayed recognition of these threats. For a return to an ordered narrative, Ann must become the subject and not just the object in the film (Figure 12.1).

FIGURE 12.1 *Following the rape, Ann feels as if she is no longer the woman she was.*

The narrative presentation of Ann's involvement with her memory of the rape trauma illustrates how the abject experience of trauma contributes to the altered representation of space and time expressed in the film. Caruth observes that "trauma does not simply serve as record of the past but precisely registers the force of an experience that is not yet fully owned."[10] Accordingly, when an individual like Ann experiences trauma, the individual lacks the ability to define subjectivity and objectivity: in that moment, the individual is often only concerned with his or her survival. There is not time to ask who (object) or what (subject) is doing this to me? The displacement of subjectivity and objectivity vis-à-vis trauma alters and confuses notions of space and time for an individual. As such, Ann is left with an inability to define or to understand the traumatic break occurring in her structure of understanding and existing.

When the structure of narrative encounters trauma, the structure of the narrative engages the profound change, the displacement of traditional positions of subjectivity, objectivity, and temporality. For example, one of the most telling lines that illustrate this narrative displacement occurs when Ann asserts that she simply cannot marry Jim nor can she return to work. In this section of the film, the sense of the effects of the traumatic is embodied in the shifting narrative presentation. This jangled shift attempts to invoke the experience of the effects of rape on all aspects of the protagonist in the structure of the narrative, ranging from the overwhelming amplification of sounds, acts, and emotion to complex representations of Ann's ongoing interactions with issues in her life prior to her traumatic sexual assault.

Sarah Projansky, in *Watching Rape: Film and Television in Postfeminist Cultures*, argues that "the versatility of rape" functions "both to define property and the family and to support new literary forms and psychological interiorization—but these are only a few of many complex ways rape has functioned historically."[11] Rape as representation often provides an interesting space for film and literary adaptation, as it necessarily becomes a weighted-contest of subjectivity and objectivity in the representation. The rape of Ann is seen both as an attack on Ann as a daughter and as a soon-to-be wife while being juxtaposed as an attack on the main arbiter of meaning in the film, Ann. She is both subject and object in and during the rape. Further, the act of rape in *Outrage* disrupts these often clearly delineated positions. Ann is viewed, following the rape, as marked as external from the structure of her own life or her own narrative arc of understanding, and the most pervasive of the views place her experience actually portrayed as being her own.

Ann is represented as seeing herself as being damaged in ways that go against some of the parameters of the cultural narrative, which include social and cultural mores and ways that victims of sexual assault are treated. As such, she must go outside of frame and off set. The film also attempts to capture a sense of her interior landscape. Lupino attempts to show a glimpse of Ann's mind as the place and space for the experience. Ann attempts to engage in establishing a sense of self outside of the confines of her family and her job. In fact, one sees her move beyond a job focused on the simple entering of numbers, and she moves more into creating and entering relationships. She becomes a subject because of the absolute need for her to try to transcend her experience of trauma. Caruth establishes a great baseline for the understanding of this type of transition when she asserts that "trauma describes an overwhelming experience of sudden or catastrophic events in which the response to the event occurs in the often delayed, uncontrolled repetitive appearance of hallucinations and other intrusive phenomena."[12] It is only in the film when Ann is portrayed as being able to reconcile, or at least approach an understanding of what has happened to her, following the tragic hallucination at the company picnic, that the viewer sees Ann truly "in frame" (Figure 12.2).

Lupino was very clever in selecting rape as the subject matter of her second film. The viewer can approach an understanding of the film because it attempts to project a sense of order in a disordered world. Lupino was adamant that Hollywood must produce "more experimentation in new film subjects."[13] She wanted to explore areas of the human experience that could bring new power and excitement to the screen. An attempt to use rape as a lens to explore new ways of creating different thoughts and experiences on screen was a risky move, especially for a woman director at this time.

FIGURE 12.2 *At the company picnic, the viewer sees Ann truly in her suffering.*

However, one should not become too quickly wrapped up in the thought that Lupino was completely going rogue in her subject matter and representation. Rape narratives have always been a dominant part of American literature and film since the inception of these media. In fact, Sarah Projansky observes that narratives with rape at their center assist in maintaining a social construction of traditional gendered understanding omits:

> [O]perating in literature, law, the courts, social activism, family, and plantation life, newspapers, paintings, and war, rape narratives help organize, understand, and even arguably produce the social world; they help structure social understandings of complex phenomena such as gender, race, class, and nation. Additionally, they help inscribe a way of looking, the conditions of watching, and the attitudes and structures of feeling one might have about rape, women, and people of color.[14]

Thus, Lupino's film references a sense of ordering in relation to how society cannot look away from yet often refuses to engage a victim of the trauma of rape. The narrative representation of the act and aftermath of rape, additionally, troubles what a victim should look, act, and be like. In the traditional narrative, good, moral, and respectful girls are not to be victims. In fact, it is because Ann is represented as a good, moral, and respectful girl that the narrative is jarring, and Ann exists well within the traditional narrative expectations. As such, the representation of her normalized existence being shaped by the act is what is so discomfiting to viewers.

FIGURE 12.3 *Ann's trauma conveyed with camera angles and close ups.*

Lupino did so well with the staging and filming of the rape scene. Working within the strict parameters provided by the Production Codes, which limited graphic representations of violence, Lupino conveyed the tension and suspension with camera angles, close-ups, and dramatic shifts in perspective and sound. The complete lack of dialogue during the sequence bolsters the very trauma of rape without so much as capturing a ripped blouse or torn skirt. Capturing the experience of trauma in a film narrative involves creating a visual and auditory structure that represents a lack of time and recognition of trauma within the fiction as presented (Figure 12.3).

However, at the time of the film's release, these issues did not appear in discussions of the narrative. In fact, many publications panned the work. However, the *Los Angeles Examiner* observed that, "with courage and frankness within the limits of good taste, *Outrage* points up the serious consequences to society . . . the story hits home to every family in that such an occurrence might happen anytime to any girl or woman."[15] While this review is not a rousing endorsement, it does capture the power of Lupino's technical voice and engineered perspective as a creative and involved director of the film. Furthermore, it also illustrates the power of her choice to create discomfort and discourse that her use of rape in *Outrage* generated. Sarah Projansky states that "rape functions as the narrative event that brings out a latent feminism in the woman (or man) who experiences rape; thus the texts make rape necessary for the articulation of feminism."[16] As such, Lupino's decision to use rape as her focus exposes a tension, a tension that allows her to express a proto-feminist viewpoint by using a very aggressive and traditionally masculine attack as the catalyst for her second film's structure.

Projansky observes that the Code's imperative that rape "should never be more than suggested, only when essential for the plot" mirrors the findings of the majority of the essays in *Rape and Representation*. Lynn Higgins and Brenda Silver observe that, in this film or films where rape is central to the structure of the film, the focus is not only on the act but also on the surrounding representations that attempt to both show the violent event and hide from the view the horrific experience omits:

> What remains is a conspicuous absence: a configuration where sexual violence against women is an origin of social relations and narratives in which the event itself is subsequently elided [...] the simultaneous presence and disappearance of rape as constantly deferred origin of both plot and social relations is repeated so often as to suggest a basic conceptual principle in the articulation of both social and artistic representations.[17]

The traumatic absence or loss of illusion is very important, as Caruth notes: "the shock of the mind's relation to the threat of death ... not the direct experience of the threat, but precisely the missing of this experience, the fact that, not being experienced in time, it has not yet been fully known."[18] Narrative portrayals, like Lupino's rape scene, of this loss or absence require a structure that embodies these qualities.

Caruth further observes that "trauma describes an overwhelming experience of sudden or catastrophic events in which the response to the event occurs in the often, delayed, uncontrolled repetitive appearance of hallucinations and other intrusive phenomena."[19] Trauma is often illustrated in fiction and in film as not simply the threatening of life but the recognition of the threat occurring as a recognition that occurs, "one moment too late."[20] In *Outrage*, this tension and delayed recognition appears as Ann attempts to integrate herself into a new small bucolic town with a kind hearted pastor. In these attempts, one sees Ann struggling with an apprehension that appears in the film as an erratic or flighty string of behaviors and interactions with others. Ann is represented as grappling with moments of an almost recognition of her experience and appears to battle with the tension between remembering and experiencing.

To explore this type of bifurcated recognition between remembering events and experiencing new moments, directors utilize a narrative structure that deploys aspects that are similar to the narrative presentation of trauma. These aspects appear in narratives in the form of disjointed narrative sequences in the film that often involve repetition and the displacement of subjectivity. For example, Ann's experience post-rape does not appear to follow a traditional narrative arc. Instead, the viewer sees her struggling to fit her new self into a fragmented sense of understanding. In the structuring of narratives of trauma, the necessity and impossibility of truly grasping the threat to life is repeatedly confronted by both the act of survival and the traumatic experience itself. The subject matter of rape thus represents an arena to play out the traumas of experience for Lupino, as evidenced in the various scenes where Ann is seen to lack an awareness or remembrance that could facilitate the ordering of her experience.

Ida Lupino interrogates and integrates trauma in her films, and the subsequent evolutions appearing in her narrative structures reflect the experiences and effects of trauma. The narrative structures of Lupino's films offer an opportunity to capture and to explore the witnessing of the experience and effects of trauma. Lupino's narrative evolution uses elements of trauma to reflect while creating a fiction that captures the external and internal experience of coming to terms with the trauma of rape.

Thus, the focus of this inquiry and reconsideration of Lupino's *Outrage* emphasizes exploring how a film narrative and structure deal with subjects who speak from *and* occupy the abject position of trauma. The experience of trauma operates as a complex interaction between knowing and not knowing that occurs in reaction to a breach in the mind's experience of time, self, and the world. This experience defies and demands attention. As such, the awareness experienced in relation to trauma is often deemed abject. Lupino's rape film narratives embody the trauma and traumatic experiences of rape through the treatment of an experience that does not occur within normal subjective or objective narrative understanding, and occurs in a third space that is self-debasing. Thus, the film narrative engages a structure that differs from previous structures of subjectivity and objectivity. In this engagement, the narrative draws on the previously silenced voice of trauma to generate a different and new presence in the cinematic representation following the act of rape.

Ultimately, the film captures rape, and not only the act of rape but the attempt at creating stable bookends to hold and to engage the experience of rape. The film attempts to explore how one might go about ordering the un-orderable. Judith Lewis Herman, in *Trauma and Recovery*, states, "traumatic events are extraordinary, not because they occur rarely, but rather because they overwhelm the ordinary human adaptations to life."[21] Thus, Ann's struggle is her attempt to reorder her understanding instead of being reordered by external forces in the face of overwhelming and tremendous personal fear and societal expectations. Perhaps that is why Richard Brody's apt observations serve interpretation so well:

> The emotional power and political vision of "Outrage" arises as much from Lupino's inspired images as from the wise and insightful script and the delicately controlled yet freely expressive performances—not the work of great actors but of attentive and sensitive ones who have the benefit of Lupino's discerning direction. It's a haunting, infuriating movie.[22]

Lupino's *Outrage* is infuriating, haunting, and demanding of attention as she addresses elements of trauma's effect on the narrative structure in such a unique yet applicable fashion that the film emphatically stands as a solid example that deserves reconsideration and, most definitely, reevaluation.

Notes

1. William Donati, *Ida Lupino: A Biography* (Lexington: University Press of Kentucky, 1996), 170.
2. Cathy Caruth, *Unclaimed Experience: Trauma, Narrative, and History* (Baltimore: Johns Hopkins University Press, 1996), 5.
3. Ibid.
4. Lynn A. Higgins and Brenda R. Silver, *Rape and Representation* (New York: Columbia University Press, 1991), 306.
5. Pam Cook, "*Outrage* (1950)," in Annette Kuhn (ed.), *Queen of the 'B's: Ida Lupino Behind the Camera* (Westport, CT: Praeger, 1995), 70.
6. Ibid., 63.
7. Carine M. Mardorossian, *Framing the Rape Victim: Gender and Agency Reconsidered* (New Bruswick, NJ: Rutgers University Press, 2014), 32.
8. Richard Brody, "Lupino's Prescient 'Outrage,'" *The New Yorker*, June 16, 2014. http://www.newyorker.com/culture/richard-brody/ida-lupinos-prescient-outrage (accessed October 13, 2014).
9. Caruth, *Unclaimed Experience*, 62.
10. Ibid., 151.
11. Sarah Projansky, *Watching Rape: Film and Television in Postfeminist Culture* (New York: New York University Press, 2001), 4–5.
12. Caruth, *Unclaimed Experience*, 11.
13. As qtd. in William Donati, *Ida Lupino: A Biography* (Lexington: University Press of Kentucky, 1996), 173.
14. Projansky, *Watching Rape*, 7.
15. As qtd. In Donati, *Ida Lupino: A Biography*, 173.
16. Projansky, *Watching Rape*, 21.
17. Higgins and Silver, *Rape and Representation*, 27.
18. Caruth, *Unclaimed Experience*, 62.
19. Ibid., 11.
20. Ibid., 62.
21. Judith Lewis Herman, *Trauma and Recovery* (New York, NY: BasicBooks, 1992), 33.
22. Brody, "Lupino's Prescient 'Outrage.'"

13

Ida Lupino, Hitchhiking into Darkness

Phillip Sipiora

> Ethos anthropoi daimon.
>
> *Character for man is destiny.*
>
> —HERACLITUS

The Hitch-Hiker (1953) is a gritty, dark disturbing film that established Ida Lupino as the first female noir director. American noir is well known for its emphasis on twisted plots, broken lives, dreary atmospheres, and a decadent primary character, coupled with uneven dispositions of justice, whether informal or jurisprudential. Noir philosophical outlook is usually bleak, often Darwinian, as individuals struggle to subvert the behavioral mores of their time.

As Darwin notes in *On the Origin of Species*, "Nothing is easier than to admit in words the truth of the universal struggle for life, or more difficult—at least I have found it so—than constantly to bear this conclusion in mind."[1] Lupino's brilliant noir art dramatizes Darwin's characterization of the universal fight for life in the lives of two very ordinary men, Roy Collins and Gil Bowen, who naïvely step into the trap of a master predator, Emmett Myers. The noir enterprise of depicting individuals coming to grips with the grim reality of life as a never-won-battle is a deeply philosophical calculus of life. According to phenomenologist Merleau-Ponty: "Philosophy does not raise questions and does not provide answers that would little by little fill in the blanks. The questions are within our life, within our history: they are born there, they die there, if they have found a response, more often than not they are transformed there."[2] Philosophy, therefore, is a necessary part of exploring what it means to probe the human experience, what it means to be human, what constitutes *being*. Lupino understands this complicated matrix of existential angst and her exposition of this phenomenon is an essential part of her film *ouevre*, particularly in her darkest film that explicitly chronicles road terror.

However, the viewer must earn the meaning, and *The Hitch-Hiker* is clearly not a typical American noir. There is no femme fatale, no mysterious incidents or urban scenes of shadowy alleys, little darkness of night, no explicit scenes of violence (although there is horrifying off-screen mayhem), and the ending of the film is relatively anticlimactic. Killer villain Emmett Myers is straight out of noir central casting: mean, disfigured, callous, and unrelentingly devoid of any ethical sensibility. So, this film is both within and outside of the American noir mainstream. The focus of my interpretation is to analyze qualities in *The Hitch-Hiker* that make it an original and valuable contribution to noir cinema, precisely because of the innovative emphases Lupino employs in her narrative, particularly her intense interest in specific expressions of the dark, Darwinian-inflected side of life, the heat and press of humanity.

Surface Structure

The storyline is relatively simple. Emmett Myers turns out to be a psychopath who has committed multiple murders while hitchhiking between Illinois and California. Engaging plot segmentation innovatively precedes his murders. The opening frame, for example, reveals a large revolver pointed directly at viewers and reveals the back of a car with an Illinois license plate, which connects the film to a well-publicized story of a murdering hitchhiker that lays the groundwork for the general narrative. The camera then pans up into the inside of the car, where we see three passengers in the convertible. The stage is set; however, all is not well. The next shot is yet another fragment of a subject: Lupino's powerful, deft use of cinematic synecdoche. We see only feet coming out of a car door.[3] We hear a woman's scream, and then a single shot pierces the darkness (presumably killing the woman as we see her purse falling out of the open car door). We then see car wheels moving, perhaps playing off of a familiar cinematic trope of moving feet, parts disconnected from the whole with no organic unity in either human or machine. Violence is off-screen, and viewers only have sounds and post-homicide fragments of evidence, such as a purse and the partially visible splayed body of the female victim, with the arm of a dead male draped over the steering wheel. These shots of displacement and disjuncture are potent metaphors at work that convey violence more violent than if viewers saw complete gore, rife with bloody bodies. These teaser tastes are not original with Lupino, of course, but they do demonstrate her sense of irony and powerfully intense visual metaphor. Five minutes into the film, we see only the lower legs of Myers, another rich synecdoche reminiscent of running feet in Hitchcock's *39 Steps*. Lupino was quite familiar with the style of Hitchcock, and her nickname on shooting set was "Mother." As Christopher Huber notes, "*The Hitch-Hiker* and her TV work had secured Lupino the moniker 'the female Hitchcock' for her 'cool hand with terror'."[4] Lupino's artisanal skills were clearly apparent to those who worked with her. Huber fondly recalls the director and her nurturing instincts: "I will always remember her as the Greatest Mother of Them All." And he declares: "One thing is for sure: on the set, Ida was Mother."[5] Lupino asserts her matronly status in unambiguous terms: "Keeping a feminine approach is vital; men hate bossy females," she explained. "You do not tell a man; you suggest to him. 'Darlings, Mother has a problem. I'd love to do this. Can you do it? It sounds kooky, I know. But can you do this for Mother?' And, they do it."[6] There can be no question that Lupino was as well versed in the art of rhetoric as she was in the art of cinema.

Lupino is a master of suspense as she orchestrates a slow, tense, tease shot of Myers' lower body, the camera following the killer's feet as he circles around the car. Later, in a gesture of *aposiopesis*, which is a pause or silence that leaves viewers' imaginations to fill in or create a "missing" scene, conveying an impression of unwillingness or inability to continue.[7] Our creative powers visualize the gruesome scene as a policeman searches the dead-of-night scene with his flashlight, illuminating the brutalized woman, legs splayed alongside her dead traveler on the road of death. Nondiegetic music envelops the scene in an eerie, foreboding atmosphere. The glare of the handheld light, in a close-up shot, creates magnified distortion. Juxtaposed newspaper headlines scream a horrific story: "Couple Found Murdered," "Nationwide Search for Hitch-Hiker Slayer," "Hitch-Hike Slayer," "Ex-Convict Myers Suspect in Hitch-Hiker Atrocities."[8] Lupino shrewdly sets the first frame in bold headlines to terrify viewers, as they sit safely in a movie theater:

> This is a true story of a man and a gun and a car. The gun belonged to the man. The car might have been yours—or that young couple across the aisle. What you see in the next seventy minutes could have happened to you.

The next scene reveals a silhouette of Myers hitchhiking on the side of the road. Two good-natured, kindly fishermen pals, Roy Bowen (Edmond O'Brien) and Gil Collins (Frank Lovejoy), invite Myers into their car with absolutely no anticipation that they have endangered their lives. Black murder *ad seriatim*. Lupino is also a master of terror, interlaced with keen emotional understanding of necessary movements in moments of terror. As Andrew Goff notes: "Absolutely assured in her creation of the bleak, noir atmosphere—whether in the claustrophobic confines of the car, or lost in the arid expanses of the desert—Lupino never relaxes the tension for one moment. Yet her emotional sensitivity is also upfront: charting the changes in the menaced men's relationship as they bicker about how to deal with their captor, stressing that only through friendship can they survive."[9] Intertwining raw terror with brief respites of relatively tranquil emotional interludes is surely an important and dynamic calculus in Lupino's masterpiece.

The surface action of *The Hitch-Hiker* is relatively uncomplicated: The two decent family men pick up a psychotic escaped convict who has already murdered two people. Lupino sets in motion a narrative trajectory that sharply contrasts images of masculinity: a lunatic sociopath versus caring, honest men. Early on, Myers calmly placidly informs Gil and Roy that he intends to murder them when the ride is over, a terrifying declaration that he repeats later in the film. The film's opening announces that it is an "actual story." This kind of narrative opening is common in crime drama, then and now, whether "true" or not, because it sets the stage for realism, which is intimately and intricately related to the genre of crime narratives, which must be accepted as realistic to viewers in order to instill authentic terror and horror. Crime drama that fails to be realistic risks the possibility of generating a comic response, which occasionally happens, for example, in hyperbolic "slasher" cinema. American audiences always seem willing to pay a premium for "truth" because narratives that relate to lived experience are close to home in instilling fear in us (Figure 13.1).

The sources of *The Hitch-Hiker* are, indeed, a series of brutal homicides of despicable cruelty, and the odd combination of psychosis intertwined with evil, akin to sociopath Norman Bates in *Psycho* (1960, Alfred Hitchcock). Ida Lupino was surely influenced by Hitchcock's work, particularly his probing into the complex matrix of evil/madness and the crafting of narratives that depict macabre and gruesome depictions of bad humanity gone mad, and Norman Bates is but one example in Hitchcock's corpus. And Lupino was a kind of cinematic hitchhiker herself, drawing upon the techniques, styles, and emphases of other artists, as do all directors, in bringing her instincts and talents to fullest fruition. In relationship to Hitchcock's crime art, psychopath/sociopath Emmett Myers is not unlike Norman Bates, both reprehensible in their depictions of primal, complex matrices of frightening and calculating synthesis of evil and sickness. Myers, like Bates, kills at will precisely because he has no ability to either self-reflect or control his horrific impulses. Myers' mind and emotions are continuously enraged, which significantly enriches *The Hitch-Hiker*. Early on in the film, Lupino cannily assembles scenes that capture Myers' moral disfigurement through synecdochal image displacement: at the beginning, we do not see Myers' face, or even his upper torso, as the camera pans only his body and feet. The camera eloquently captures the physical detachment of a subhuman character, illustrating a fearful detachment from sanity and morality. "When Talman enters the protagonists' back seat," observes Michael Atkinson: "it's a black abyss, and the film grabs onto the very cinematic uneasiness

FIGURE 13.1 *Terrorizing the audience.*

when you look into a man's shadowed face and see absolutely nothing."[10] Myers kills coldly with calm nerves, and his acts of violence become particularly powerful precisely because we do not witness them. Myers is eerily reminiscent of Hans Beckert (Peter Lorre) in Fritz Lang's *M* (1931), a haunting portrait of a sadistic, soulless pedophilic murderer who preys on prepubescent girls. Myers is similar to Beckert and Bates in that they are all complex outsiders, aliens in their own culture yet also aliens within their twisted, disjointed selves, disenfranchised from their connection to their communities. Myers is clearly disconnected from the ethical codes and cultural bonding and that bind Gil and Roy together. For example, Lupino shrewdly reveals Myers' lack of cultural connection (and knowledge) in the scenes in Mexico, where Myers not only has no knowledge of Mexican mores, but he does not even know that their language is Spanish, referring instead to it as "Mexican." Myers is just as contemptuous of Mexican citizens as he is of average Americans, particularly Gil and Roy as exemplars, and, of course, Myers has contempt for law enforcement. Unredeemable sociopaths often rely upon impulsive scorn for anything "normal" in order to fuel their debased, despotic, and paranoid desires.[11] Indeed, in the final scene Myers stupidly attempts to assault Mexican police as they arrest him, revealing his perpetual state of impulse gratification and arrested development. He is pure ID in the worst sense of the term, as revealed from the very beginning of the film, evidenced by his impulsive behavior and rash decisions.[12]

An early scene presents an imageless sound of a woman's scream, punctuated by gunfire, which forces us to engage macabre horror, and the result is a particularly foreboding form of terror. Lupino surely learned a few things from Hitchcock about creating horror, and her approach to terror and horror facilitates her penetrating treatment of the mind's fragile inscape, as noted by Atkinson: "[I]n *The Hitch-Hiker*, arguably Lupino's best film and the only true noir directed by a woman, two utterly average middle-class American men are held at gunpoint and slowly psychologically broken by a serial killer."[13] Indeed, Roy and Gil are in the process of being broken minute by minute.

Lupino's compactly written and directed noir appears, on the surface, to be a straightforward tale of abduction and terror. Yet there is a deeper noir narrative structure, rich in nuance, technique, and philosophical implication. This black film is much more than a tale of dangerous highways, bad luck, and tangled love. Indeed, there is no romantic love whatsoever in the film (beyond casual references to the fishermen's generic love for their families): "The Hitch-Hiker is not just another existentialist noir parable about bad fortune and men with crushed hearts and a rapacious world consuming the innocent schmuck."[14] Myers is a crazed, shadowy sociopath, relatively uncommon fare in noir, with some exceptions such as Tommy Udo (Richard Widmark) in *Kiss of Death* (1947, Edmund Goulding) (Figures 13.2–13.4).

FIGURE 13.2 *Norman Bates (Anthony Perkins) in* Psycho.

FIGURE 13.3 *Tommy Udo (Richard Widmark) in* Kiss of Death.

FIGURE 13.4 *Emmett Myers (William Talman) in* The Hitch-Hiker.

Gallery of Sociopaths

Myers, like Udo, derives pleasure in taunting and emotionally torturing his captives. One striking example is when Myers forces Gil to shoot at a can held by Roy near his head in a "William Tell" game, further revealing Myers' unhinged and unethical core nature. Gil struggles to do what he is told, fearful of killing his friend, but also mindful that Myers will kill him if he does not shoot and risk Roy's life. This "game" is a form of sadistic portraiture that reveals a morally insane narrative and thematic configuration, once again distinguishing Lupino as a protégé of Hitchcock. *The Hitch-Hiker* is a series of scenes of descriptive vignettes that reveal characters in search of shards of ontological meaning. This quest pattern is not limited to cinematic and literary characters, of course, but extends to viewers and readers as well. The audience is inextricably intertwined with Lupino in the investigation of subjects and various contexts of subjectivity. As Howard Pearce articulates, "We connect with other subjectivities; we apprehend structures of relationships that are not simply perceived; we engage in acts of the imagination that interpolate, extrapolate, extend, confirm meaningfulness and purposefulness, in art as in life. As reflectors of the artist, we contribute to his patterning of events and images by seeing meaningfully."[15] Pearce's sentient insight emphasizes viewers' dual (and symbiotic) roles in creating *and* participating in cinematic "reality" (Figure 13.5).

The film is structured on a matrix of phenomenological dependencies. Myers depends on Gil and Roy, and they codepend on him (and each other), all for the same reason: they desperately need one another to stay alive. Codependency is one of the film's driving motifs, and plot segmentation is relatively simple in the diurnal experiences of captor and captives. Myers methodically controls the lives of Roy and Gil under the constant threat of killing them, and they know, all too well, of his pragmatic experience in murder. Myers requires safe haven in their car en route to Santa Rosalia, where he hopes to elude a massive international manhunt. So, the narrative quickly becomes a thriller in a race against time. Yet Myers only has power over Gil and Roy because he has a gun and the will to use it. The ongoing threat of death gives the film an urgency and tension that is intensified by drab scenes in Mexican desert rural areas (actually filmed in southern California). Dry parched desert scenes create an atmosphere of loneliness and detachment that is well within the noir tradition, even though a number of scenes are shot during the day. The bleakness of the film is exacerbated by a general lack of tension-releasing interludes providing any respite from the calamity of road trip terror.

The film's unceasing dread reminds us that Lupino is so very talented in portraying victims, as contributors to this volume have so effectively articulated. As Martin Scorsese argues, "What is at stake in Lupino's films is the psyche of the victim."[16] Lupino's powerful film, *Outrage* (1950), is an

FIGURE 13.5 *Gil Bowen forced to channel William Tell.*

excellent illustration of victimhood. A sexual assault victim, Ann Walton (Mala Powers), is a young woman who lives with her family and works in an office, a typical portrait of a young professional woman in the 1950s. Early in the film, Ann is brutally sexually assaulted, and the narrative addresses the way that sexual assault victims were treated at the time. Sadly, victims were not always treated as victims deserving compassion and respect. Ann experiences from severe trauma and leaves her family to relocate to a rural life. Later in the film, without consent, a ranch worker kisses Ann, and, in defending herself, she nearly kills him. She is arrested but is released when the full circumstances of her assault become known. The interpretive of her legal resolution is clear: society carries significant responsibility for helping victims of sexual assaults.

Lupino's empathic portraiture is clearly a major motif in *The Hitch-Hiker*, as Roy and Gil are sympathetically depicted in direct response to the barbarity and irrationality of Myers. Lupino's scripting is savvy because she understands the potential challenges of a crime drama involving only three men. There is no significant female presence to distract from the bleakness of this noir. As Atkinson notes, "It's a very dark movie: when Talman enters the protagonists' back seat, it's a black abyss, and the film grabs onto the very cinematic uneasiness when you look into a man's shadowed face and see absolutely nothing."[17] Myers clearly does not care if he kills or not. Self-preservation is the only expediency that he knows, and his selfishness defines and influences the surface and deep structure of the film (Figure 13.6).

FIGURE 13.6 *Terror on the road.*

Deep Structure

The deep structure of the film reveals a complexity more interwoven and philosophical than superficial, storyboard representations. Although *The Hitch-Hiker* was a low-budget film made over roughly six weeks, it is not without its complications and subtle textures. There are interwoven layers of meaning that may offer a glimpse into Lupino's treatment of noir and simultaneous reaction against noir, particularly against black cinema as commonly reduced to fundamental human failings: evil and crime. Lupino offers us a kind of film that is representative of American noir, so very popular in the 1940s and 1950s. Lupino also articulates complex psychological, intellectual, and emotional sensibilities. More specifically, Lupino probes fundamental issues of cinematic subjectivity. Film subjectivity is always a complex issue, and in *The Hitch-Hiker* (as well as in *Outrage* and *The Bigamist*) Lupino surgically probes fundamental issues of agency, intersubjectivity, and the ways in which they interrelate to call to attention two fundamental interpretive questions: How does one learn from experience and how does one act based on that acquired knowledge? How does Lupino represent *being*? Hence, Lupino creates two competing stories within a general narrative trajectory. First, the surface of the film depicts the abduction of two citizens by a bloodthirsty murderer. Second, the narrative chronicles an evolving relationship between Gil and Roy, a friendship whose metamorphosis into a much stronger bond is the direct result of their abduction and their responses, collectively and individually, to their plight of terror. Parallel tracks of actions and verbal exchanges in this seventy-one-minute thriller reveal qualities of character that define Roy and Gil as two good men who value loyalty to each other above all else, and they build upon it to forge something greater than it was at the beginning of the film. According to Merleau-Ponty, there is a psychological and philosophical wall between us and others, but it is a wall that we build together, each putting a stone in the niche left by the other.[18] Roy and Gil fill in those interstices. Ethical responsibility is a cornerstone code in this film, and it is the result of a vacuum that resides at the heart of the two decades of American noir: "[A]t the heart of the noir mood or tone of alienation, pessimism, and cynicism we find, on the one hand, the rejection or loss of clearly defined ethical values."[19] A phenomenological approach to interpretation is not explanatory and can only be exploratory in examining human relations and probing for meaningful connections, as Merleau-Ponty characterizes the phenomenological act as phenomenology as "a matter of describing, not of explaining or analysing."[20] The ordeal of Gil and Roy is an illustration of how their collective, defining responses to the sociopathy of Myers transforms them individually as well as their relationship to each other. Lupino deftly presents through description their analytical and interpretive experiences in a series of scenes demonstrating her rich cinematic powers, which lead viewers to salient interpretive inferences. Cinema would seem to be a continuous, concentric series of analytical and interpretive loops, from writer to actor to director to viewer.

The Hitch-Hiker chronicles the loss of ethical values, but also depicts the reclamation of those values through narrative encounters, lending to the illustration of demonstrated ethics as a direct result of cinematic encounters. "Ethics," as Emmanuel Levinas and Merleau-Ponty suggest, exists necessarily in relationships and encounters as Levinas examines human interactions in terms of personal interfacement: "[T]he face [is] a source from which all meaning appears."[21] As Levinas argues, summarily, in *Totality and Infinity*, a collaborator or participant in a discourse exchange necessarily undergoes some level of ethical transaction precisely as a result of the encounter. Levinas notes the importance of daily ritual in response to a contaminated, dangerous world: "At the very moment when the world seems to break up we still take it seriously and perform reasonable acts and undertakings, the condemned man still drinks his glass of rum. To call it everyday and condemn it as inauthentic is to fail to recognize the sincerity of hunger and thirst."[22] The daily rum for Gil and Roy is the continual reinforcement of their bond of friendship, with some occasional setbacks, as noted. And it is precisely the chain of interactions (interfacings) among Myers, Gil, and Roy that determine the meaning they come to know, particularly in the case of the fishermen. Lupino erects this wall, scene by scene, as she chronicles the evolution of the complex relationship among Myers, Gil, and Roy. However, it is the relationship between Roy and Gil that becomes the epicenter of this phenomenological narrative. These portraits offer insight into Gil and Roy's respective qualities of character and ethics as revealed through their verbal and physical encounters. The interactions of the fishermen are striking examples of the importance of "interfacing" and its strategic role in determining meaning in interrelationships, necessarily with powerful ethical implications. The interactions of Roy and Gil reveal their essential natures, which are further contextualized by their responses to the exigencies of their capture. Lupino deftly reveals a metamorphosis of character, catalyzed by dramatic events, such as an attempted escape, a serious ankle injury, and repeated psychological torture. We learn much about Roy and Gil as we witness their adapting coping mechanisms in dealing with their bizarre plight. After Roy has injured his foot, Gil gives an oath to his friend: "I'll never leave you out here alive." These words exemplify a sacred bond of loyalty, which comes forth as a result of the constant threat of death, revealing the phenomenological power of cinema. As Vivian Sobchack argues, "Cinema thus transposes, without being completely transforming, those modes of being alive and consciously embodied in the world that count for each of us as *direct* experience: as experience 'centered' in that particular, situated, and solely occupied existence sensed first as 'Here, where the world touches,' and then as 'Here, where the world is sensible, here, where I am'."[23] Hence the power of phenomenological moments that catalyze and define act(s) of being. Gil and Roy, moment by moment, are shaped by their transformative experiences.

Lupino astutely portrays emerging inner sides of these characters as they grow through their harrowing experiences. Indeed, Gil and Roy become just as compelling as the sociopath, and perhaps even more so. Their change in character development is notable by the film's end as they clearly are different from what they were before Emmet Myers. The infrastructure of this formidable film represents human existence as a common man journey of interrogation, a search of not what life "is" or "means," but rather an ongoing, yet unachievable, quest for tiny shreds of meaning imbedded in words and actions that sometimes function as stepping stones into some small moments of momentary insight into shared experience. This process is emphatically phenomenological.

Sobchack's deep structure theoretical analysis is a useful tool in examining *The Hitch-Hiker* because it provides a probing, exhaustive analysis of the complexity and interpretive insight of phenomenological phenomena in cinema generally. Although Sobchack does not specifically discuss Lupino or *The Hitch-Hiker*, her seminal analysis opens the door for a phenomenological exploration of Lupino's masterpiece. My specific approach of phenomenological subjectivity refers to Lupino's depiction of Roy and Gil in their struggle to know (epistemology) and their search for how to function (ontology). Their interactions with each other and with Myers reveal much about character of the two endearing (and enduring) pals in their Darwinian struggle to survive, which requires an ability to quickly adapt to changing circumstances as they do with a sociopathic killer. Each and every encounter with Myers is a series of kairic moments, "special, threatening time," that carries the potential for immediate death at any time, thus potentially intensifying terror, trauma, and horror in viewers.

Gil and Roy's quest begins with the fishermen driving at dawn. They have planned a routine, unadventurous adventure: two husbands off for a safe male retreat of fishing and camaraderie. As they drive along the California highway, the naïve vacationers see a hitchhiker, stop, and wave the hitchhiker into their car, a simple, friendly gesture that describes and defines the quality of the men. There is no audible dialogue. The scene is a common occurrence in mid-1950s America on the highway: two good men helping out a stranger. Yet five minutes into the film, once again, we see only the lower legs of Myers in the dark of night, standing next to a car, presumably the one that picked him up, sans living driver. When Gil and Roy pick up Myers, he is standing next to a car and he has murdered his ride, William Johnson. Myers proudly announces to Gil and Roy that he used the empty chamber in his revolver on "the last guy." At this moment, the pals clearly recognize their plight in the hands of a sociopath.

In the back seat of the car, the hitchhiker pulls a gun, but still shows no face, creating an ominous mood. Suddenly the sharply, illuminated face of Myers appears as he barks orders at them. His prisoners meekly acquiesce to his commands. They are not hardened, like their captor, and the two pals are only two suburban husbands off for a getaway weekend fishing retreat (a trip based on lies told to their wives). Fate intervenes, as it so often does in the world of noir. The verbal exchanges with Myers are staccato, surreal, and unnatural. Lupino calls our attention to this trope of asymmetry: a world and society in disorder, intertwined in disjointed human experience. Myers' eyes come straight out of mid-1920s German Expressionism: unnatural, piercing, soulless, freakish windows into derangement, not unlike the eyes of psychopathic fiend, Hans Beckert (Peter Lorre) in *M*. The effect on viewers is one of piercing horror, a Lupino trademark as she sets forth successive frames of human depravity. No dialogue is necessary to complement these images, which stand alone in revealing and eliciting terror, shared by the captives and their viewers. As John Krewson observes, "As a screenwriter and director, Lupino had an eye for the emotional truth hidden within the taboo or mundane, making a series of B-styled pictures which featured sympathetic, honest portrayals of such controversial subjects as unmarried mothers, bigamy, and rape. . . . [I]n *The Hitch-Hiker*, arguably Lupino's best film and the only true noir directed by a woman, two utterly average middle-class American men are held at gunpoint and slowly psychologically broken by a serial killer."[24] I think that it is important to note that they are broken; yet, they do not break, an important distinction (Figure 13.7).

Lupino consistently presents experience through dynamic, usually emotional exchanges, which are not limited simply to characters with other

FIGURE 13.7 *Eyes of derangement.*

characters, yet also include the director with characters, and intertwine the audience, which is an essential part of complex configuration that generates meaning in this multi-textured noir. We share the terror that Gil and Roy experience in our interfacing with them and their plight.

In the tradition of noir, crime and punishment are governing criteria and Emmet Myers is obviously the dark film's requisite central character, and he must, of course, be punished. However, Roy Collins and Gil Bowen are subjects of considerable emphasis, not only as victims of Myers but, more important, as evolving characters. The husbands are simple, middle-class men. They love their families, their work, and spending time together. Whatever character flaws they may have, such as lying to their wives about the trip, are relatively less important in the film than their growth as loyal friends. And some of their male pattern weaknesses have an ironic and comic undertone. For example, prior to the Myers' encounter with the men, they arrive at the front of a gentleman's club in Mexicali (a familiar stomping ground), and the street barker attempts to coax the men inside for some excitement. However, Gil has fallen asleep in the car, oblivious to the bawdy enticement, and he is probably beyond the days of his bawdy youth. These men are not wild carousers at heart, and they prefer the company of each other and their fishing gear, a .22 rifle, and camping equipment to enrich their lives. Friendship and shared experience are the goals of this vacation.

After the men have been taken prisoner by Myers, they drive to a grocery store and a revealing encounter takes place. As Myers directs the actions of

Roy and Gil, he encounters a little Mexican girl, and Myers is gruff with her. Roy instinctively pats the little girl on the head, a gesture of consolation. Roy performs a minor, yet important, rescue of her from Myers. Roy says to the girl, "*Vaya con Dios.*" When Myers asks what he said, Roy responds, "You wouldn't understand." Roy's sharp retort is semantic, moral, and metaphysical. Myers' words in this encounter reveal him to be a misanthropic psychopath, also revealed by his facial expression, and simultaneously illustrates Roy's compassionate nature. Myers' contempt for the girl is not disconnected from his reaction to everyone and everything. For example, as Roy and Gil later break open the lock on a gas pump, Myers kills a barking dog without a second thought, and this act of cruelty, once again, reflects his basic nature. The antisocial, ethically corrupt nature of Myers is further illustrated when Myers later examines Gil's inscribed wristwatch, an important token of affection that is left behind by Gil as a clue to their location. Sentimentalism is not in Myers' nature as he sharply informs the men: "I had a watch like this once when I was seventeen. Nobody gave it to me. I just took it. I knocked off a broken down jewelry store." So, another Lupino synecdoche, another exemplum of character differentiation that Lupino deftly intertwines into her narrative that reveals essential character.

There is never any question about Myers' solipsism, isolation, and sociopathic egotism. In a burst of faux cultural philosophy, Myers taunts his prisoners: "You guys are soft. You know what makes you that way? You're up to your necks in IOUs. You're suckers. You're scared to get out on your own. You always had it good for yourself. Well, not me. No one ever gave me anything. So I don't owe nobody. . . especially if you got them the point of a gun. That really scares them." Myers' ontological code is simple: survival by any means necessary with no regard for the ethical implications of his behavior, which is in stark contrast to the nurturing fishermen, whose ever-present ontological code is one of compassion and care for others, demonstrated in large and small ways, including (and especially) in their conversations. Some scenes in the film are set at night, when fear and terror become magnified because of mysteries associated with the dark unknown. At one night camp, Myers tells Collins, "You haven't got a chance. You guys are going to die, that's all. It's just a question of when." This noir thriller contains occasional deadpan exchanges, which can turn on a dime from vicious confrontation to banter, such as Myers' offer to buy the men a beer so that they can relax. The series of exchanges reveal Lupino's deft hand in coauthoring the script with Collier Young as they continually emphasize the instinctive, pervasive cruelty that dominates Myers' nature as he uses fear and terror to control his subjects. Unlike other hommes fatales, Myers reveals almost no sense of humor, when, for example, he chides Gil and Roy for deceiving their wives and going to Mexico for "dames." Myers is pathetic, and there is no indication that he has ever had a "normal" relationship with dames or anyone else. Myers as outcast is illustrated by his awkward presence as the trio heads South into another country. The social environment of the Mexican setting is warm and kindly (in contrast to stark and foreboding physical settings). Everyone the threesome encounters is friendly: a gas station attendant, storekeeper, and a couple in a convertible, for example. There is, at times, a comforting presence in the Mexican universe, yet there is also concomitant danger in the air. As the three men search for fishing opportunities, a police plane and a helicopter circle overhead, reminding us of the vultures seen earlier. Death is in the camera's viewfinder as we see the ground perspective of the plane pilot. The three men scurry among the desert bushes and rocks, like frightened mice hiding themselves from a cat on a staircase. Gil desperately yells to the pilot for help, his words lost in the engine noise. As Roy falls to his knees in despair, Myers' commands to Gil are ironic and callous: "Leave him alone. Can't you see that he's praying." Yes, indeed, Roy is praying precisely because the situation is so perilous in dealing with a psychotic killer in a noir jungle. Myers' disregard for the values the men hold is yet another example of his total disconnection with the "normal" world, which makes him all the more dangerous.

Against the serene interactions with local residents, there is a chilling counter background, dramatically illustrated by the growing intensity of the international manhunt. For example, a radio news announcer screams "Race against death," pouring fear into the ears of Myers, Roy, and Gil. Lupino intensifies the frenzied atmosphere with her use of nondiegetic music, typical of the noir tradition: jarring horns, violins, trumpets, and so forth. There are several close, cramped shots of the characters in the car, revealing and intensifying dramatic tension. These scenes are systematically balanced by panoramic, topographical long shots that provide a respite to the claustrophobic atmosphere of the automobile holding cell. Action and inaction are syncopated, as Lauren Rabinovitz keenly notes, "The editing style shifts emphasis from mounting suspense through crisp action to the strain on the characters of passively waiting" (98).[25] A little more than halfway through the film, Lupino increases dramatic tension with an escape plan scene. The conversation between the men becomes intense as Roy explains to Gil his plan to physically confront Myers, which foreshadows the impending physical confrontation between Gil and Roy. Gil is reticent about Roy's plan and tells Roy that "we got to stay together." Gil responds, "I will go it alone if necessary." This encounter reveals a dramatic and unexpected fissure in the relationship between the men, who were in agreement about nearly everything before the escape plan was hatched. This temporary rupture infuses additional tension to the film, and it reveals the power that Myers has in severely affecting the relationship between the pals. Yet events are in a state of flux, and, soon after escaping to the highway in the middle of the night, they are recaptured by Myers as he chases them down by car, creating a near-comic scene of an automobile pursuing escapees, as if they were the guilty ones. The recapture episode with Myers clearly influences the evolving relationship between Roy and Gil, and it is a poignant moment of epiphany. This kind of cinematic infrastructure reveals and emphasizes human existence as an infinite journey of interrogation, a search of not what life "is" or "means," but rather an ongoing, yet unachievable, quest for fragments of suspended knowledge that function as stepping stones for yet further probing. Hitch-Hiker is a series of transactions that do not fit neatly into a simple cause and effect narrative pattern, yet each encounter undoubtedly leaves a distinctive residue. In the acrimonious encounters between Gil and Roy, for example, they do not lead to estrangement and disintegration, but rather to an intense, deeper relationship that becomes enhanced precisely because of the stress and tension they experience in their conflict with Myers, leading to the consolidation and enrichment of their relationship. This dynamic calculus is an example of productive conflict. This specific pattern of phenomenological cause and effect is a recurring, signature gesture in Lupino's best work and it characterizes her legacy as a director.

Myers' overriding control of the two friends leads to a range of unexpected effects. For example, when Roy threatens Myers, Gil knocks out Roy, facilitating Myers' reassertion of control over them. This scene shows Lupino's continuing complication of Gil and Roy's ability to function within a chaotic matrix of emotion and reason. They are so terrorized that sometimes they act and react without thought or consequences. Ultimately, they become unified, but the road is long and bumpy, and friend-on-friend violence reveals a breakdown in their common bonds of beliefs/values. The immediate effect is to increase dramatic tension by calling attention to the stress both within and outside of their relationship, thus energizing the narrative trajectory. When Roy falls to his knees in desperation, Myers' words to Gil are ironic and callous: "Leave him alone. Can't you see that he's praying." Yes, indeed, Roy is praying. He has no other options at this point in time. The friends have run out of natural resources in dealing with the barbarism of Myers.

Adjudication

As the film progresses toward the dramatic conclusion, the action becomes as ominous and foreboding as the black night in which the characters are barely visible, mere human shadows groping in the dark. Once they arrive at the dock, Myers desperately attempts to evade encroaching Mexican police. The threesome hide under a bridge traversed by law enforcement as a doppelgänger motif is woven into the scene. Myers comes up with a plan to switch clothes, and therefore identities, with Roy. Myers states, "You know, Collins, you'd look just like Emmet Myers." The obvious implication is that Roy would *be* Myers in the eyes of the police and, therefore, would probably be killed, as Myers informs Collins. Gill wryly responds to Myers,

FIGURE 13.8 *German Expressionist angst in* The Hands of Orlac.

"And that would solve all of your problems, wouldn't it?" This scene is yet another example of Lupino's touch of irony, brilliantly set and scripted in the murky fog of night. As the three men proceed to the shore, Myers continues to taunt Roy and Gil. He is very specific in ridiculing their bonds of friendship and loyalty: "You guys are really fools. If you weren't, one of you would have gotten away. But you kept thinking about one another, so you missed some chances." Myers then announces that he is now going to kill them as they have outlived their usefulness. As they progress toward a bleak denouement, Myers has decided that this is the time for Roy's murder by cop, and Myers orders Roy to walk toward the waiting police, who nervously wait with weapons drawn. As the police commence firing, Roy screams, "I'm not Myers." However, good fortune is with Roy, and he is not killed. Gil knows that he must act, and he springs into action, viciously punching Myers, knocking the revolver out of his hand. The killer no longer controls either man, and the Mexican police quickly subdue him. The dynamic of the situation has radically changed, and it is now Gil who gives orders to Myers: "Do as he tells you. You're all through." For the first time in the film, Myers has a discernibly frightened look in his eyes, once again akin to German Expressionist figures, such as Paul Orlac in *The Hands of Orlac* (1924) when Orlac comes to believe that he possesses murderous hands, which define him (Figure 13.8, *The Hands of Orlac*). Killer Myers recognizes that he truly is "finished off," and he becomes frenzied once he is under police control. In an act of desperation and still in handcuffs, Myers lunges violently at the police. Fuelled by pent-up rage, Roy viciously punches Myers twice while he is held by police. Myers' moment of destiny has expired. At the film's end, Gil consoles his friend with words that sum up their relationship: "It's all right, Roy, it's all right," as the buddies walk off into the good night. This rough and rumble noir pits savage Darwinian survivalism versus bonds of loyalty, and human friendship wins out in the end, a reaffirmation of the ethical, ontological, and social order. *The Hitch-Hiker* ends where it begins—in the dead of night—which is the inevitable destination to which Myers has hitchhiked himself. Gil and Roy, involuntary passengers into the darkness of night, are now safe and can anticipate the light of day—and maybe even go fishing.

Notes

1 Charles Darwin, *On the Origin of Species*. A Facsimile of the First Edition (Cambridge: Harvard University Press, 1964), 62.

2 Maurice Merleau-Ponty, *The Visible and the Invisible*. Ed. Claude Lefort. Trans. Alphonso Lingis (Evanston, IL: Northwestern University Press, 1968), 105.

3 The camera focusing only on moving feet in this scene is reminiscent of Alfred Hitchcock's treatment of motion; the synecdochic shot adds an element of suspense and terror to the scene. What we do not see is often more frightening than what we do see because of our imaginations. There are no limits on human imagination.

4 Christoph Huber. Available at http://cinema-scope.com/features/mother-of-all-of-us-ida-lupino-the-filmaker (accessed July 18, 2016).

5 Ibid.

6 Ibid.

7 Richard A. Lanham, *A Handlist of Rhetorical Terms* (Berkeley, Los Angeles, CA: University of California Press, 1991), 20.

8 These headlines are not unlike those that chronicled the actual murders that provided the background for *The Hitch-Hiker*.

9 Geoff Andrew, "The Hitch-hiker," *Time Out London*, 2017. Available at www.timeout.com/london/film/the-hitch-hiker (accessed September 8, 2017).

10 Michael Atkinson, "A Noir Journey into No-Woman's Land: Ida Lupino's *The Hitch-Hiker*," January 21, 2011. Available at https://web.archive.org/web/20170114062203/http:/www.fandor.com/keyframe/a-noir-journey-into-no-womans-land-ida-lupinos-the-hitch-hiker (accessed August 16, 2017).

11 Characteristics of a Sociopath. Available at http://www.healthguidance.org/entry/15850/1/Characteristics-of-a-Sociopath.html (accessed August 24, 2017).

12 Ibid.

13. Atkinson, "A Noir Journey into No-Woman's Land: Ida Lupino's *The Hitch-Hiker*".
14. Ibid.
15. Howard D. Pearce, "*The Shining* as *Lichtung*: Kubrick's Film, Heidegger's Clearing," in Jan Hokenson and Howard D. Pearce (eds.), *Forms of the Fantastic* (Westport, CT: Greenwood, 1986), 54–5.
16. Martin Scorsese, "Behind the Camera, A Feminist," *New York Times* (December 31, 1995), SM43.
17. Atkinson, "A Noir Journey into No-Woman's Land: Ida Lupino's *The Hitch-Hiker*".
18. Maurice Merleau-Ponty, *Signs*. Trans. Richard C. McCleary (Evanston: Northwestern University Press, 1964), 19.
19. Annette Kuhn, *Queen of the 'B's: Ida Lupino Behind the Camera* (Westport, CT: Praeger, 1995).
20. Maurice Merleau-Ponty, *Phenomenology of Perception*. Trans. Colin Smith (London: Routledge & Kegan Paul, 1965), ix.
21. Emmanuel Levinas, *Totality and Infinity: An Essay on Exteriority*. Trans. Alphonso Lingis (Pittsburgh: Duquesne University Press, 1969).
22. Emmanuel Levinas, *Existence and Existents*. Trans. Alphonso Lingis (The Hague: Martinus Nijhoff, 1978), 45.
23. Vivian Sobchack, *The Address of the Eye: A Phenomenology of Film Experience* (Princeton: Princeton University Press, 1992), 4.
24. John Krewson, "The editing style shifts emphasis from mounting suspense through crisp action to the strain on the characters of passively waiting". Available at *The A.V.Club*, DVD review, March 29, 2002 (accessed August 17, 2017).
25. Lauren Rabinovitz, "*The Hitch-Hiker* (1953)," in Annette Kuhn (ed.), *Queen of the 'B's: Ida Lupino Behind the Camera* (Westport, CT: Praeger, 1995), 90–102.

14

Unsolicited Bequest

Ambivalent Inheritance in Ida Lupino's 1960s Mysteries

Ann Torrusio

In *The Twilight Zone* episode "The Sixteen Millimeter Shrine," written by Rod Serling and directed by Mitchell Leiden, Ida Lupino plays the role of Barbara Jean Trenton, an aging actress "whose world is a projection room."[1] The episode opens with Lupino sitting in the dark with shades drawn, a cigarette in one hand and a drink in the other. Only the light of the flickering projection screen illuminates her. She is the subject of her own interest, transfixed by her performances from twenty-five years earlier. Serling and Leisen present the audience with "a picture of a woman looking at a picture," providing a meta-theatrical quality to Lupino's performance as an actress aware of her own theatricality. Lupino grapples with the complexity of an actress playing not only an aging film star, but an actress who watches—and is seduced by—her younger self performing on the movie screen. In a move only possible inside *The Twilight Zone*, Lupino's character wishes herself onto the screen, inserting herself in the aging film reel through sheer will, in essence, managing to redirect the film's ending.

During the episode, Lupino's character is offered, and subsequently rejects, a role in a motion picture. When her agent explains that the role is that of "a mother"—described only as a "very vibrant" forty-something—Lupino storms out of the casting office insisting, "I don't play mothers." Ironically, in Lupino's real life, she proudly embraced the role of a mother figure during her years as a director. Lupino famously referred to herself as "Mother" on set, and even had the phrase "Mother of Us All" embroidered on the back of her director's chair. The rhetoric of maternity fosters a sense of identity only in relation to others, an individuality that exists only in connection to kin. The concept of "mother" also implies a sense of citizenship that likely helped to reinforce her position on the set, directing others, as rightful and natural. The very role of mother implies a legacy to pass down, and the name itself exists only in relation to a successor. Indeed, even Lupino's very first film role was an unintended gift from her mother. In 1933, her mother brought Lupino to an audition, and daughter, not mother, ended up with a part in the film, *Her First Affaire*. The attributes and talents passed down from mother to daughter provided Lupino with her first big break.

Lupino was not ignorant to complexities of her inheritance. This chapter will examine several made-for-television mysteries that Lupino directed during the early 1960s, including "Sybilla" (1960) from *Alfred Hitchcock Presents*, "Trio for Terror" (1961) from the *Thriller* series, and "The Masks" (1964) from *The Twilight Zone*, all of which demonstrate a preoccupation with the unsolicited—even abject—aspects of inheritance. Throughout Lupino's tenure as a television director, she constantly delved into problems of inheritance, employing them as tropes to explore the futility of those attempting to sidestep their legacies or, worse, the dangers of those claiming legacies that are unearned. This chapter attempts to trace that thematic thread woven through a small selection of her television dramas as a way to better understand her precarious position as a woman working in the early years of television. The question of ambivalent inheritance depicted in Lupino's television mysteries reflects the postwar ideological tension over gender norms and Lupino's position as a pioneering female director during the formative years of American television.

The Making of Mother Directress

The unapologetic conviction with which Lupino's character in "The Sixteen Millimeter Shrine" (Season 1, Episode 4, October 23, 1959) wills herself into her own production is a stark contrast to the way Lupino often described her transition from actor to director. Lupino claims she fell into directing television in much the same way that she claims to have started directing movies. According to one of many stories concerning Lupino's origin as a director, George Diskant, a cameraman on her film *The Bigamist* (1953), invited her to try her hand as a television actress on CBS's *Television's Four Star Playhouse* in 1953. Although Lupino initially considered the new medium inferior to film, she eventually claimed to love it. Later, when approached by her ex-husband to direct Joe Cotton in the television show *On Trial* (Season 1, Episode 8, 1956), she took him up on his offer.

As a director, Lupino was well known for her soft manner. In her article "Me, Mother Directress," originally written in 1967 for the Director's Guild of America's in-house magazine *Action*, Lupino explained her gentler approach to directing:

> I would never shout orders to anyone. I hate women who order men around—professionally or personally. I think it is horrible in business or in the home. I've seen bossy women push their men around and I have no respect for the gal who does the shoving or the man who lets himself get pushed around. I wouldn't dare do that with my old man. When we were married they said it would last three months. It's now seventeen years. It's because I don't ever order him around. I learned that. And I don't do it with the guys on the set.[2]

What is notable—perhaps unsettling—about Lupino's description of her directing style was her willingness to consciously conflate life on the set with life at home, mirroring her relationships with the actors that she directed and her relationship with third husband, actor Howard Duff. Despite her placid description of their marriage, the turbulence of their relationship was well known, and they separated soon after her interview with *Action* magazine, divorcing in 1984. The persona Lupino constructed for the Actors Guild interview compromised her demanding directorial efforts, and it pandered to the misogynistic anxiety over women assuming work previously reserved for men, planting her firmly in the domestic sphere as passive wife.

Many of Lupino's statements, like the one in *Action* magazine, have colored the ways that critics have interpreted her major films. Indeed, her adamant rejection of the "bossy" woman makes it difficult to fit her within an easily definable feminist framework. Despite addressing taboo topics in her films such as polio (*Never Fear*, 1949), illegitimacy and unwed motherhood (*Not Wanted*, 1949), rape (*Outrage*, 1950), and bigamy (*The Bigamist*), her directorial contributions have received only limited serious critical attention.

Before tackling the director's chair, Lupino was, of course, an actress, and her ability to direct so effectively is due, in part, to her time in front of the camera. Lupino's acting career was sparked by the flames of her family's legacy as stage performers. Descended from a long line of entertainers, Lupino once confessed that "I became an actress just to show my father I wouldn't let him—or the other Lupinos—down."[3] The Lupino lineage of acting talent can be traced back to the Italian Renaissance, and the family continued to occupy the stage as its second home ever since. Lupino's father, Stanley, was a renowned comedian, and her mother, known as Connie Emerald, was a respected tap dancer. The weight of the Lupino legacy was an inspiration and an encumbrance that she would grapple with during her entire life.

Lupino was driven by the desire to prove herself worthy of the family name that had been bequeathed to her. Much like the Derridian notion of hauntology and the paradoxical notion of the "non-present present,"[4] Lupino's professional life was in constant comparison to the successful Lupino legacy. As author Louise Heck-Rabi points out: "Pleasing the family and living with the constant expectation of having to perform . . . prodded Lupino to explore all avenues of her seemingly inexhaustible compass of talents."[5] According to Derrida, there is no opting out of inheritance. Rather, inheritance is necessary: "the *being* of what we are *is* first of all inheritance, whether we like it or know it or not."[6] Derrida contends that we all see within ourselves the "figure of the heir" but that we must not assume a "secure comfort" from this position; rather, we must address the "contradictory assignation" it provides us.[7] Inheritance is never something that we receive as a possession to use as we see fit. "Inheritance is never a *given*," he warns, "it is always a task."[8] This "task" of inheritance was a weight that Lupino felt throughout her life, both as a positive, creative force and the oppressive ghost of expectation. Although she clearly earned her professional reputation and became the most famous Lupino of them all, there lurked an apparent anxiety of being heir to the family name.

There are critics who have asserted that approaching Lupino's directorial work for television as that of an auteur is dangerous. Kearney and Moron argue that assuming Lupino "had the freedom to call her own shots and the status of an auteur . . . is rather misleading within the context of a television industry whose creative efforts are shaped and controlled almost exclusively by producers rather than by directors."[9] Annette Kuhn also sees the danger in tracing Lupino's motifs: "even if certain authorial marks are traceable through the film and television she directed, to what extent are these attributable solely to the director?"[10]

Although the criticisms are well warranted, there is evidence to suggest that Lupino was selective in choosing the scripts that interested her. For instance, when Alfred Hitchcock approached Lupino to act in an episode of *Alfred Hitchcock Presents* (1955–62), Lupino informed him she was not interested in playing the role, but that she would love to direct the episode, which she did.[11] From the mid-1950s into the early 1960s, Lupino directed well over 100 television shows. Critic Louise Heck-Rabi has pointed out that after directing an episode of *On Trial* (Season 3, Episode 38, June 11, 1960), television directing jobs "just flocked to her."[12] Author Ally Acker argues that it is imperative to examine Lupino's television work in order to evaluate her talents because it is through television where she developed them most clearly: "Although her filmmaking gave her much acclaim, it was her directorial work in television that brought her craft into its maturity."[13] Heck-Rabi goes further to point out that not only did Lupino find satisfaction in directing for television, she argues that it gave her "the opportunity to express a personal viewpoint."[14] These critics suggest that, although Lupino may not have written her own scripts, she did operate with autonomy in selecting projects once she had made a name for herself. Indeed, Lupino's television efforts were so notable, particularly in the suspense genre, that after 1960 she became known as "the female-Hitch."

Tracing the Theme of Inheritance

Lupino directed her first episode of *Alfred Hitchcock Presents*, entitled "Sybilla" (Season 6, Episode 10, December 6, 1961). The episode opens with Horace, a forty-year-old bachelor, finally taking a wife named Sybilla. When Horace enters his home with Sybilla following their wedding, Horace remarks: "Thanks to my mother's providence I've had the means to keep up this house." The implication is that Horace's means are the result of his mother's inheritance. Horace is fully set in his ways, and Sybilla promises she will never be a "nuisance" to him. She is a dutiful wife and agrees to respect his specific request that she never enter his study. As the episode progresses, it becomes apparent to the audience that Horace has failed to emerge from the shadow of his overbearing mother, the memory of whom he projects onto his new wife. "She was always so gentle, so agreeable," Horace, recalls. He begins to suspect that his mother's amiability was, in fact, her sly way of asserting control over him.

As the episode progresses, Horace begins "feeling like a man beating against air, imprisoned by invisible walls," and fantasizes about killing Sybilla, writing out several nefarious plots to do so in a diary that he keeps in his study. When Horace discovers Sybilla walking out of his study one afternoon, he panics and botches an attempt at causing her death through an overdose of sleep medicine. Complicating Horace's dilemma, Sybilla subsequently reveals to him the premise of a mystery novel she has been reading: a man reads the diary of someone who wants to kill him. He makes a copy of the diary and gives it to his lawyer to be read upon his death. Then, he lets the would-be murderer know that he has distributed copies of the diary in the event that anything should happen to him (Figure 14.1).

Horace suspects that Sybilla is coyly advising him that she has been reading the diary he keeps in his study. In an effort to ensure her silence, Horace begins waiting on Sybilla, hand and foot. However, despite his efforts to keep her alive, Sybilla soon becomes very ill and dies suddenly. Following her death, Sybilla's attorney asks to meet with Horace, presumably to confront him with incriminating passages from his diary. Instead, Horace learns that Sybilla bequeathed to him a few bonds, as well as the mystery of whether or not she actually knew of the schemes contained in his diary. He

FIGURE 14.1 *An overdose of sleeping medicine in* Alfred Hitchock Presents, *"Sybilla."*

is also grief-stricken with the realization and the regret that he never told his wife that he loved her.

Although Sybilla's death imposes upon Horace the catastrophic repercussions that both he and the audience are left to contemplate, it also delivers its own unique set of disappointments. Sybilla left Horace with not only a new framework for understanding their marriage but also a new means of interpreting the actions of his life. Through death, Sybilla enables Horace to bury the oppressive specter of his mother and replace it with the benevolent spirit of his bride.

In 1961, Lupino directed "Trio for Terror," an episode of the *Thriller* (Season 1, Episode 25, March 14, 1961), hosted by Boris Karloff. The episode was divided into three vignettes, each telling an independent, macabre tale. The first story in the "Trio for Terror" is based on the short story "The Extra Passenger" by August Derleth (written under the pseudonym Stephen Grendon). The episode begins in the middle of a conversation between a young man named Simon and his beloved. The beloved talks Simon into murdering his uncle for his inheritance, convincing him under threat: "If you don't go through with it I'm through with you.... Money I've got to have."

In the next scene, Simon boards a train to carry out a plan to kill his uncle. He intends to sneak off the train at its first stop, where he will drive in a car he has left waiting to get to his uncle's home, commit the crime, and then travel by car to reboard the same train at its next stop without being detected by the conductor. In an effective use of panning out, Lupino begins the scene when he arrives at his stop cropped tightly around Simon's unreadable face. The camera slowly pans out to reveal his fists tightly clenched on top of his thighs. When Simon enters his uncle's home, it is apparent that the uncle dabbles in the occult: there is a table with the zodiac etched on top, a memento Mori skull, potions, even a crowing rooster. Lupino reveals the uncle through a bell jar, distorting his face as he reads an ancient-looking text. Simon sneaks up behind his uncle and hits him over the head with a large pestle, killing him with one blow. The rooster crows as Simon slips out to his getaway car. Simon reboards the train and believes that the plan was a success until he discovers an old man with him in his compartment. The old man reveals to Simon that his uncle was, unbeknownst to his family, a mage with the ability of exacting revenge in the afterlife. Simon initially disbelieves the old man but falls into a trance when the old man beckons him closer. The scene ends with the claw of a rooster enclosing around Simon's throat. When his body is finally discovered, Simon's neck has been clawed out (Figure 14.2).

Although the climax is disappointing, the filming techniques and pacing of the suspenseful buildup of the story are effective. Simon has an incomplete understanding of his uncle's nature, dismissing his capabilities. Simon openly denies his uncle's power, laughing it off as an old man's hocus-pocus. The moral seems a bit on the nose: one cannot obtain what one has not earned. However, the uncle's ability to avenge his death from beyond

FIGURE 14.2 *Killed for inheritance money in* Thriller, *"Trio for Terror."*

the grave speaks to larger concerns that surround the theme of inheritance. Inheritance can enrich but it can also oppress. Simon failed to understand his uncle's true nature and pays for it with his life. Blinded by the powerful lure of what he will inherit, Simon disbelieves in the power of the legacy from which he descends.

The second story in the "Trio for Terror" (Season 1, Episode 25, March 14, 1961) is based on the short story "A Terribly Strange Bed," by Wilkie Collins. A young man visits a casino to play roulette and seems unable to lose. As the night progresses, the young man befriends a veteran of the Crimean War, who is enamored with his lucky streak. During a spin of the wheel, Lupino employs a great cinematic effect as the camera slowly spins around with a slight tilt from the perspective of the roulette wheel, with the whir of the ball as the only audible sound. The camera spins past the faces of each of the gamblers who are, in turn, hypnotized by the wheel. The scene's disorienting effect reinforces the young man's intoxication after a long night of drinking and gambling. After cashing out his winnings, the veteran and a member of the casino's staff help the young man into one of the casino's guest rooms. As he is lying in bed, the young man realizes that the canopy is slowly and ominously descending on him. He manages to escape when, as the canopy slams with a thud on top of the mattress, he realizes that someone intended to smother or crush him to death. Having determined that he is no longer safe at the casino, the young man grabs his winnings, which are tied up in a cloth, and escapes through the window. When he finally arrives at a safe place, the young man opens the package containing his winnings but finds only a cannon ball from the Crimean War. Yet again, in the second episode, the dream of acquiring easy money is thwarted by the unanticipated cleverness of others. Both the first and second tales offer the false promise of success, only to have that promise dashed by a lack of perception.

Although the final episode in the "Trio of Terror" (Season 1, Episode 25, March 14, 1961) is not a direct commentary on the complexities of inheritance, it does open with a warning against not remembering the past. Before the beginning of the final tale, Karloff warns his audience of the hazards of forgetting history:

> I sometimes think—perhaps you do, too—how outrageous it would have seemed to anyone a hundred years ago, if they had been told that someday men would be doing exactly what you're doing now. Listening to a voice, watching a picture plucked as if, uh, out of the air. We've learned a lot in the last hundred years. But how much do you suppose has been forgotten in the past five thousand? You know how scientists scoff at folklore and ancient beliefs. But every now and then they amaze themselves with a discovery that our remote ancestors were right after all. Our third tale of terror contains the echo of an ancient fable that may

not be a fable at all. It begins with a manhunt, a search for a murderer. A strangler, if you will.

The tale is based on the short story "The Mask of Medusa" by Nelson Bond, and depicts a serial murderer known as "The Strangler" trying to escape police. He enters the first open door along the street and, as luck would have it, steps into what appears to be a museum of wax figures. The museum has just closed, and the curator is in the process of locking up for the night. The curator asks his guest if he would like a tour, which The Strangler readily accepts. As the tour proceeds, the curator reveals two pieces of information: before he devoted his life to his museum, he devoted his life to Greek archeology, and that all the figures in his museum are murderers. The figures are exceedingly lifelike and The Strangler is unable to conceal his increasing unease. He begins questioning the curator, whom he suspects may be a murderer himself, accusing him of displaying dead petrified bodies or corpses treated with plaster. The curator, however, denies that he killed his exhibits. They killed themselves, he insists, "by looking" because "they didn't believe." When The Strangler accidentally reveals himself as the subject of the manhunt and demands that the owner help him escape, the owner reveals the Mask of Medusa, which turns The Strangler to stone, making him the newest piece in the gallery of murderers.

Although the thematic connection to inheritance is not in the forefront of the tale's narrative, it does address the repercussions of twisting the lessons of history into an inconsequential or harmless mythology. The curator insists to—and thereby warns—The Strangler that Medusa was not just a myth, but also a queen whose mask he excavated during an archeological dig in Greece. The irony, of course, is the curator's warning against social amnesia: his exhibits were turned to stone because they looked upon the mask. They looked because they did not believe.

Lupino makes a strategic decision at the conclusion of the episode by revealing the Medusa mask to the audience. After an entire episode of buildup concerning the sinister artifact, it is finally and dramatically unveiled to the audience. However, instead of an ancient object of terror, the audience is presented with a funny-looking mask with plastic snakes gyrating from the face. Like Odysseus bound to his ship as he travels past the Sirens, Lupino allows us to survive beyond the moment of terrible revelation: the moment in which we should, like The Strangler, be turned to stone. It is another dimension of Lupino's ambivalence toward the past: a birthright of fear and a mythology to be mocked.

Lupino had the distinction of being the only person to both act and direct episodes of *The Twilight Zone* series. In her episode "The Masks" (Season 5, Episode 25, 1964), Lupino yet again revisits the problems of inheritance and its potentially unsavory consequences. The episode opens with the elderly and wealthy Jason Foster, who is dying in his New Orleans home during Mardi Gras. He invites his greedy daughter Emily, her husband, and her two teenage children to his estate for a final farewell. Lupino's use of mirrors in this episode alone could have earned her the title of "the female Hitch." In the opening scene, the dying patriarch gazes at his fading body in his upstairs bedroom mirror, while his teenage granddaughter applies and reapplies foundation in a compact mirror downstairs. It is a juxtaposition that exemplifies the contrast between the contemplative dying man and the vain and greedy young woman, and reinforces the episode's examination of the inheritors' duplicity and fractured personalities

After eating dinner, Foster's guests are coaxed into each selecting a Mardi Gras mask with special "properties" that they feel represent the antithesis of their character. After a chorus of grumblings and protests, the old man quotes his demand from a proviso contained within his will—unless all four of his beneficiaries select masks and wear them until midnight, they will all be disinherited.

The restrictive atmosphere in the parlor stands in stark contrast to the merriment on the streets outside. In Mikhail Bakhtin's famous analysis of the carnival and the grotesque, he argues that the carnival provides an arena for the values of high culture to be inverted and ultimately debased. Marked by drunkenness and rowdiness, the carnival allows a freedom that contrasts with the regimented morality of everyday life. Moreover, the utopian elements of Mardi Gras are expressed in material bodily form, depicting images of sexuality and violence, birth and death. Using the body to represent these extremes brands the body grotesque. The fundamental trait of the grotesque body is its promise of metamorphosis, the transgression of its boundaries from one grotesque body "a new body emerges in some form or another."[15] Foster's family does not realize that they are playing a larger role in the carnivalesque atmosphere in the streets than they bargain for.

The episode's tension builds as the family waits for the approach of midnight, the transitional moment in time that will usher one day into the next. It becomes increasingly clear to the audience that midnight will also be the pivotal moment when Foster's life ends and his fortune is usurped by the legatee. Indeed, the success of the episode's suspense is in part due to the perverse satisfaction we derive when, at the stroke of midnight, Foster passes away and the family removes their masks only to discover that their faces have been transformed to mock their elevated perceptions of themselves. Foster's daughter's face is contorted in physical pain, her husband's face epitomizes his avarice and greed, their daughter dons the nose of a swine, and their son possesses the sadistic look of a tormenter. In death, Foster mocks his family's inheritance by condemning them to wear the shameful flaws they foolishly believed that they concealed. The ambivalent space occupied by the grotesque body is echoed in Lupino's ambivalence toward

FIGURE 14.3 *The price of inheritance in* The Twilight Zone, *"The Masks."*

inheritance and the possibility that acknowledging our inheritance often shines an unflattering light on the blind spots that keep us blissfully ignorant of our faults (Figure 14.3).

The Lupino Film Legacy

In the 1970s, feminist scholars fervently scrambled to rediscover forgotten female contributions to the arts and Lupino's work was rediscovered only to be condemned as "conventional, even sexist."[16] Feminist film critics ultimately felt that Lupino failed to serve as a figure that could help reshape an understanding of women's contribution to cinematic studies. Critic Annette Kuhn opined that Lupino's work "is something of a disappointment for feminist film criticism: not only does the filmmaker quite unapologetically cast herself as a man's woman, her work has also appeared to many critics difficult to claim for feminism."[17] Indeed, the tendency of critics to evaluate Lupino's work outside of the context of its time has contributed to the scant attention paid to her work and the hesitancy of feminists to claim her as a leading lady of Hollywood's feminist canon. However, this critical viewpoint glosses over Lupino's ability as a scriptwriter, the success of her independent production company, her uncanny ability to thrive as the only female director in Hollywood in the 1950s, and the sheer volume of television programs that she directed during the 1960s. The failure of critics to evaluate her directed works beyond the major films that were intentionally written to be palatable to a mid-twentieth-century America denies Lupino's hustle and adaptability. Clearly, Lupino wanted to work and knew how to find it.

Feminist film critics have also criticized Lupino's directorial career on the basis that she explained her transition into directing in such a way as to deny her own agency. Although some critics have speculated that Lupino's move to directing was due to her frustration from feeling "[powerless] as an actress" and a desire to "control her own career,"[18] Lupino's own explanation was far more allusive and sphinxlike. "I never planned to become a director." Lupino famously claimed, "The fates—good and bad—were responsible."[19] Lupino would become famous for insisting that her transition into directing both movies and television was a product of luck, a gift from her professional male contemporaries, rather than a calculated professional decision arising out of her own talent and success. Authors Mary Celeste Kearney and James M. Moran speculate that Lupino's modesty was, at least in part, a calculated rhetorical move. Her anecdotal tone and the nuances in her diction (luck, fate) "couch what may have been Lupino's recognition of the nascent television industry's opportunities for career advancement in the polite language of society columns, wherein traits of hospitality and glamour would be considered more suitable than blatant directorial ambition to describe an established female star working in Hollywood."[20] Perhaps Lupino understood that being forthright with her professional desires would have appeared unsavory within her industry and to her public, particularly during the late 1950s and early 1960s, when America was struggling with ideological tensions over gender during the postwar years.

There is little doubt that Ida Lupino wrestled with what it meant to be a Lupino and to be respected as an artist in her own right. Throughout her life she struggled to fulfill her family legacy while making a name for herself. Her struggle was compounded with the difficulty of being one of the first women in a predominantly male profession during a time when concepts of gender were under an intense scrutiny arising from the anxiety marking the beginning of the sexual revolution. Lupino embodies the tensions surrounding the role of a working woman during the postwar years. It is perhaps because of her awareness of these tensions that inspired her to adopt the nickname of "Mother," thereby inventing a persona that entitled her to both respect and protection within patriarchy's powerful grasp. Even if we must ultimately renounce labeling Lupino as a trailblazing feminist in the arts, we cannot deny the sheer magnitude of her professional efforts. As a director she might have had a soft touch, but it was both effective and prodigious.

Notes

1. "Sixteen Millimeter Shrine," *The Twilight Zone* (CBS, 1959).
2. Ida Lupino, "Me, Mother Directress," *Action*, 2, no. 3 (1967): 15.
3. Molly Haskel, *Reverence to Rape: The Treatment of Women in the Movies* (Chicago: University of Chicago Press, 1987), 201.
4. Jacques Derrida, *Specters of Marx: The State of the Debt, the Work of Mourning, and the New international* (New York: Routledge, 1994), 6.
5. Louise Heck-Rabi, *Women Filmmakers: A Critical Reception* (Metuchen: The Scarecrow Press, 1984), 223.
6. Derrida, *Specters of Marx*, 54.
7. Jacques Derrida and Elisabeth Roudinesco, *For What Tomorrow: A Dialogue* (Stanford, CA: Stanford University Press 2004), 3.
8. Derrida, *Specters of Marx*, 54.
9. Kearny and Moran, "Ida Lupino as Director of Television," in Annette Kuhn (ed.), *Queen of the B's: Ida Lupino Behind the Camera* (Westport: Greenwood Press, 1995), 138.
10. Annette Kuhn, "Introduction: Intestinal Fortitude," in Annette Kuhn (ed.). *Queen of the B's: Ida Lupino Behind the Camera* (Westport: Greenwood Press, 1995), 8.
11. Dwight Whitney, "Follow Mother, Here We Go, Kiddies!," *TV Guide*, October 8, 1966, 18.
12. Heck-Rabi, *Women Filmmakers*, 224.
13. Ally Acker, *Reel Women: Pioneers of the Cinema 1896 to the Present* (New York: Continuum, 1991), 74.
14. Heck-Rabi, *Women Filmmakers*, 243.
15. Mikhail Bakhtin, *Rabelais and His World*. Trans. Helene Iswolsky (Bloomington: Indiana University Press, 2009), 26.
16. Cary O'Dell, *Women Pioneers in Television: Biographies of Fifteen Industry Leaders* (Jefferson: MacFarland and Co. 1997), 165.
17. Kuhn, "Introduction: Intestinal Fortitude," 5.
18. Acker, *Reel Women*, 74.
19. Whitney, "Follow Mother, Here We Go, Kiddies!," 15.
20. Kearny and Moran, "Ida Lupino as Director of Television," 137.

15

A Subtle Subversion: Ida Lupino Directing Television

Adam Breckenridge

When researching the literature on Ida Lupino's work as a director, it is a common sentiment to lament the neglect Lupino has received in the annals of critical scholarship, a complaint that the publication of this volume may render outdated. However, even within the body of literature surrounding her work, her time as a television director truly does receive scant attention and warrants considerable new scholarly attention.

The reasons for this neglect are numerous and, in some cases, self-evident. In regard to auteur theory, television directing brings little to the table as television has always been the terrain of producers and writers. The director is more of a workhorse, sometimes bringing little more than personal style and workmanship to the production, and even the former is restricted, as even in the post-*Sopranos* era of high-concept television, stylistic flourishes are rarely seen in television directing, and such was the case under the much tighter restrictions of the 1950s and 1960s, when Lupino was working in television. Any significant kind of signature style was very difficult to implement. This situation, coupled with the fact that many of the best-known television shows that Lupino worked on, such as *Gilligan's Island* (1964–6) and *Bewitched* (1965), offer little of substance for critical analysis, making more problematic the task of focusing in on this part of her *oeuvre*.

However, if we plumb the depths of her television work, we find that Lupino did much of her best work in this medium, and her television directing can be seen as an extension of the motifs and style that she explored in her film work, especially when we bear in mind that Lupino was free to choose which scripts and shows she directed, and, therefore, she was free to choose scripts that explored ideas that were of interest to her, which makes it much easier to argue for her television work as an extension of the themes explored in her cinema.

Lupino deserves serious commendation for the remarkable variety of her television work. She was involved in directing approximately thirty different shows that span many genres, including Westerns (*Tate* (1960), *Hotel de Paree* (1959–60), *The Rifleman* (1961), *Have Gun, Will Travel* (1959–61), *The Virginian* (1966), *Dundee and the Culhane* (1967)); sitcoms (*The Donna Reed Show* (1959), *Bewitched* (1965), *Gilligan's Island* (1964–6), *The Ghost and Mrs. Muir* (1968)); horror/suspense (*The Twilight Zone* (1964), *Thriller* (1961–2), *Alfred Hitchcock Presents* (1960–1)); crime/gangster (*77 Sunset Strip* (1959), *Hong Kong* (1960), *The Fugitive* (1963–4), *Sam Benedict* (1962–3), *The Untouchables* (1962–3), *The Rogues* (1964–5)); detective shows (*Honey West* (1966)); medical dramas (*Dr. Kildare* (1964)); and historical adventure (*Daniel Boone* (1967)). Further, Lupino directed a number of "teleplay" shows such as *Screen Director's Playhouse* (1956), *Climax!* (1956), *General Electric Theater* (1961–2), *Kraft Suspense Theater* (1964), and *Bob Hope Presents the Chrysler Theater* (1966). In considering this range, one cannot help but call to mind the fact that many of the studio system's most celebrated directors had to show similar versatility to thrive in a system where the wishes of the director were often secondary to the desires and whims of producers and or stars.

Considering the sheer variety of her television work, one may also wonder how it could be possible to locate a thread connecting them to Lupino's work in film. It may seem a redoubtable task but, if we look carefully, we indeed find some common threads connecting at least most of these works together into what we may perhaps refer to as the "Lupino touch."

Two of the principal reasons Lupino's directing work has been neglected stems from the rather ironic combination of sexism and feminism. The former, I presume, requires no explanation, as Lupino is hardly the only artist to be neglected because of her gender. However, when feminist critics began to dig through the annals of film history to develop a narrative of women filmmakers, Lupino is largely overlooked as not being "feminist" enough. This judgment stemmed from two issues. The first was that Lupino's films were seen as rather unfeminist: they make no large statements on women's rights and do little to challenge patriarchal mores. The second was Lupino herself, whose story is a far cry from those of many other feminist pioneers: she did not have to fight the patriarchy for the right to direct films, and publicly she maintained the face of a meek woman who knew her place, as evidenced by public statements such as this one:

> I retain every feminine trait. Men prefer it that way. They're more cooperative if they see that fundamentally you are of the weaker sex even though [you are] in a position to give orders, which normally is the male

prerogative, or so he likes to think, anyway. While I've encountered no resentment from the male of the species for intruding into their world, I give them no opportunity to think I've strayed where I don't belong. I assume no masculine characteristics, which can often be a fault of career women rubbing shoulders with their male counterparts, who become merely arrogant or authoritative.[1]

If one's aim is to build a narrative of women asserting their authority and right to a place in the male-dominated world of filmmaking, such proclamations hardly make for an ideal poster woman. Thus, did Lupino languish in relative obscurity, although we are now seeing a second revival: exploring a more nuanced look at Lupino's filmography that is less interested in trying to create a fixed narrative that Lupino clearly does not fit into. Dan Georgakas, in his essay "Ida Lupino: Doing it Her Way," addresses this matter while also suggesting a way she fits into the film canon as a feminist:

> She unapologetically believed in romantic love as much as she believed that there was considerable social and gender injustice. Her director's gaze was that of a woman, but she was not ideologically feminist in terms of an activist agenda. In that sense she is like minor poets who bridge two artistic eras. Their work breaks with the past but contains only in rudimentary form the elements and attitudes that will exemplify the new era. Such artists till new soil but do not bring in a prize crop even though their crop is not without merit.[2]

Open defiance was not Lupino's style but, in the context of her time period, it should also be noted that if she had acted with the kind of open defiance that many today wish that she had exhibited, she would almost certainly have been shut out of the studio system entirely. It is a point of historic fact that Lupino was the only woman directing in the Hollywood studio system in the 1950s. There was, however, another woman directing films in America during this time: the avant-garde filmmaker Maya Deren, whose defiant nature and overtly feminist films are far more befitting to the narrative of the defiant woman that some feminist critics sought. Deren, however, was forced to operate well outside the studio system and her experimental films are far too rarified for all but the most discerning viewers. Deren, then, is a director whose works could never have had more than a limited impact, but to work within the system, putting on the performance of a meek and feminine woman who just so happened to have found her way behind the camera, while wreaking a subtle subversion in her works, that is, an approach that draws viewers' attention to your work.

There is indeed a subtle subversion to Lupino's films, but the question that must be posed is how her television directing fits into this. Slavoj Zizek's ideas on fantasy and ideology provide a useful framework for the reading I wish to undertake. Zizek grounds his ideas of fantasy in his own critique of ideology, which he sought to complicate through Peter Sloterdijk's *Critique of Cynical Reason*, which undermines the notion of ideology as inherently naive by arguing that people practice ideology despite being aware of its effects.[3] One of Zizek's most important claims in *Sublime Object*, however, is that even this idea is problematic, because it operates from the assumption that ideology lies in knowing, but one of the great declarations that Zizek makes in *Sublime Object* is that ideology does not exist in knowing but in doing: "But such a reading of the Marxist formula leaves out an illusion, an error, a distortion which is already at work in the social reality itself, at the level of what individuals are *doing*, and not only what they *think* or *know* they are doing"[4]

Zizek, in trying to move us away from the "post ideological world" is also trying to move us toward the idea that fantasy also lies, not in the knowing, but in the doing. In *Sublime Object*, he demonstrates this through the example of money:

> When individuals use money, they know very well that there is nothing magical about it--that money, in its materiality, is simply an expression of social relations. . . . The problem is that in their social activity itself, in what they are *doing*, they are *acting* as if money, in its material reality, is the immediate embodiment of wealth as such. They are fetishists in practice, not in theory.[5]

From here he explains that the illusion at work is that we pretend not to be aware of this when in fact we are or, to continue on with the aforementioned analogy, we are aware that we only act as if money is the embodiment of wealth but we ignore the fact that we are aware of it.[6] We mask our own awareness.

This desire to construct ideological fantasies to mask a kernel of the Real can be transferred to an analysis film and television. Is it not the work of much of our popular entertainment to weave ideological fantasies for us, to let us believe that the good guy always wins, that wrongs are always righted, justice always served, even as we are bombarded everyday by news and experiences that overwhelmingly inform us that this scenario is not even remotely the case? The first critics to reconsider Lupino's directing work were seeking a woman who worked to destroy these fantasies and discarded her when they confronted someone who was not working to wreak havoc on the fantasies of the patriarch. But these critics, in their own fashion, were weaving their own ideological fantasy: the idea that for a woman to be a feminist she had to openly challenge the system, not work within it. She had to defy classical notions of femininity, not embrace them; she had to aggressively assert her authority, not politely ask for it. Lupino, however, did challenge our ideological constructs, and she did so in much the same manner in which she fashioned her directorial career, by putting on the air of conformity while making mischief with her subject matter.

Consider her work in one of her earliest television efforts: *The Donna Reed Show*, one of the many family sitcoms of the 1950s and 1960s that portray the kind of idyllic households that are often the object of the ideological fantasies of those who have deluded themselves into believing that the 1950s were a golden era. The one episode she directed, "A Difference of Opinion" (1959), focuses around Donna Stone (Donna Reed) and her husband Alex (Carl Betz), who learn from their son at the beginning of the episode that children who grow up in households where the parents never fight are much more likely to grow up as well adjusted. The couple, becoming alarmed at this news, decide that they must never fight in front of the children. However, a little later they find themselves in a running dispute over whether or not to attend a dinner party being hosted by a couple they despise. Yet it is always when their arguments are at their most heated that their two children suddenly show up, and the parents are forced to put on a façade of a happy couple who never fights. The episode ends, of course, with the usual life lesson typical of such shows that sometimes couples can argue and still love each other.

The episode, overall, involves low stakes; both the subject and tone of their conflict are mild and everything ends happily, but there are some significant issues. The 1950s were a time when the ideal of the nuclear family was at its peak. Our culture was bombarded by images of the happy and idyllic suburban American family, and, even more so than now, there was an expectation of an image of idyllic happiness in one's own family. What we see here then is a couple who, every time they are confronted with an audience for their relationship, are forced to uphold this fantasy, lest any sign of imperfection be allowed to show through (and, to use another Lacanian term, the fantasy is also being upheld for the sake of the Big Other). It is subtle but the episode does thumb its nose at the absurdity of the ideal of a perfect family and the expectation to appear as such.

It is worth noting that this work is not the first time that Lupino challenged our cultural obsession with the happy family. *The Bigamist* (1953), perhaps her best known film, tackles this very notion by showing us a man who, by all appearances, is an upstanding member of society but who secretly has two families in two different cities. I bring this point up to suggest that many of the themes Lupino explored in her television directing work can be seen as extensions of the work she did in film.

She would revisit the theme of unhappy families in some of the other shows she directed. In the first of three episodes of *The Fugitive* (1963–4) that she directed, "Fatso," we encounter a far more dysfunctional family than we see in either *The Donna Reed Show* (1959) or even *The Bigamist*. *The Fugitive* was a dramatic show with some powerful elements of noir it, focusing on Dr. Richard Kimble (David Janssen), who was falsely accused, convicted, and sentenced to death for murdering his wife, yet he escaped and went on the run after a prison transport crashes, which is the source material for a 1993 Harrison Ford film. "Fatso" chronicles his arrest for a minor offense that puts him in a cell with Davey "Fatso" Lambert (Jack Weston), a simple-minded and kind man who takes an immediate liking to Kimble. When Kimble breaks out of the jail (in fear that his true identity will be discovered), Fatso tags along and offers his family farm as a hiding place. As they approach the farm and have an encounter with Fatso's brother, Frank (Burt Brinkerhoff), it becomes apparent that this return home after a long absence is not a pleasant one, and soon Kimble learns that some years ago Fatso had set fire to the barn and killed most of the livestock, a crime that only his mother is willing to forgive.

As the episode unfolds, we begin to sense the dynamics of this family. Fatso's brother is mercilessly abusive toward him, taking pleasure in whipping him without provocation. The father, bedridden, is equally ruthless with his words, and still holds a grudge against his son for what he did. Kimble, after confessing his own story to Fatso, becomes suspicious about events after Fatso finds out that the police are closing in on Kimble, and he turns himself in to them, concocting a half-baked claim that he was actually the one who murdered Kimble's wife, a ludicrous claim that the police quickly dismiss. After some investigation, Kimble discovers that it was actually Frank who burned the barn down and that Fatso took the blame to cover for his brother, which destroyed Fatso's life while Frank continued to be the favored son. The episode ends with the truth being revealed to the entire Lambert family, after which Kimble goes on the run again.

This configuration is a far more sadistic portrayal of the American family than what *The Donna Reed Show* would offer us: Fatso, wanting only to be loved and accepted by his family, was mercilessly abused by them his entire life, mostly for his "slowness." To the rest of the townspeople, they are an upstanding family burdened with a failure of a son, a son whom they cast out of their lives for failing to live up to the ideals of the American family. If *The Donna Reed Show* gave us the fear that every wrinkle in the façade of happiness can expose the whole lie, "Fatso" shows us how the façade can mask the savage cruelty of family.

Although I commend Lupino for the variety of her directing work (and not without reason), it must be noted that she had a strong attraction toward stories of suspense, crime, and noir, which represent a substantial proportion of both her television and the film work. The very subversiveness of a woman working in these genres in itself should not be overlooked as, even to this day, in the struggle for women to gain a foothold in directing films, there is the additional trouble of the "coding" of genres, which is to say of women wanting to direct films in genres that are considered "masculine." Even the briefest of Google searches reveals an extensive debate on both the popular and the academic level over Kathryn Bigelow directing "male" movies, a fact that seems to anger both misogynists, who are angry that she is breaking into their "man's world," and feminists, who are angry that the most prominent female director in the world is not making feminist films.[7] Given how much consternation this seems to cause everyone on both sides of the debate even today, it seems all the more remarkable that Lupino worked so extensively in these genres. In fact, what among her television work other than the three female-led sitcoms she worked on (*The Donna Reed Show*, *Bewitched*, and *The Ghost and Mrs. Muir*) could really be seen as "female" shows?

We should resist speculating on what drew her to these genres but we may certainly observe that these are genres that are inherently subversive because, for all of them, exposing the darker aspects of human nature is inherent to them. The discussion of her work on *The Fugitive* here has perhaps already elucidated that, but some of her other television work should be considered as well.

Lupino directed three episodes of *The Untouchables* (1962–3), and the first episode she directed, "A Fist of Five," is particularly notable for the way it flips the conventions of the crime genre on its head. The episode guest stars Lee Marvin as Mike Brannon, a cop who, at

the beginning of the episode, is seen being forced to hand over his badge and gun for being "out of line" for beating up a known gangster. Disgraced, he arranges a meeting with his four brothers, and, after a speech about how he has tried to fight the gangs for years and

has gotten nowhere with his life, he is ready to commit a crime of his own. He arranges with his brothers to kidnap the head of one of the crime families, Tony Lamberto (Frank DeKova), and hold him for $150,000 ransom (Figure 15.1).

FIGURE 15.1 *Mike Brannon (Lee Marvin) outlines his plan to his four brothers in* The Untouchables, *"A Fist of Five."*

Lamberto, however, had secretly been making arrangements with Elliot Ness (Robert Stack) to close up his entire organization if Ness can get him out of serving any jail time, declaring that he is through with crime. Shortly after Tony is introduced, we are also introduced to his wife Angie (Phyllis Coates), who was left paralyzed in a bombing that was intended for Tony. Tony shows genuine love and affection toward his wife, giving him a level of sympathy that is rare for characters like him. By contrast, Brannon becomes increasingly corrupted as he and his brothers carry out their scheme, even going so far as to kill one of Tony's henchmen in cold blood and dismissing his actions as killing someone unworthy to live. The end of the episode sees Tony being shot by Mike as Ness and his men are attempting to rescue him. Tony absolves himself before his death by telling Ness the location of his account books while Mike Brannon is taken into custody.

This reversal of the classic hero/villain role is quite novel and complicates these roles in a way that is quite sophisticated for a television show. By 1963 (when "Fist of Five" aired), there had already been a decades-long tradition of making gangsters into "heroes," although this portraiture was something that ran against the Hayes Code in Hollywood, which is why the code mandated that criminals could never get away with their crimes, although the punishments they receive in film and television is, of course, doing little more than paying lip service to the Big Other which, if anything, allowed the audience to more thoroughly revel in the *jouissance* of their beloved antiheroes. Tony Lamberto, however, is genuinely heroic. He is determined to right his past wrongs and become a good man, and, while the Big Other's notion of justice is still served (all the more so when he learns in his dying conversation with Ness that the Justice Department refused to offer him immunity), his death is not adjudication or even heroic (in the "blaze of glory" sense) but is rather tragic.

Meanwhile, Mike Brannon is, for the time, a rare example of a corrupt cop in popular media. Mainstream media was uncomfortable with corrupt police officers (although it was not an intractable rule the way punishing criminals was), and examples before the dissolution of the Hayes Code are rare. However, what is more notable is just how much of a transformation Brannon undergoes. The scene that opens the episode of Brannon being forced to hand over his gun and badge quickly codes him as a rebellious hero, although there is an added menace to the scene when Brannon hands over his gun and, for a moment, looks as though he is going to shoot his chief. Thus, from the beginning we see that Brannon's rogue behavior is possibly not heroic but psychotic. However, even as he plans the heist he still elicits our sympathies: the blue-collar Joe fed up with working hard his whole life and getting nowhere is another trope that audiences are often quick to identify with. It is only when he shoots the henchman in cold blood that the rug is pulled from under us, and we see just how twisted he really is. This slow unveiling of a "heroic" character's inner psychosis was a rare direction for a narrative to develop in this time, and, when Brannon is arrested, it really is justice being served. Through it all, however, we still have Elliot Ness in the lead, and his character always remains an incorruptible force of good, yet "Fist of Five" presents us with quite a sophisticated inversion of hero and villain roles and, in so doing, calls into question notions of good and evil in a way that is quite remarkable for mainstream television of the early 1960s.

Have Gun, Will Travel gives us another incorruptibly heroic character: that of Paladin (Richard Boone), a gun for hire in the Old West. Lupino directed eight episodes of *Have Gun, Will Travel*; the only show for which she directed more was Boris Karloff's *Thriller* (nine episodes). Outside of these two shows, there is no show that she directed that showed as much dedication. This context would suggest that the very premise of *Have Gun, Will Travel* was something that appealed to her. Paladin, whose very name invokes the heroism and nobility of the Chivalric era, is a classic grizzled loner with a strict code of honor. Each episode begins with him in a hotel in San Francisco (where he presumably lives), being called upon to right some injustice that has been committed (Figure 15.2).

Perhaps the most compelling exploration of justice we see in any of Lupino's episodes of *Have Gun, Will Travel* comes in "The Trial." In this episode, Paladin is hired by a man named Morgan Gibbs (Robert F. Simon), who wants Paladin to go after his son, who murdered Morgan's fiancée. Paladin asks why Gibbs refuses to go after his son himself (as he knows where

FIGURE 15.2 *Paladin (Richard Boone) defends himself at a sham trial for a crime he didn't commit in* Have Gun, Will Travel, *"The Trial."*

his son is hiding out), and Gibbs tells Paladin, "because I'll probably kill him, or he'll kill me." Paladin tells him that if he retrieves Gibson's son, "it'll be to the law." "Don't trouble yourself about the law," Gibbs says, "the boy killed a woman, a woman I was set to marry and he'll hang for it. But no Gibbs is gonna be drug skinned through the rocks like some savage, not even him."

Gibbs' position is fundamentally absurd: he wants his son to die but, somehow, he believes that the hangman's noose (a public spectacle) is more dignified than being shot in the wilderness (where no one would bear witness to it). Paladin accepts Gibbs' terms, though, and heads out to the location where his son is hiding out. However, another bounty hunter shows up as Paladin is trying to apprehend Gibbs' son, and the hunter kills him. When Paladin returns to the saloon with his son's body, Gibbs' only response is to tell him not to forget his $500 reward for the dead body. "I'll be here in the morning," Paladin responds. The scene cuts to Paladin descending the stairs the next morning to find Gibbs with several armed men waiting for him. Gibbs accuses Paladin of murdering his son and tells him he will stand trial for it. Gibbs has arranged for the townspeople (over whom Gibbs has significant influence) to sit in on a sham trial. We watch as Gibbs bullies the townspeople into serving their roles in the trial, many of whom do not even know the proper terminology they are supposed to be using for a trial that is dictated by Gibbs' whims.

Observant viewers will note the similarities to the court of criminals in Fritz Lang's *M*. Both present trials that purport to uphold the ideals of justice, while making a mockery of them. Gibbs is a man who thinks nothing of abusing his power and twisting all notions of justice to exact the revenge he wants, remaining adamant in his belief that Paladin murdered his son, despite all evidence to the contrary. While it is difficult to imagine anyone being disturbed by this episode, the implications certainly become disturbing if you think about them long enough. Gibbs coaches the witnesses on what answers to give throughout the trial and openly manipulates everything to obtain the results he wants, to the amusement of the townspeople, who make no effort to oppose him in his ploy to kill an innocent man. Paladin, however, begins to figure out that this sham trial is a way for Gibbs to hide guilt of his own which, through his questioning is revealed to be a deep-rooted hatred for his "half-breed" son (who was half Native American) and whose actions were forced by Gibbs' cruel treatment of him. This episode then, becomes a way of exposing the darkest aspects of the American justice system: the way it so often serves as a system for punishing the innocent for the crimes of the culture.

Many of the other episodes of *Have Gun, Will Travel* that Lupino directed show a similar interest challenging notions of justice in our culture, suggesting that the scripts exploring these issues were something that Lupino was drawn to. There is clearly a need for a full-length analysis of the work that Lupino did for *Have Gun, Will Travel*.

I would be remiss if I were to write a defense of Lupino as a feminist director without considering the way that women are portrayed throughout her television work. I wish I could say that Lupino was dedicated to fighting for the rights of women through all the television directing work she did but, alas, the truth is always far more complicated than we want it to be. By no means do I wish to suggest that Lupino's television work only upheld female stereotypes. In fact, when reviewing her television filmography, we see that she often chose to focus on episodes dealing with women's issues or featuring more complex female characters. However, there is no denying that the portrayal of women in her television work is very scattershot.

However, there is still a clear streak in her television work of choosing scripts that challenged gender stereotypes, at least for their time (they may not all seem quite so progressive now). *Honey West* is the only female-led show she worked on that was not a sitcom (the sitcoms do admittedly advocate for the domesticity of women). *Honey West* is a detective show with something of a *Mission Impossible* twist (high-tech gadgets are a key element), with the titular character working as the head of the organization with mostly men working for her. To see women working in such positions of power was rare in the popular entertainment of this time but Honey West (Anne Francis) is also smart, resourceful, and usually the one who rescues her male employees. In the context of the mid-1960s, the show is positively progressive.

Lupino only directed one episode of it: "How Brillig, O, Beamish Boy." It is not a particularly notable episode but it does possess all of the qualities outlined earlier. The episode depicts West charged with the task of delivering half a million dollars to a client, but a shady character by the name of Mr. Brillig (John McGiver) kidnaps one of West's men, Sam Bolt (John Ericson), and threatens to kill him if she does not turn the money over to him. It is hard not to observe that this episode is an inverse of the classic damsel-in-distress scenario with the brave woman charged with the task of rescuing a helpless man (Sam is one of her detectives but all his attempts to escape on his own are woefully ineffective). When West finds her way to Mr. Brillig's hideout, she, too, is taken captive and the money stolen but, unlike Sam, she is able to escape almost immediately and she is able to track down Brillig, apprehend him, and retrieve the money before the police show up. Unlike some of the other shows that Lupino directed, where she seemed to gravitate to scripts that appealed to her, it is the very premise of *Honey West* that fits our framework. *Honey West* may not have lingered in the public consciousness the way more regressive shows like *Bewitched* and *Gilligan's Island* have, but it deserves commendation for being ahead of its time in its portrayal of women and is perhaps worth a reconsideration because of it.

Lupino's work on *The Virginian*, however, is much more likely to be in the appeal the script held for her. *The Virginian* was a Western focusing on an ever-shifting cast of characters on the Shiloh Ranch in Wyoming.

The Virginian (James Drury) and Trampas (Doug McClure) were the only recurring characters through the entire series. Both are cowhands on the Shiloh Ranch, and they bear witness to the characters who pass through. The episode that Lupino directed, "Dead Eye Dick," is notable not just for having a strong female lead in the teenage tomboy Marjorie Hammond (Alice Rawlings) but it also highlights the absurdity of masculine standards. Marjorie, who comes to town with her mother, is obsessed with dime novels telling the tales of a Western hero named Dead Eye Dick. In town she meets a boy her age named Bob Foley (David Macklin), who quickly becomes smitten with her but she is not interested in him because Foley, a small and scrawny teen who plans to be a lawyer, possesses none of the qualities of Dead Eye Dick that she pines for. Because of this misfitting quality of character, Foley abandons his dream of being a lawyer and tries to learn to be a cowhand instead, a job he is woefully inadequate for, much to his frustration.

Usually a man's inability to perform the tasks expected of a man is played off as comedy in entertainment, and, while there is some humor in Foley's failures to perform the basic task of a cowhand, it is his frustration that takes center stage. Marjorie falls in love, instead, with the Virginian, who does possess all of the qualities of Dead Eye Dick. The Virginian's efforts to refocus Marjorie's affections toward Bob Foley becomes a major focal point of the episode, and it is because of Marjorie's stubborn determination that her character comes through. It is the woman who is the pursuer, dogged in her determination to get her trophy man, and it should be emphasized that she does not view the much-older Virginian as a father figure but as a potential mate.

This toying with gender tropes is unfortunately reversed late in the episode when Marjorie becomes the primary witness to a bank robbery. One of the robbers is caught but the other two get away. The one who is captured is put on trial but before Marjorie can testify and the other two return and kidnap her, intending to hold her for a swap for their partner. When this plot is discovered, a posse is sent out after her but the two robbers easily thwart them. Bob Foley, however, goes out for the first time on a solo hunting expedition (another phase in his attempts to prove his masculinity) when he stumbles across the robbers' hideout, subdues the one stationed outside, and shoots the gun out of the hand of the one holding Marjorie hostage. Impressed by his heroics, Marjorie winds up falling for him, after all, and he returns to his plans to study law. Marjorie thus becomes reduced to the status of damsel in distress while Bob Foley, having his archetypal masculinity affirmed, is able to return to his old self. There is some small relic of the episode's original mischievousness in the final line when the Virginian compliments Foley on the remarkable shot he took and Foley responds "What shot? I had my eyes closed," revealing his macho bravura to have been little more than dumb luck.

It is unfortunate that an episode so willing to have fun with conventional gender roles had to, by the end, revert to the status quo. Marjorie, although she had to be rescued at the end, does at least maintain her character (she never "learns her place" so to speak), and Foley's affirmation of his conventional masculinity is dubious. Still, this ending, at the very least, explores a fundamental flaw in the very nature of trying to challenge cultural values through the classical structure of a television show. Before the advent of long narrative television shows, it was essential that each self-contained episode resolve all conflicts and, by consequence, return the narrative to the status quo before the credits roll. This formula required writers to undo whatever cultural transgressions they have committed in the episode. But we can perhaps still salvage some progress by observing that the willingness to experiment with this kind of transgression holds some merit.

I have focused only on two of the more interesting portrayals of women and gender roles in Lupino's work. She directed many other episodes where the roles of women, if they are not always outright progressive, are at least complicated enough to warrant some reflection on their merit. A sampling of such episodes include the following: *Have Gun, Will Travel*'s "The Lady on the Wall" and "Lady With a Gun"; her sole episode of *Daniel Boone*, "The King's Shilling"; her episode of *Kraft Suspense Theater*, "The Threatening Eye," which has one of the more compelling femme fatales to show up in her television work[8] and her first television job; and an episode of *Screen Director's Playhouse*, "No. 5 Checked Out." There is limited space for an analysis of these episodes here, but I would like to focus on two of the most famous shows she directed: *Bewitched* and *Gilligan's Island* (Figure 15.3).

FIGURE 15.3 *Samantha (Elizabeth Montgomery) using her magic to wait on her husband Darrin (Dick York) hand and foot in* Bewitched, *"A is for Aardvark."*

Bewitched, perhaps more than any other show that Lupino worked on, threatens to undermine my theory of her as a subtly subversive director. It is a show with a female lead, but one who becomes a model for the belief that a woman's place is in the home serving her husband. Marriage means having to give up on her own desires, since her husband strictly forbids her to practice magic, a request that she acquiesces to, echoing the sentiment that it is her place as a woman to accommodate his wishes. It is, of course, the running joke of the show that she is constantly having to use her magic to get her husband out of the messes he gets himself into, a theme played upon to great extent in the one episode Lupino directed, "A is for Aardvark," which depicts Samantha (Elizabeth Montgomery) and her husband Darrin (Dick York), who is laid up in bed with a sprained ankle. Samantha finds herself forced to wait on him hand and foot and forbidden to use magic to aid in her work. Eventually, however, she disobeys and Darrin becomes so enraptured by how much easier her magic has made things that he wants to start using it for everything. This development, in its own way, starts to become a drain on Samantha, who wishes for things to return to the way they were. She then begins to use her magic to take the joy out of the fun Darrin was having with it until he asks her to bring things back to the way they were before, a request to which she acquiesces. The episode ends with her meekly serving her injured husband without the aid of her magic, thus reverting to the status quo, without even the complexity that "Dead Eye Dick" left us with.

This show should have been as popular as it was and, as such, is more likely to become the focus of attention in a consideration of Lupino's directorial work for television. *Gilligan's Island* is similarly inane, although the issue is not so much an upholding of the status quo, like *Bewitched*, as not holding up any sort of positioning at all. *Gilligan's Island* is a show resistant to any sort of meaningful criticism outside of its archetypes and cultural impact, neither one of which has a place in my thesis. The four episodes that Lupino directed is more likely a commentary on the paycheck she probably received for it more than on any appeal the material may have had for her. There is, however, one episode that is at least worth briefly mentioning—"The Producer," which she directed shortly after finishing work on her last feature film, *The Trouble with Angels* (1966).

This episode sees a producer named Harold Hecuba (Phil Silvers) come to the island looking for new and exotic talent for a Broadway production. Hecuba is spoiled and demanding, reducing Thurston Howell (Jim Backus) and his wife (Natalie Schafer) to the status of servants while making the other residents of the island beckon to his every whim. Seeing Hecuba as an opportunity to escape the island, they stage a musical adaptation of *Hamlet*. When Hecuba watches it, he begins coaching them on how to perfect the production and, when he is pleased with the idea, he flees the island with plans to strike it rich off his stolen idea, leaving the castaways, as always, still stranded on the island.

The temptation to read this episode as Lupino's disenfranchisement with Hollywood is hard to resist. She said many times in her life that she preferred directing for television, claims that are usually dismissed as her covering for what has traditionally been seen as a back step in her career.[9] Perhaps it is true that television directing allowed Lupino to explore the themes that she was interested in without the rabble rousing that was inherent in her studio productions, which did tend to incite controversy even with their relatively mild exposition on the themes that she pursued in them. Thus, a stronger case can be made for viewing her television work as an extension of her film work and, therefore, an important key to understanding Lupino's interests and motivations as a director.

Notes

1. Wheeler Winston Dixon, "Great Directors: Ida Lupino," *Senses of Cinema* (Senses of Cinema Inc., n.p.).
2. Dan Georgakas, "Ida Lupino: Doing It Her Way," *Cineaste*, 25, no. 3 (2000): 32–6.
3. Slavoj Zizek, *The Sublime Object of Ideology* (Brooklyn: Verso Books, 2008), 26.
4. Ibid., 28.
5. Ibid.
6. Ibid., 30.
7. Anyone interested in reading a discussion of this very debate should look at Katherine Barscay's essay "Kathryn Bigelow's Gen(d)re" in *Cinephile* for a superb analysis of both the debate and her films.
8. One interested in the study of femme fatales may also want to look at her work in *The Untouchables* and *The Fugitive*.
9. This reasoning would have been especially true in the 1950s and 1960s, when television was still seen as an inferior art form to movies.

16

Ida Lupino's Thrillers: The Terror of the "Lethal Woman"

Fernando Gabriel Pagnoni Berns

Confirmed bachelors often enjoy a carefree and enviable reputation in the classic films and television shows of the 1950s and 1960s. These men generally are funny and upbeat, attracting the suspicion of homosexuality only in the more cynical films of the early 1970s. The older women, who have never been married and presumably are virgins, however, and are generally perceived negatively and depicted in films of the period as tense and unnatural, a threat to the men they encounter. These women, in previous decades known as "spinsters" or "old maids," have always been threats to the social status quo, and, unmarried and childless, they refuse to fulfill the socially expected female role by submitting to men and continuing the masculine lineage.[1]

Classic films tend to categorize women either as the femme fatale or as the sacrificing wife and mother without allowing for more subtle variations of these roles. The "spinster" generally falls outside these categories and hence is pathologized as deviant.[2] Just as relatively few roles have been available to older female actors, so the question is asked: Are aging female characters in film marginalized to the threshold of invisibility?[3]

Ida Lupino, as a director, depicted such unmarried women in the foreground of several episodes of the Boris Karloff-hosted anthology series *Thriller*, produced by Hubbell Robinson Productions for MCA's Review Studios and broadcast by NBC between September 13, 1960, and April 30, 1962. Such women sometimes appear either as immature and unconcerned with their own physical attractiveness or even directly subversive as witches, lesbians, and even Medusa herself. Their nonsexual nature is central to the characters' prominence in these episodes and, in "The Closed Cabinet," this context plays a role in resolving the main riddle of the story.

I would argue that, in the Lupino-directed *Thriller* episodes, beautiful and sexually active women are subjugated by men and used as a commodity for the exchange of wealth, while women of indeterminate sexuality exhibit a certain freedom of action and have self-determinacy. I also analyze the various ways that these empowered women engage with men to provoke the quality of terror in Karloff's series. Ultimately, such agency displaces Lupino's characters from the binary categories of good woman/bad woman that patriarchy has forced upon society and the masculine/feminine distinction that feminism, as an intellectual movement, attempts to deconstruct and destabilize.[4]

Overall, I will examine six of the nine stories that Lupino directed for *Thriller*. First, I will consider two of Lupino's *Thriller* episodes depicting aggressive and sexuality-charged women and then explore the differences between these tales and other episodes, which focus on more passive women who fulfill society's expectations of womanhood and sexuality.[5]

Women as Commodity: "Guillotine" and "The Bride Who Died Twice"

Both "Guillotine" (Season 2, Episode 2, September 26, 1961) and "The Bride Who Died Twice" (Season 2, Episode 25, March 19, 1962) deal with women who are exchanged as a commodity between men. In "Guillotine," Babette Lamont (Danielle De Metz) is a married and thus sexualized woman in nineteenth-century France who has an affair only to have her husband, Robert Lamont (Alejandro Rey), discover the indiscretion and murder her lover. He is imprisoned for his crime and sentenced to death by guillotine, thus reinforcing Babette as a classic femme fatale who brings destruction to men, a figure exemplifying "male anxieties about women's sexual and economic freedom."[6] Although a decidedly sexual female and thus potentially threatening to men, Babette nevertheless is vulnerable to manipulation and communalization by her husband. As the story explains a French tradition of the period, if the executioner dies, then the next prisoner in line for execution is summarily pardoned. Robert agrees to forgive Babette if she will poison the executioner, Monsieur de Paris (Robert Middleton), to secure his release, even implying that she may seduce the executioner to promote her mission. Robert thus exchanges his wife's sexuality for his own benefit, preying upon her feelings of guilt and remorse, even though he has been less than an ideal husband throughout their marriage. As Gerda Lerner argues, "women are no mere things. Their sexuality is what is commoditized," thus depriving them of their autonomy and subjectivity.[7] Babette nevertheless may display a dark side, such as when she kills a cockroach to assess the potency of the poison, yet she remains hesitant and nervous at the prospect of killing another human being. Her efforts finally are thwarted, and she is arrested, while Robert goes to his execution as a man even further compromised by his wife's agency and sexuality. Babette remains a complex character, a combination of the commoditized female victim and the unfaithful femme fatale eluding both of these polarized, stereotypical categories.

Perhaps more consistent with *Thriller*'s emphasis upon passive women, Consuelo De La Verra (Mala Powers), the daughter of the nineteenth-century Spanish General De La Verra (Eduardo Ciannelli) in "The Bride Who Died Twice," becomes a commodity for two different men. While her father essentially exchanges her to Colonel Sangriento (Joe De Santis) in a business transaction intended to spare the father's life, Consuelo is motivated to consume a drug simulating rigor mortis to escape violation by the Colonel on her wedding night. Consuelo not only has no say in the forced marriage, submitting to the masculine deal that determined her fate, but also effectively objectifies herself by faking death, a physical representation of the passive nature of many women in her social order (Figure 16.1).

Consuelo, revived, attempts to escape with her lover Captain Bartolomeo Antonio Fernandez (Robert Colbert), but they are captured and Antonio is executed by the Colonel in Consuelo's presence. Consuelo runs to embrace the fallen Antonio and, while kissing him, stains the wedding dress she is wearing with his blood. In some cultures, the stain of blood on a white

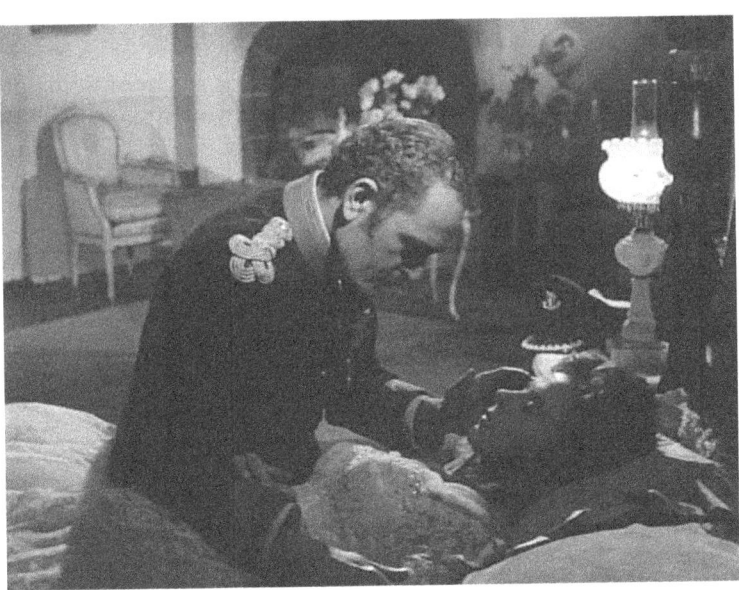

FIGURE 16.1 *A body without a soul in* The Bride Who Died Twice.

dress affirms the purity of the bride before her wedding night, but here this nearly ceremonial revelation reflects the inevitability of death.[8] "I have brought back to you everything that you have ever owned," she tells the Colonel as she collapses in his embrace, thus rejecting any suggestion that he once dominated her incomparable spirit. Consuelo dies from the effects of poison passed to her by her lover and the white dress becomes a shroud, the bloodstain symbolizing the end of life rather than the beginning of marriage.

Nonsexual Women as Threat

While Babette and Consuelo exhibit little agency of their own, other female characters in Lupino's *Thriller* episodes demonstrate the subversive independence most challenging to the masculine social order. "The Last of the Sommervilles" (Season 2, Episode 7, November 6, 1961) and "Mr. George" (Season 1, Episode 32, May 9, 1961), in particular, share so many common elements related to the notion of the empowered woman that the episodes effectively present twin stories. Both tales involve murder as a means of gaining an inheritance, and they share similar characters: the childish woman, the older, unmarried woman who regrets her secluded life and who seeks relief in a windfall bequest, and the man emotionally emasculated by the aggressive women's power. Lupino, in fact, wrote ,"The Last of the Sommervilles," after directing "Mr. George," adapted by Donald S. Sanford from a story by August Derleth, a frequent collaborator with H.P. Lovecraft and an important author of horror and the macabre in his own right. The characters apparently resonated so powerfully with Lupino's own sensibilities that she appropriated them for her own, perhaps more successful script.

"Mr. George" tells the story of Priscilla (Gina Gillespie), a child whose inherited fortune is in trust until she reaches adulthood. Priscilla's guardians, the Leggetts, are outraged that the family money is reserved for the child alone and plot to murder Priscilla to gain the inheritance. Edna (Virginia Gregg), along with Jared (Howard Freeman) and Adelaide (Lillian Bronson), are unaware that Priscilla has a more beneficent but invisible fourth guardian, Mr. George (voiced by Les Tremayne), the ghost of her mother's attorney and, probably, the girl's true father. Mr. George successfully thwarts the Leggett's attempts to kill Priscilla and, in the process, begins systematically exterminating them in creative ways that mimic the Leggetts' own homicidal attempts. While Mr. George, from beyond the grave, may be morally compromised by these acts, the Leggetts emerge as the real villains of the episode through their coldhearted and mercenary collusion. Mr. George's acts are mitigated as he has Priscilla's protection in mind, and, after all, the ghost eliminates some very nasty characters from the physical plane.

Edna, the most malicious of Priscilla's three corporeal guardians, decides that the child must die not only to secure the family fortune but to avoid the odious task of guardianship. "What do we know of raising children?" Edna rhetorically asks as Adelaide somewhat passively agrees, thus confirming the isolation and limited prospects of the aging, unmarried and sexually inactive woman in a masculine-dominated culture. As critic Richard Dyer maintains, "the notion of women's only fulfillment being achieved through marriage and childbearing is central to the culture," and therefore avoiding these social requirements adds elements of intentional evil to the already-marginal characters of Priscilla and Edna.[9]

The evil, childless woman may be a prevalent stereotype in both literature and film, perhaps bringing order to the narrative and allowing the artist to communicate character and motivation in a succinct way. Stereotypes, however, generally are based upon rigid concepts used to preserve the existing social order.[10] Lupino's own use of stereotypes certainly supports the status quo in this manner, but she also uses the narrative to give visibility to a group that otherwise would be ignored, immune from discussion, criticism, or revision. Although hardly commendable characters, Edna and Adelaide also display a peculiarly feminine form of preservice and conviction, eclipsing the tenuous and wishy-washy personality of the only male member of the family. Jared initially may be horrified at Edna's plot but, as she so readily points out, he already had considered, silently, a similar plan yet was too sanctimonious to acknowledge his base motives. Both women, overall, may be represented negatively, but nevertheless depict a kind of forthrightness and honesty characteristic of the more-empowered post–Second World War woman.

The motif of strong, unwed women with evil intent is repeated in "The Last of the Sommervilles," yet another episode directed by Lupino and featuring a plot structure and characters similar to that of "Mr. George." Aunt Celia Sommerville (Martita Hunt) is the temperamental counterpart of Adelaide, an unmarried and childless woman, who is both emotionally infantile and unwilling to confront her diminished social status. Celia's life has been spent in misanthropy and avarice, and she shamelessly flirts with Dr. Albert Farnham (Boris Karloff), the only man who regularly visits her house. Like Adelaide, she is socially deviant, not only through her failure to advance the female expectations of marriage and motherhood, but also by her rejection of the real world in favor of imagination and fantasy.[11] When Celia's nephew, Harvey Parchester (Chet Stratton), comes to visit, Celia suddenly confronts a real-world crisis for which she is sadly unprepared: Harvey's intention is to borrow money for a business deal rather than to express love for his aging relative. Ultimately, she refuses the loan, and Harvey then plots with Ursula Sommerville (Phyllis Thaxter), a distant relative and Aunt Celia's unwelcome live-in partner, to murder Aunt Celia and inherit her presumably meager estate.

While Celia replicates Adelaide in her infantilism and moral compromise, Ursula mirrors the aging Edna from "Mr. George." Both women have spent their lives living reclusively in big houses, isolated not only from other people but from the possibility of romantic relationships. Celia physically projects moral ambiguity through her grotesque appearance, dressing with a genteel shabbiness and talking in a shrill, affected voice. Yet Ursula is even more representative of evil, a cold-blooded murderer who further adds to the negative attributes associated with the unmarried, sexless woman as a social type. At the episode's end, Ursula's character is undermined, somewhat abruptly and, with perplexing narrative inconsistency, when the audience learns that she is romantically involved with the family attorney and the true last Sommerville, Rutherford (Peter Walker).[12] Ultimately Ursula's character transitions from the typical film representation of the spinster to another classic female type, the femme fatale. This surprising conclusion has provoked critical discussion, and ultimately Ursula's success may result from previously obscure sexual urges.

Both Celia and Ursula are nonsexual women whose failure to have husbands and children, and consequently their perceived lack of femininity, positions them as monsters in the classical negative stereotype. Lupino will again use the nonsexual woman in "The Closed Cabinet" (Season 2, Episode 10, November 27, 1961), a more thematically complex episode of *Thriller*. Here the main female character is neither an aging spinster nor a sacrificial virgin willing to submit to men, but a strong-willed woman whose very virginity makes her able to resolve the tale's narrative mystery.

This gothic episode begins on a stormy sixteenth-century night in a brooding English castle where Lady Beatrice (Patricia Manning), sick of her husband's physical and mental tortures, decides to kill him using a dagger that also becomes the instrument of her dramatic, storm-drenched suicide (see Figure 16.2). Dame Alice (Doris Lloyd), enraged by her son's murder and frustrated by Lady Beatrice's escape from punishment through death, invokes a curse upon the family. As she dictates through occult measures, each generation will "see a Mervyn bring shame and death" to the family. The curse will continue until someone discovers the murder weapon that she has hidden in a secret cabinet drawer. When the castle maid (Myra Carter) convinces her to allow for an end to the curse, Dame Alice agrees: "An end there shall be," she proclaims, "but it is beyond the wisdom of man to fix it, or the wit of man to discover it" (Figure 16.2).

The agency of women is the primary subject and main theme of the story, binding the narrative and adding a feminine-centered pretext at once both thrilling and courageous for a 1960s television episode. Dame Alice's son is an inert, sleeping body in the bed when he is murdered by his wife, who a moment later makes the decision to end her own life. Both corpses are found by another woman, the maid, who then calls Dame Alice and inadvertently leads to the invocation of the family curse. Even the curse presents a female-centered pretext, as only the agency of a woman may find the dagger and thus end the generational hex.

Three-hundred years after Lady Beatrice's fatal act, Evie Bishop (Olive Sturgess) visits the castle to visit her cousin Lucy Mervyn (Jennifer Raine),

FIGURE 16.2 *Lady Beatrice's fatal act in* The Closed Cabinet.

who is married to the castle's owner, George Mervyn (Peter Forster). Upon her arrival, Evie reports hearing about the curse from "a funny little woman on the train," and although Lucy is skeptical, Evie seems excited about the prospect of uncovering the truth behind a supposedly supernatural event.[13] Only two characters, George and Alan Mervyn (David Frankham), fear the curse as they are the modern-day masculine representatives of the Mervyn family and thus the lineage seems to end with them. Yet both men lack the motivation to help Evie resolve the presumably supernatural enigma, even as she consistently reminds them of the curse with her insistence upon spectral appearances and stormy nights that only she seems to hear. During the second day of her stay, Evie tours the castle and grounds with Alan and finds a locked door that may be the entrance to the dungeons that Evie so insistently wants to find. When Alan retires in search of a key, the door automatically opens for Evie, and she impulsively descends a dark stairwell and through cobweb-laden passages to the crypt where Hugh, Lord of Mervyn, the cruel husband killed by Lady Beatrice at the beginning of the episode, is interred. On Lord Hugh's coffin lies a symbol of his masculinity: a whip that Evie briefly inspects with horror before letting it drop a moment later. When a stone wall in the crypt mysteriously opens, Evie finds the hidden tomb of Lady Beatrice. The cryptic inscription above her coffin is especially troublesome for Evie:

Where the Woman Sinned
The Maid Shall Win

But God help the Maid
Who Sleeps Here-in

As Dame Alice's curse ordains, the mystery may be solved only by a woman, and the inscription further implies that the woman also must be a maid, a virgin who has not yet "sinned" by having sexual intercourse, and one with the will and sense of empowerment to "win." Evie is, at least implicitly, a virgin, and Lupino communicates the young woman's purity through the white, flowing dress she wears and the bouquet of flowers she carries as she descends into the dungeons of the castle. The mystery is hers to solve, and the doors and secret passages naturally open for her in recognition of her status.

George exemplifies the masculine dominance and tyranny that has suppressed women for centuries and that Evie, in her purity of intent, seeks to disrupt. When George finds out that the secret crypt of Lady Beatrice has been discovered, he reacts violently, for the tomb is a reminder of the family curse. He impulsively attacks his brother with a whip similar to the one Evie earlier found on Lord Hugh's coffin, thus demonstrating the male dominance and suppression that is pervasive in the castle as well as in society. George at one point even advises his brother to remain single, despite Alan's obvious attraction to Evie, citing the dangers that may happen through continuing the Mervyn line. George thus affirms masculine dominance and views women only as commodities to be used and then abandoned.

Evie, led by the benevolent apparition of Lady Beatrice, eventually finds the hidden dagger and is confronted by the inert body of Lord Hugh, preternaturally materialized on the chamber bed. She refuses to reenact the ancient homicide, and the ghost of Lady Beatrice, relieved of guilt and satisfied to see the family curse end, dissolves with a smile. When Evie looks toward the bed, the specter of Lord Hugh has disappeared as well.

Evie's agency and courage represents a powerful depiction of the feminine psychology, one notably at odds with the common television portrait of women as malleable servants intended nearly exclusively to support the goals of a masculine culture. In both "Mr. George" and "The Last of the Sommervilles," the male-centered social structure remains threatened by the nonsexual woman and her power and agency. Lupino uses the medium of anthology television to both entertain and to tell the story of a social and sexual identity challenge that continues to affect us all, over fifty years after the episode's initial broadcast.

Monstrous Women: Lesbians, Witches, and Gorgons

While many of the Lupino-directed episodes of *Thriller* are concerned with female sexual deviance as monstrous, subversive to a patriarchal social order, other episodes focus on a more literal representation of monsters, an extension of the popular horror film motifs of the mid-twentieth century. As Jeffrey Jerome Cohen argues, a deviant sexual identity is "susceptible to monsterization."[14] Certainly in the broadly homophobic period when *Thriller* episodes were broadcast, the figure of the sexually degenerated homosexual implied socially transgressive and even "monstrous" behavior. Freedom and democracy were the ostensible political standards used by politicians to combat the communist menace, but in fact many

American citizens were expected to conform to expected homogeneity, and any deviation was viewed as unpatriotic and, by extension, monstrous.

"The Lethal Ladies" (Season 2, Episode 29, April 16, 1962), the penultimate *Thriller* episode, features two separate stories dealing with timid people confronted by challenging situations. The first tale, "Murder on the Rocks," the most relevant to this discussion of Lupino's work, not only deals with malicious intent and murder, mainstays of Karloff's series, but also with lesbianism, a remarkably courageous departure from the typical TV expectations of the period. Here Myron Sills (Howard Morris) decides to kill his wife Lavinia (Rosemary Murphy) during a trip through the mountains, and succeeds in pushing her over a cliff, presumably to her death. Lavinia remarkably survives the fall and returns to enact revenge upon her husband, taking him to the same mountainous location and intending to shove him over the same cliff. Ultimately, in the type of twist ending common to both EC Comics and the *Thriller* series, both Lavinia and Myron meet unexpected and terrifying ends.

The story is bland and the climax is patently moralizing, but the episode remains one of the few early 1960s representations of a lesbian character broadcast on nationwide television. Indeed, Lupino emphasizes Livinia's covert sexual orientation by masculinizing her physical features and revealing her testosterone-fueled outdoor hobbies. As Elaine Lawless maintains, audiences in a patriarchal culture only recognize lesbianism in the masculine form, the so-called "butch" persona clearly codified as "women disguised as men with manly behavior."[15] Lavinia consequently is strong and athletic, a masculine presence who takes up rock climbing as a hobby. When Myron characterizes their upcoming weekend hike in the mountains as an unusual way to relax, Lavinia dismisses his evaluation and implies that, for her, outdoor physical exertion is routine. In fact, Lavinia exhibits the physical characteristics that Lawless identifies as the cultural codification of lesbianism: she sports a short hairstyle and dresses in plaid shirts, baggy pants, and cowboy boots.[16] She is always on the edge of aggression, even in polite conversation. Myron's lover, Gloria (Pamela Curran), presents a sharp contrast with her overtly feminine wardrobe and bubbly mannerisms. While Lavinia's clothes tend to obliterate her curves, adding to her explicit masculinity, Gloria favors a tight black-and-gold dress that is short and revealing and accentuates her "bimbo-lover" aspect with her platinum hair, heavy makeup, and girlish giggle. Lavinia is perceived as a cultural monster because she is a murderer and, especially, a lesbian. She represents a dual threat to manhood, and, therefore, according to the early 1960s television codex, she must die with her emasculated husband in the moralizing ending of the episode.

While the established social order may identify deviant individuals as monsters, and *Thriller* regularly deals with these perceived aberrations, other episodes in the series move into *Twilight Zone* territory and present real monsters with an occult or supernatural basis. For example, "La Strega" (Season 2, Episode 17, January 15, 1962) begins in the eighteenth-century Italian countryside with the young and beautiful Luana (Ursula Andress) being brutally attacked by three men who accuse her of witchcraft. The nature of the scene implies gang rape, with Luana protecting her breasts as the men approach her with malicious smiles (Figure 16.3).

The men eventually toss Luana into the river, expecting her to drown but, instead, she is rescued by a visiting Spaniard, Tonio Bellini (Alejandro Rey). Romance blossoms, and Luana agrees to stay in Tonio's room, allowing him to paint her portrait, but the arrangement soon is spoiled by the arrival of La Strega (Jeanette Nolan), who demands that Luana, her granddaughter, return home. Tonio refuses, and La Strega seeks revenge by invoking a curse. Tonio at first is skeptical of the spell, but soon begins to drift into hallucinations and nightmares, eventually culminating when Tonio apparently strangles the witch.

FIGURE 16.3 *Luana dreading the attack in* La Strega.

Luana, like Consuelo in "Bride" and Babette in "Guillotine," is an erotized creature whose sexuality is objectified by the male villagers as a means of control. Sexual desire is commonly associated with the accusation of witchcraft, and transgressive women thus suffer physically as men, seeking dominance, disguise their lust as cultural outrage. In this social ruse, the woman loses her humanity and becomes an object inviting violation, while the community moralistically looks the other way. In contrast, La Strega exhibits the characteristics typically associated with witches in Western folklore: long nose, afflicted skin, malevolent voice, tattered black dress, matted hair, and long, dirty fingernails. Lupino once again emphasizes the type of female that creates profound social anxiety among men, a monstrosity evoking castration and the disruption of masculine cultural dominance.[17] As Monica Germanà maintains, "much like the madwoman, the witch signifies . . . at least two things: the destabilizing power of woman's self-determination, and, as a result of such dissidence, her enforced relegation to the peripheries of social spectrum."[18] The witch, like other cruel female monsters from Lupino-directed *Thriller* tales, has self-determination and a strong-willed personality allowing her to be feared, especially by men. Her power of speech is so strong that Tonio eventually becomes convinced of the curse and, in his delirium, is unable to distinguish imagination from reality.

Ultimately, Tonio discovers that he has been the victim of an occult ruse—a seemingly psychotic transference—allowing La Strega to project her physical form onto Luana. His portrait of the lovely young Luana transforms into the image of the witch, and the lifeless body of the dead woman becomes Luana, murdered by a confused and delirious Tonio. This surprise ending exemplifies masculine anxieties and paranoia, the almost innate fear and distrust expressed by a patriarchal society towards the self-determined and confident woman.

The witch as an "other" and as an agent of castration represents the masculine fear of women, but other supernatural female figures incite a similar fear.[19] The Gorgon, the malevolent female monster from ancient Greek mythology whose gaze turns men to stone, also mirrors the witch as a socially excluded agent of castration, a symbol of the "dread of women."[20] Lupino extends her study of the supernatural female outsider by briefly including a Gorgon in the last tale of "Trio for Terror" (Season 1, Episode 25, March 14, 1961), a multipart episode of *Thriller*. The segment, titled "The Mask of Medusa," deals with Shanner (Michael Pate), a serial killer of young women. Escaping from the police, Shanner takes temporary refuge in a museum filled with lifelike statues sculpted from stone. At the climax of this short tale, the sculptor, Kriss Milo (John Abbot), reveals the secret of his art: he has acquired the mask of the Gorgon Medusa, and all of the sculptures on display are in fact men who had the misfortune to encounter that monster. Shanner, too, becomes an object d'art in Milo's gruesome exhibit, a fitting end for a man who embodies the masculine desire for revenge upon the social threat of emerging womanhood.

Conclusion

Lupino, in her directorial accomplishments with Karloff's *Thriller*, uses negative female stereotypes to demonstrate the many ways that women have been socially suppressed through the centuries, thus motivating the audience to contemplate this marginalization and support a more positive view of woman's role in society. Of the nine episodes that Lupino directed for the show, six involve "lethal ladies": killer spinsters, hags, infantilized old ladies, and even Medusa herself. Two episodes, "Mr. George" and "The Last of the Sommervilles," employ the same set of stock female characters. Lupino certainly seems to concentrate on the female outsider, consistently choosing to direct episodes that examine the feminine "other" and her role in society. These characters live at the margins of society, resisting the culture-bound expectations of woman as the heterosexual nurturer of children and servant to men. Adrienne Rich, examining those women who do not surrender to male suppression, provides a list that reinforces Lupino's selection of characters. As she maintains, "witches, *femmes seules*, marriage resisters, spinsters, autonomous widows, and/or lesbians" all have managed to resist collaboration with male oppression. Rich omits only the Gorgon, Lupino's mythological creature and perhaps the archetype and mother of all female outliers.[21]

As a director, Lupino certainly was on dangerous artistic ground by seeking a positive audience reaction to these negative female stereotypes. Was the early 1960s television audience able to understand and appreciate the complex implications of her statement? Or did her use of negative stereotypes effectively reinforce the unfavorable perception of transgressive women prevalent at that time among audience members who may have been culture-bound on gender issues? Lupino takes a more traditional approach with "The Closed Cabinet," arguably one of her more feminist episodes, examining Evie, a female character who is both strong-willed and decidedly princess-pure. Every plot element is resolved by women while men look on, whip in hand, fearing the feminine threat to patriarchal domination. Evie may not be a monster per se, but she certainly seems like one to the threatened and domineering men of the story. Nevertheless, Evie emerges as a sympathetic character and one perhaps communicating Lupino's vision of strong womanhood most effectively to an audience accustomed to straightforward messages in popular culture. Lupino finally delivers an imposing challenge to women of her era: either demonstrate self-determination and confidence in all thought and action or prepare to be labeled as a monster, a social outcast subject to emotional marginalization and physical outrage.

Notes

1. Patricia Vertinsky, *The Eternally Wounded Woman: Women, Doctors, and Exercise in the Late Nineteenth Century* (New York: Manchester University Press, 1994), 95.
2. Jane Garrity, *Step-Daughters of England: British Women Modernist and the National Imaginary* (New York: Manchester University Press, 1994), 156.
3. Sara Lennox, *Cemetery of the Murdered Daughters: Feminism, History, and Ingeborg Bachmann* (Amherst: University of Massachusetts Press, 2006), 87.
4. Sophia Phoca, "Feminism and Gender," in Sarah Gamble (ed.), *The Routledge Companion to Feminism and Postfeminism* (New York: Routledge, 2001), 46.
5. The episode "What becoming ghost" is not included in this discussion as it generally does not deal with female representation. Two of the three tales that compromise "Trio of terror" also are omitted for the same reason.
6. Helen Hanson, *Hollywood Heroines: Women in Film Noir, and the Female Gothic Film* (New York: I.B. Tauris, 2007), xv.
7. Gerda Lerner, *The Creation of Patriarchy* (New York: Oxford University Press, 1986), 213.
8. Lisa Wedeen, *Ambiguities of Domination: Politics, Rhetoric, and Symbols in Contemporary Syria* (Chicago: University of Chicago Press, 1999), 64.
9. Richard Dyer, *The Matter of Images: Essays on Representations* (New York: Routledge, 2013), 84. Emphasis in the original.
10. Ibid., 12.
11. Diana Tietjens Meyers, "The Rush to Motherhood: Pronatalist Discourse and Women's Autonomy," *Signs*, 26, no. 3 (Spring, 2001): 735.
12. See, for example, two online sites dedicated exclusively to the series *Thriller*. In the review of this episode, both sites agree that the episode's ending appears to be an afterthought and is not consistent with the main story. See http://athrilleraday.blogspot.com.ar/2010/10/last-of-sommervilles-season-2-episode-7.html and https://www.facebook.com/BorisKarloffsThriller/posts/627694227268020.
13. Evie's comment is an important indication that the story of the Mervyn curse primarily circulated among local women while men, particularly Alan and George, generally refused to discuss this threat to their masculinity.
14. Jeffrey Cohen, "Monster Culture (Seven Theses)," in Jeffrey Jerome Cohen (ed.), *Monster Theory* (Minneapolis: University of Minnesota Press, 1996), 9.
15. Elaine Lawless, "Claiming Inversion: Lesbian Constructions of Female Identity as Claims for Authority," *The Journal of American Folklore*, 111, no. 439 (Winter, 1998): 14.

16 Ibid., 12.
17 Ibid.
18 Monica Germanà, *Scottish Women's Gothic and Fantastic Writing: Fiction Since 1978* (Edinburgh: Edinburgh University Press), 66.
19 Barbara Creed, *The Monstrous-Feminine: Film, Feminism, Psychoanalysis* (New York: Routledge, 2007), 74.
20 Nancy Sorkin Rabinowitz, *Anxiety Veiled: Euripides and the Traffic in Women* (New York: Cornell University Press, 1993), 85.
21 Adrienne Cecile Rich, "Compulsory Heterosexuality and Lesbian Existence," *Journal of Women's History*, 15, no. 3 (Autumn 2003): 15.

CONTRIBUTORS

Fernando Gabriel Pagnoni Berns (PhD in arts, PhD candidate in history) works as professor in the Universidad de Buenos Aires (UBA)—Facultad de Filosofía y Letras (Argentina). He teaches courses on international horror film and is director of the research group on horror cinema "Grite." He has published chapters in the books *To See the Saw Movies: Essays on Torture Porn* and *Post 9/11 Horror*, edited by John Wallis, *Critical Insights: Alfred Hitchcock*, edited by Douglas Cunningham, *Dreamscapes in Italian Cinema*, edited by Francesco Pascuzzi, *Reading Richard Matheson: A Critical Survey*, edited by Cheyenne Mathews, among others. He has authored on Spanish horror TV series *Historias para no Dormir* (Universidad de Cádiz) and has edited a collection on director James Wan (McFarland).

Adam Breckenridge is an assistant professor of speech and writing in the Overseas Traveling Faculty program at the University of Maryland Global Campus, where he teaches writing, speech, and film classes to overseas US military. His scholarship is focused on the intersections of film and rhetorical theory. His latest article, "A Path Less Traveled: Rethinking Spirituality in the Films of Alejandro Jodorowsky," was recently published in the *Journal of Religion and Film*.

Ashley M. Donnelly is a professor of telecommunications at Ball State University. Her book *Renegade Hero or Faux Rogue: The Secret Traditionalism of Television Bad Boys* (MacFarland Press) is available in print, and her latest book *Subverting Mainstream Narratives in Reagan's America: Bringing Power to the People* (Palgrave Macmillan) is available in print as a full manuscript and online through Springer Publishers. She publishes primarily on issues related to media and contemporary American culture, and her work can be found in a variety of journals and edited collections.

Julie Grossman is Professor of English and Communication and Film Studies at Le Moyne College. She has published numerous essays on film and literature in scholarly journals and edited collections. She is coeditor (with R. Barton Palmer) of the book series *Adaptation and Visual Culture* (Palgrave Macmillan) and the essay collection *Adaptation in Visual Culture: Images, Texts, and Their Multiple Worlds* (Palgrave Macmillan, 2017). Other books include *Rethinking the Femme Fatale in Film Noir* (Palgrave Macmillan, 2009, 2012), *Literature, Film, and Their Hideous Progeny* (Palgrave Macmillan, 2015), *Ida Lupino, Director: Her Art and Resilience in Times of Transition* (coauthored with Therese Grisham, Rutgers UP, 2017), *Twin Peaks* (coauthored with Will Scheibel, Wayne State UP, 2020), and *The Femme Fatale* (Rutgers UP, 2020).

Curtis LeVan is a visiting instructor at the University of South Florida. His areas of interest include early English drama, physiognomy, film adaptations, and acting/performance history.

Valerie Barnes Lipscomb is Professor of English at the University of South Florida. Her monograph, *Performing Age in Modern Drama*, was published in 2016 by Palgrave Macmillan. Her work also has appeared in such journals as *Modern Drama*, *Comparative Drama*, *International Journal of Ageing and Later Life*, and *Age, Culture, Humanities*. She is treasurer of the North American Network in Aging Studies and has chaired the Modern Language Association's Age Studies Forum.

Karen McNally is Senior Lecturer in Film and Television Studies at London Metropolitan University and a specialist in American Film, television, and culture. She is the author of *The Stardom Film: Creating the Hollywood Fairy Tale* (Wallflower Press, 2020) and *When Frankie Went to Hollywood: Frank Sinatra and American Male Identity* (University of Illinois Press, 2008), editor of *Billy Wilder, Movie-Maker: Critical Essays on the Films* (McFarland, 2011), and coeditor of *The Legacy of Mad Men: Cultural History, Intermediality and American Television* (Palgrave Macmillan, 2019). Karen has published and presented widely on topics such as stardom, masculinity, race, and musicals, and has been interviewed on television and radio and at a variety of media events. Her edited volume *American Television in the Trump Era* is forthcoming with Wayne State University Press.

Mary Lynn Navarro is an associate professor at Kingsborough Community College, CUNY. She teaches composition, literature, film, and journalism courses. She has written creative nonfiction and articles on popular culture and race and class representation in film.

Gary D. Rhodes currently serves as Associate Professor of Film and Mass Media at the University of Central Florida, Orlando. He is the author of *Emerald Illusions: The Irish in Early American Cinema* (IAP, 2012), *The Perils of Moviegoing in America* (Bloomsbury, 2012), and *The Birth of the American Horror Film* (Edinburgh UP, 2018), as well as the editor of such anthologies as *Edgar G. Ulmer: Detour on Poverty Row* (Lexington, 2008), *The Films of Joseph H. Lewis* (Wayne State University, 2012), and *The Films of Budd Boetticher* (Edinburgh UP, 2017). Rhodes is also the writer-director of such documentary films as *Lugosi: Hollywood's Dracula* (1997) and *Banned in Oklahoma* (2004). His latest book, coauthored with Robert Singer, is *Consuming Images: Film Art and the American Television Commerical* (Edinburgh UP, 2020).

Kathleen "Kat" Robinson teaches in the General Education program at Eckerd College. She also is the Scholarship and Fellowship Adviser at Eckerd College. In addition to a number of articles on various authors such as Ernest Hemingway and Norman Mailer, she works with theories of trauma, narrative structure, and gender perspectives.

William T. Ross is former chair and professor emeritus of English at the University of South Florida, where he taught courses on silent and early sound films. In addition to a number of articles on rhetoric and the discursive prose of George Orwell and Bertrand Russell, he is the author of books on the American poet Weldon Kees and the historical works of H.G. Wells.

Courtney Ruffner Grieneisen is Professor of English at State College of Florida. She has studied Ezra Pound's *Cantos* in Northern Italy, and has also researched and studied Pound in Madrid, Spain. She has published on Italian-Americana, Ezra Pound, Edgar Allan Poe, and John Donne, and has presented her work on Italianity and on Pound nationally and internationally. Her work on Donne has been translated into Portuguese and has been published in the Brazilian journal, *Revisto Espaço Acadêmico*. She earned her doctorate in Literature and Theory from Indiana University of Pennsylvania. She is the vice president of Marketing and Communications for the Italian American Studies Association, and is an associate editor for the association's journal, the *Annual*.

Marlisa Santos is Professor in the Department of Humanities and Politics and Honors College Faculty Fellow at Nova Southeastern University. Her research focuses on *film noir* and classic film studies. She is the editor of *Verse, Voice, and Vision: Poetry and the Cinema* and the author of *The Dark Mirror: Psychiatry and Film Noir*. She has also published numerous articles on various topics such as Cornell Woolrich, film noir aesthetics, the James Bond franchise, and American mafia cinema, and on directors such as Martin Scorsese, Edgar G. Ulmer, and Joseph H. Lewis.

Michael Shuman is a senior instructor in the Department of English at University of South Florida. He teaches classes in the "Professional Writing, Rhetoric, and Technology" program and coordinates the department's internship program. While primarily teaching technical communications, his research interests include film studies, especially film noir of the late 1940s and early 1950s, the psychoanalytic theory of Otto Rank, and contemporary speculative fiction. His latest project is an essay on *Jack Armstrong, The All-American Boy*, a 1947 science adventure film serial directed by Wallace Fox. He is Deputy Editor of *The Mailer Review*.

Phillip Sipiora is Professor of English and Film Studies at the University of South Florida. He is the author or editor of five books, and has published approximately three dozen scholarly essays. He has published essays on the films of Wallace Fox, Joseph H. Lewis, Ida Lupino, Stanley Kubrick, Robert Wiene, Billy Wilder, and Edgar Ulmer. He has lectured nationally and internationally on twentieth-century literature and film and is the founding editor of *The Mailer Review*. He is currently working on a book on Martin Scorsese.

Ann Torrusio is an associate teaching professor in the Pierre Laclede Honors College at the University of Missouri–St. Louis, where she teaches composition, American literature and film. She also serves as a faculty adviser.

INDEX

77 Sunset Strip 228

Accused, The (1988) 181
Acker, Ally 216–17
acting, Lupino, Ida 8–9, 147–62
   American studio 151–7
   cinematic context(s) 147–62
   Ghost Camera, The
     (1933) 148–51
   High Sierra (1941) 151–7
   method 157–62
   Private Hell 36 (1954) 157–62
   in *Twilight Zone, The*
     (episodes) 213–15
Adams, Dorothy 65–6
Adam's Rib 179 n.15
Adler, Stella 158
Affron, Charles 152
African Queen, The 179 n.15
age conventions manipulation,
   Lupino's 127–43
   mid ages 138–43
   older ages 130–4
   younger ages 134–8
Alfred Hitchcock Presents 11, 165,
   214, 216–17, 228
Alice in Wonderland 128
Allen, Robert C. 152
American films 148, 151–7; see also
   specific films
American Girl 99
American studio acting 151–7,
   162 n.7
Anderson, Mary Ann 44, 127–8,
   177 n.5
Andre Kostelanetz Orchestra 39
Andrews, Tod 83, 141

aposiopesis 195
Artists and Models (1937) 96
Atkinson, Michael 169–70, 197–8
Axmaker, Sean 41

backstage characters 19–21
Bad and the Beautiful, The
   (1951) 19–20
Baise Moi/Rape Me (2000) 182
Bannion, Katie 98
Barsam, Richard 159–61
Basinger, Jeanine 21, 25
Bates, Norman 196
Beaumont, Charles 88
Berns, Fernando Gabriel
   Pagnoni 12–13
Betz, Carl 231
Bewitched 165, 227, 228, 237,
   239–40
Bigamist, The (1953) 3, 5–9, 11, 16,
   19, 44, 78–80, 95–110, 114–21,
   127, 131–4, 138, 141–2, 166–
   76, 177 n.4, 214–15, 231
   advertisements for 99–100
   agency in 95–110
   audience associations 99
   as classic noir 114–21
   flashbacks in 97
   genre in 95–110
   intertextuality of things 100
   Italian neorealism in 117–18
   low-budget shooting 117
   Lupino's direction, characteristics
     of 114–16
   moral uncertainties of in 109–10
   script 118–20
   shooting location 117

shortcomings 108
visual technique in 115–16
voice-over narratives, use of 97
bigamy 107, 118
Bigelow, Kathryn 232–3
Big Knife, The (1955) 19–21
black films 95, 193–211
Black Snake Moan (2007) 182
Blake, William 64–5
Bob Hope Presents the Chrysler Theater 228
Bogart, Humphrey 37, 151–3, 162 n.7, 176
Bond, Anson 18, 42
Bond, Nelson 221
Bond, Raymond 82
Bond, Ward 54
Bonnie and Clyde (1967) 36
Boone, Richard 46, 85
Bowen, Gil 193
Brando, Marlon 158
Braverman, Joan 178 n.7
Breckenridge, Adam 11–12
Breillat, Catherine 182
"Bride Who Died Twice, The" 88–9, 245–6
British films 148–9
Britton, Laura 23
Brody, Richard 134, 184–5, 191–2
Brown, Clarence 41
Bryna Productions 18
business of show 17–33

Caruth, Cathy 182, 186–7, 190–1
Castle, Charlie 20
Catholicism 123–4
Chambers, Wheaton 65–6
"Charley Red Dog" 86–8
Chivers, Sally 132
Ciannelli, Eduardo 88
Cinematographic Films Act (1927) 148
Clarke, Robert 83
Clifton, Elmer 42–3, 64, 96
Climax! 228
Cohen, Jeffrey Jerome 251
Colbert, Robert 88
Coleman, Ronald 38

Collins, Paul 24
Collins, Roy 193
Conard, Mark T. 95
Conversation, The 168
Cook, Pam 135, 141–2, 183–4
Cook, William, Jr. 138
Cotton, Joe 215
Crawford, Joan 132
Critique of Cynical Reason (Sloterdijk) 230
Crow, The (1994) 182
cult films 36
culture 4, 9–10, 12, 65, 68, 71
American 166
bus 74
patriarchal 127
rape 184
shamateurism in tennis 29
women and 132–4
Curtiz, Michael 38

Daniel Boone 228
Darwin, Charles 193–4, 204–5, 211
Davis, Bette 132
"Day of the Bad Man" 86–7
"Dead Eye Dick" 238
DeKova, Frank 233–4
De Metz, Danielle 89
DeNiro, Robert 60
Deren, Maya 229
Derleth, August 246
De Santis, Joe 88
De Sica, Vittorio 130
Despente, Virginie 182
Dietrich, Marlene 37
Dietrichson, Phyllis 30
Diskant, George 214
Dixon, Wheeler Winston 88, 122
Doctor Zhivago (1965) 36
documentary films 40–2
Donati, William 35, 41, 43, 47–8, 58–9, 91, 120, 128, 155–6, 182
Donna Reed Show, The 85, 228, 231–3
Donnelly, Ashley M. 7
double-consciousness, Lupino's 165–77, 177 n.3

Bigamist, The (1953)   170–7, 177 n.4
Hitch-Hiker, The (1953)   167–70, 177 n.4
role as woman director   166
as unaffiliated feminist   166–7
Double Indemnity (1944)   30
Douglas, Kirk   18, 20
Dr. Kildare   228
DuBois, W. E. B.   177 n.3
Duff, Howard   39, 128
Dundee and the Culhane   228
Dussere, Erik   72–3
Dwan, Allan   16, 38

Easy Rider (1969)   36
Eggenweiler, Robert   42
Emerald, Connie   2, 215–16
Emerald Productions   18

Farley, Florence   27, 136–7
Fat Girl (2001)   182
Father Knows Best   45
Feldman, Charles K.   41
Ferguson, Bruce   141
Film Acting (Pudovkin)   158
Filmakers, production company   3, 7, 18–19, 21, 27, 34 n.2, 96, 99–100, 121, 127, 159, 165, 169
film noir   95–6, 100, 114, 182; see also *Bigamist, The*
film nudity   36
Flynn, Errol   37
Ford, John   37
Forrest, Sally   64–70
Four Star Playhouse   45
Fourth Age   130
Frank, Nino   95
Freud, Sigmund   185
From Here to Eternity (1953)   44
Frye, William   47
Fugitive, The   165, 228, 231–3
Fuller, Sam   169

gender   4–6, 51–2, 63–74; see also *Bigamist, The*
General Electric Theater   85, 228
Gentlemen Prefer Blonds   45

Gentlemen's Agreement (1947)   41
Georgakas, Dan   18, 27, 78–9, 99, 104, 108, 110, 229
Ghost and Mrs. Muir, The   228
Ghost Camera, The (1933)   8, 148–51
Gilligan's Island   47, 227, 228, 240
Gillis, Joe   97
Girl with the Dragon Tattoo, The (2011)   182
Glancy, H. Mark   148
Goff, Andrew   195–6
Gomery, Douglas   152
Graduate, The (1967)   36
Graham, Harry   8, 78–9, 93, 97, 100–1, 106–9, 115–16, 119, 123, 131, 168–73, 176
Gravagne, Pamela H.   129–30
Grieneisen, Courtney Ruffner   4
Grisham, Therese   104, 165
Grossman, Julie   4–5, 104, 165
"Guillotine"   88–9, 244–5
Gwenn, Edmund   98, 132
Gypsy (1962)   22–3

Haastrup, Helle Kannik   97–8
Hands of Orlac, The (1924)   210
Haralovich, Mary Beth   122
Hard, Fast and Beautiful (1951)   3, 7–8, 16, 18–19, 21, 27–33, 40, 99, 127, 134–41
Harding, June   122
Hard Way, The (1943)   3, 21–8, 32–3, 40
Harlow, Jean   38
Haskell, Molly   79
Hathaway, Henry   38
Have Gun, Will Travel   46, 85, 88, 228, 235–7, 239
Hayes Code   234
Hecht, Harold   18
Heck-Rabi, Louise   216–17
Hepburn, Katherine   179 n.15
Her First Affaire (1932)   2, 38, 214
Herman, Judith Lewis   191
Higgins, Lynn   183, 190
High Sierra (1941)   9, 16, 51–2, 151–7
Hill, James   18

INDEX

Hill-Hecht-Lancaster 18
Hitchcock, Alfred 216
Hitch-Hiker, The (1953) 6–7, 9–11, 16, 40, 44, 51–2, 85, 96–7, 127, 134, 138–9, 165–70, 175, 177 n.4, 193–205, 209
   adjudication 209–11
   deep structure of 202–9
   ethics 203
   sociopaths, gallery of 200–2
   sources of 196
   subjectivity 202
   surface structure 194–9
Hoff, Stanley 20
Hollywood, Lupino, Ida in 4, 35–49, 165
   with Bond, Anson 42
   documentary films 40–2
   on film nudity 36–7
   Four Star Playhouse 45
   income 40
   New York Film Critics' Best Actress award 40
   Not Wanted (1949) 4, 16, 43–5, 63–74, 96, 129
   Paramount Pictures 38–9
   in show business 37–8
   television works 45–9
Hollywood studios 163 n.9
Homeward Bound 68
Honey West 12, 228, 237
Hong Kong 228
Hopper, Hedda 37, 41
Hotel de Paree 228
Howe, James Wong 43
Hubbell Robinson Productions 243
Huber, Christopher 195
Hughes, Howard 3, 39, 99
Hurd, Mary 78

Ida Lupino, Director: Her Art and Resilience in Times of Transition (Grisham) 13, 165
Ida Lupino Beyond the Camera 177 n.5
idealized masculinity 72–3
I Lived With You (1933) 38
I'll Cry Tomorrow (1955) 22–3

Inge, William 65
inheritance 216–23
Intruder in the Dust (1950) 41
Irving, Richard 53
Italian neorealism 117–18

Jakobsen, Janet 122
Janssen, David 231–2
Junior Bonner (1972) 129

Kaplan, Jonathan 181
Karloff, Boris 88
Kawin, Bruce F. 36
Kazan, Elia 65, 158
Kearney, Mary Celeste 46–7, 224
Kiss Me Deadly (1955) 92
Kiss of Death (1947) 198–9
Kolker, Robert 52–3, 60
Kraft Suspense Theater 228
Krewson, John 205
Kristeva, Julia 97
Kubrick, Stanley 114
Kuhn, Annette 37, 63–4, 128, 216, 223

"Lady on the Wall, The" 85–6
"Lady with a Gun" 85–6
Lancaster, Burt 18
Land of the Pharaohs 45
Last House on the Left (1979 and 2009) 182
"Last of the Sommervilles, The" 91–2, 246–50
"La Strega" 252
Lean, David 36
Leave Her to Heaven 179 n.15
Leiden, Mitchell 213
LeRoy, Mervyn 52
"Lethal Ladies, The" 89–91, 251–2
Letter to Three Wives, A (1950) 43
Levinas, Emmanuel 203
Light that Failed, The (1939) 38
Lipscomb, Valerie Barnes 7–8
Little Caesar 52
Litvak, Anatol 38
Lorre, Peter 197
Los Angeles Philharmonic 39
Lovecraft, H. P. 246

INDEX

Lovejoy, Frank 139, 195
Love Race, The (1932) 2, 37
Loving Cup 99
Lupino, Ida 1–3
  1960s mysteries 213–24
  acting of 8–9, 147–62, 213–15
  age conventions, manipulation of 127–43
  Alfred Hitchcock Presents 11, 165, 214, 216–17
  American stages and 8, 17–33
  with Anderson 177 n.5
  Artists and Models (1937) 96
  Bad and the Beautiful, The (1951) 19–20
  Bigamist, The (1953) 3, 5–9, 11, 16, 19, 44, 78–80, 95–110, 113–21, 127, 131–4, 138, 141–2, 166–76, 177 n.4, 214–15, 231
  Big Knife, The (1955) 19–21
  biography on 51, 128
  with Bond, Anson 42
  in British films 37–8
  and business of show 17–33
  career 3–4, 17, 51–2, 64, 213–24
  cinematic context(s), situating performance in 147–62
  on culture 4
  On Dangerous Ground (2019) 4, 13, 52–62, 62 n.6
  as director 3, 7–8, 35, 166, 213–24, 227–41
  documentary films 40–2
  double-consciousness of 165–77
  fans 165–6
  female perspective 51–3
  in Film Comment 102
  film legacy 223–4
  Four Star Playhouse 45
  gender trauma, analysis of 4–6, 51–2, 63–74
  Georgakas comments on 78–9
  Ghost Camera, The (1933) 8, 148–51
  Gilligan's Island 47, 227, 240
  as go-to actor 96
  Hard, Fast and Beautiful (1951) 3, 7–8, 16, 18–19, 21, 27–33, 40, 99, 127, 134–41
  Hard Way, The (1943) 3, 21–8, 32–3, 40
  Have Gun Will Travel 46
  Her First Affaire (1932) 2, 38, 214
  High Sierra (1941) 9, 16, 51–2, 151–7
  Hitch-Hiker, The (1953) 6–7, 9–11, 16, 40, 44, 51–2, 85, 96–7, 127, 134, 138–9, 165–70, 175, 177 n.4, 193–205, 209
  hitchhiking into darkness 193–211
  in Hollywood 4, 35–49
  as humanist 5
  I Lived With You (1933) 38
  Junior Bonner (1972) 129
  Light that Failed, The (1939) 38
  Love Race, The (1932) 2, 37
  men, portraits of 77–93
  middle ages characters, portrayals of 138–43
  moral filmmaking 113–24
  as mother directress 214–17
  Never Fear (1949) 16, 18, 42–4, 52, 57–8, 61, 62 n.6, 215
  No. 5 Checked Out 46, 239
  Not Wanted (1949) 4, 16, 43–5, 63–74, 96, 129
  older characters, portrayals of 130–4
  One Rainy Afternoon (1936) 96
  Outrage (1950) 5, 7–12, 16, 18, 30, 39, 42, 80–5, 127, 131–42, 181–92, 200–2, 215
  overlooked/underrepresented 51–61
  performance, interest/experience in 3
  Private Hell 36 (1954) 9, 157–62
  professional control 17–18
  reception/reputation 3
  with Reed, Barbara 39
  Road House (1948) 19, 41–3, 77

with Rossellini, Roberto 40
Scorsese's eulogy to 3, 15–16, 51
Screen Director's Playhouse 46
in *Search for Beauty* (1934) 2, 96
Sunset Boulevard (1950) 19, 97, 132
teleplay shows 12
television works 11–13, 45–9, 85–93, 177 n.1, 213–24, 227–41
Thriller series 11–12, 85, 88–91, 200, 214, 218, 243–54
Trouble With Angels, The 7, 35, 113–15, 122–4, 240
Twilight Zone, The 9, 11, 51, 132, 165, 168–70, 213–15, 221, 252
Two Weeks in Another Town (1962) 19–20
Where Angels Go Trouble Follows 47
works 51–2, 127–43, 147–62 (*see also specific works*)
young characters, portrayals of 134–8
with Zanuck 18, 41
Lupino, Stanley 1–2, 37

McCarthy, Clifford 152
McNally, Karen 3–4
male authoritarianism 135
Mamoulian, Rouben 38
Man I Love, The (1947) 16, 19
Mankiewicz, Joseph 43
Marcus, Larry 118
Mardorosssian, Carine M. 184
Marriage of Heaven and Hell 64–5
Marvin, Lee 233
"Mask of Medusa, The" 92, 221–3
"Masks, The" 9, 11, 165, 168–9, 214, 221–3
Mast, Gerald 36
Mean Streets (1973) 168, 259
men, portraits of 77–93
Merck, Mandy 29, 136
Merleau-Ponty, Maurice 193–4, 203
method acting 157–62

Middleton, Robert 89
Mildred Pierce (1945) 21, 28
Milestone, Lewis 38
Miller, Ann 98
Miller, Arthur 158
Mills, Hayley 122, 142–3
Mines, Harry 43
Mintz, Stephen 65, 68–9
Miracle on 34th Street (1947) 98, 132
Monahan, Dave 159–61
monstrous women 250–4
Moore, Cleo 53
moral filmmaking 113–24; *see also Bigamist, The; Trouble With Angels, The*
Moran, James M. 46, 224
More than Night: Film Noir in Its Contexts (Naremore) 95
Morra, Anne 60
mother 214
"Mother of a Champion" 99
Mr. Adams and Eve 45, 128, 167
"Mr. George" 246–50
Mulvey, Laura 178 n.8

Naked Kiss, The (1964) 169, 178 n.13
Napper, Lawrence 148–9
Naremore, James 20, 95–6
Navarro, Mary Lynn 9
Neale, Steve 97
Neff, Walter 30
Negulesco, Jean 36, 38
Nerenberg, Ellen 29
Never Fear (1949) 16, 18, 42–4, 52, 57–8, 61, 62 n.6, 215
New Yorker, Outrage, The 184–5
Nichols, Mike 36
No. 5 Checked Out 46, 239
noir films 95–6, 100, 114; *see also Bigamist, The*
Not Wanted (1949) 4, 16, 43–5, 63–74, 96, 129
childlike affectation in 71–2
fear foregrounded in 68
female longing in 68–70

INDEX

gender and family roles in 65–6
ideology of childhood in 64
love and marriage in 65
men in 67–8
romanticism in 71–2
women in postwar America 66–74
Novello, Ivor 37–8
Now, Voyager 179 n.15

O'Brien, Edmond 78, 101, 139, 195
On Dangerous Ground (2019) 4, 13, 52–62, 62 n.6
One Rainy Afternoon (1936) 96
On the Origin of Species (Darwin) 193
Orgeron, Marsha 17, 127, 129
Orlac, Paul 210
Out of the Past (1947) 98
Outrage (1950) 5, 7–12, 16, 18, 30, 39, 42, 80–5, 127, 131–42, 181–92, 200–2, 215

Palance, Jack 20
Paramount Pictures 38–9
Paris, Jerry 84
Parsons, Louella 37
Pearce, Howard 200
Penn, Arthur 36
Penn, Leo 66–8
philosophy 194
Pinky (1949) 41
pornography 36
postwar America's children 63–74
Powers, Mala 80, 88, 135, 141
Private Hell 36 (1954) 9, 157–62
Projansky, Sarah 187–90
Psycho (1960) 196
psychosocial dysfunction 64
Pudovkin, Vsevolod I. 158

Quart, Barbara 58–9
Queen of the 'B's: Ida Lupino Behind the Camera (Kuhn) 63, 178 n.6, 183
quota quickies 148–51

Rabinovitz, Lauren 139

Raging Bull (1980) 60
Rainmaker, The 179 n.15
rape 9–10, 181–92; *see also Outrage*
  culture 184
  films on 182
  as representation 187
  as trauma 9–10, 181–92
Rape and Representation 190
Ray, Nicholas 13, 45, 52, 68–9
Raymond, Paula 85–6
Rebel Without a Cause (1955) 68–9
Reed, Barbara 39
Rey, Alejandro 89
Rifleman, The 228
Road House (1948) 19, 41–3, 77
Robinson, Kathleen "Kat" 9–11
Rogers, Ginger 22
Rogues, The 228
Ross, William T. 4
Rossellini, Roberto 40
"R"-rated movie 36
Run for the Roses 48
Russell, Rosalind 47, 122
Russian silent films 158
Ryan, Robert 52

Saks, Sol 47
Sam Benedict 228
Santos, Marlisa 5–6
Scheib, Ronnie 30, 74 n.3, 102, 134–5
Schor, Lou 118
Scorsese, Martin 3, 15–16, 51, 60
Screen Director's Playhouse 46, 228
Search for Beauty (1934) 2, 96
Second Age 131
Seiter, Ellen 99–100
Selznick, David O. 41
Serling, Rod 213
sexual assault 187
sexual exploitation 19
sexual otherness 83
shamateurism, in tennis 29
Sherman, Vincent 3, 20–3
Shields, Jonathan 20, 23–4
shows, business of 17–33
Shuman, Michael 6

Siegel, Don 45
Silver, Brenda 190
Simon, Robert F. 235–6
Sipiora, Phillip xii
"Sixteen Millimeter Shrine, The" 214
Sloterdijk, Peter 230
Smith, Betty 65
Smith, Darr 43
Sobchack, Vivian 204
Souls of Black Folk, The (DuBois) 177 n.3
spinsters 243
Splendor in the Grass 65
Stack, Robert 234
stage mother 3, 21–2, 27, 32–3
Stage Mother (1933) 22
Stallone, Sylvester 60, 61
Stanislavsky, Konstantin 157–8
Stanwyck, Barbara 30
Stevens, Leith 102
storytelling intertextuality 97–8
Stout, Archie 43
Strangers on a Train 74
Sublime Object 230
Summertime 179 n.15
Sunset Boulevard (1950) 19, 97, 132
Supreme Court Paramount Decision (1948) 18
Suspense, radio series 39
Swanson, Gloria 132
"Sybilla" 11, 214, 217–20

Talman, William 139, 193–211
Tate 228
Taxi Driver (1976) 60
television works, Lupino's 11–13, 45–9, 85–93, 177 n.1, 227–41
  77 Sunset Strip 228
  1960s mysteries 213–24
  Alfred Hitchcock Presents 11, 165, 214, 216–17, 228
  Bewitched 165, 227, 228, 237, 239–40
  Bob Hope Presents the Chrysler Theater 228
  "Bride who Died Twice, The" 88–9

"Charley Red Dog" 86–8
Climax! 228
Daniel Boone 228
"Day of the Bad Man" 86–7
Donna Reed Show, The 85, 228, 231–3
Dr. Kildare 228
Dundee and the Culhane 228
Fugitive, The 165, 228, 231–3
gender roles, exploration of 85–6
General Electric Theater 85, 228
Ghost and Mrs. Muir, The 228
Gilligan's Island 47, 227, 228, 240
"Guillotine" 88–9
Have Gun, Will Travel 46, 85, 88, 228, 235–7, 239
Honey West 228, 237
Hong Kong 228
Hotel de Paree 228
inheritance, theme of 217–23
Kraft Suspense Theater 228
"Lady on the Wall, The" 85–6
"Lady with a Gun" 85–6
"Last of the Sommervilles, The" 91–2
"Lethal Ladies, The" 89–91, 251–2
on masculinity 86
"Mask of Medusa, The" 92, 221–3
"Masks, The" 9, 11, 165, 168–9, 214, 221–3
as mother directress 214–17
with Powers, Mala 88
Rifleman, The 228
Rogues, The 228
Sam Benedict 228
Screen Director's Playhouse 228
"Sixteen Millimeter Shrine, The" 214
"Sybilla" 11, 214, 217–20
Tate 228
Thriller series 11–12, 85, 88–91, 200, 214, 218, 228, 243–54
"Trio for Terror" 11, 91–3, 214, 218, 220–1, 253

Twilight Zone, The   9, 11, 51, 132, 165, 168–70, 213–15, 221, 228, 252
Untouchables, The   228, 233–5
Virginian, The   228, 237–8
"What Beckoning Ghost"   91
They Drive by Night (1940)   77
Third Age   130
Thoroughbreds, The (1976)   48
Thriller series   11–12, 85, 88–91, 200, 214, 218, 228, 243–54
   "Bride Who Died Twice, The"   245–6
   "Guillotine"   244–5
   "Last of the Sommervilles, The"   246–50
   "La Strega"   252
   "Lethal Ladies, The"   89–91, 251–2
   on monstrous women   250–4
   "Mr. George"   246–50
   on nonsexual women as threat   246–50
   "Trio for Terror"   253–4
   on women as commodity   244–6
Torrusio, Ann   11
Totality and Infinity   203
trauma   16, 40, 58, 135, 141
   film's narrative structure, effect on (*see Outrage*)
   rape as   9–10, 181–92
   sexual   84
   war   83–4
Trauma and Recovery (Herman)   191
Trauma: Explorations in Memory (Caruth)   182
Tree Grows In Brooklyn, A (1945)   65
"Trio for Terror"   11, 91–3, 214, 218, 220–1, 253–4
Trouble With Angels, The (1966)   7, 35, 113–15, 122–4, 240
   Catholicism in   123–4
   introduction to   122–3
   Lupino's direction, characteristics of   115, 122–3

   as mainstream comedy   122–4
   queer approach to   122
   social issues in   123–4
   women, relationships between/among   123–4
Tunis, John   99
Twilight Zone, The   9, 11, 51, 132, 165, 168–70, 213–15, 221, 228, 252
Two Weeks in Another Town (1962)   19–20
Tyler, Elaine May   68

Umberto D. (De Sica)   130
underground cinema   36
Untouchables, The   228, 233–5

Vaccarino, Maurice   42
Van, Curtis Le   8–9
violence   19
Virginian, The   228, 237–8
"Visual Pleasure and Narrative Cinema," (Mulvey)   178 n.8

Wager, Jans B.   78
Wald, Malvin   18, 96
Waldman, Diane   42
Walsh, Raoul   16, 36, 38
Warner, Jack   37
Warner Brother Studios   36, 152
Watching Rape: Film and Television in Postfeminist Cultures (Projansky)   187
Wellman, William   36, 38
Weston, Jack   85–6, 232
"What Beckoning Ghost"   91
Whatever Happened to Baby Jane (1962)   132
Where Angels Go Trouble Follows   47
White, Susan   122
Widmark, Richard   198
Wild Bunch, The (1969)   36
Wilson, Jim   4
Winters, Shelley   20
Woman of the Year   179 n.15
women

as commodity 244–6
  film genre 163 n.9
  monstrous 250–4
  movement 36
  nonsexual, as threat 246–50
  in postwar America 66–7
  responsibility 36
Woolrich, Cornell 88

Wyatt, Jane 45

Young, Collier 3, 18, 41–2, 96, 118

Zanuck 18, 41
Zinnemann, Fred 44
Zizek, Slavoj 229–30

www.ingramcontent.com/pod-product-compliance
Lightning Source LLC
Chambersburg PA
CBHW052217300426
44115CB00011B/1727